Humanistic Capitalism

Ricardo Sayeg and Wagner Balera
Translation Rafa Lombardino

HUMANISTIC CAPITALISM

1st Edition
POD

K

KBR
Petrópolis
2013

Text editing **KBR**
Copyediting **Marco Antonio Beck e Carla Marcondes Hasson Sayeg**
Translation **Rafa Lombardino**
Cover design **Luciano de Abreu Tavares**

ISBN: 978-85-8180-128-5

KBR Editora Digital Ltda.
www.kbrdigital.com.br
www.facebook.com/kbrdigital
atendimento@kbrdigital.com.br
55|24|2222.3491

340 - Legal

Ricardo Hasson Sayeg is an Associate Professor of Economic Law at the School of Law at the Pontifical Catholic University of São Paulo (PUC-SP), with a Master's Degree and PhD in Business Law by PUC-SP. He coordinates the PhD, Master's and Bachelor's programs, as well as the Research Center, and teaches Economic Law at the Department of Tax, Economic, and Business Law at the School of Law with PUC-SP. He is the leader of the Humanistic Capitalism Research Group with PUC-SP, registered with the National Council of Technological and Scientific Development (CNPq) Research Directory and immortalized as holder of Seat # 32 at the São Paulo Academy of Law.

Wagner Balera is a Full Professor of Human Rights at the School of Law at the Pontifical Catholic University of São Paulo (PUC-SP). He is an Associate Professor of Social Security Law, PhD in Social Relations Law, and Master of Tax Law by PUC-SP. He coordinates the Sérgio Vieira de Melo Pontifical Chair, dedicated to the International Rights of Refugees and the result of a partnership between PUC-SP and the United Nations High Commissioner for Refugees (UNHCR), in addition to coordinating the PhD, Master's and Bachelor's programs, as well as the Social Security Law Research Center, and teaching Human Rights at the Department of Individual and Collective Rights with the School of Law with PUC-SP. He is the leader of the Humanistic Capitalism Research Group with PUC-SP, registered with the National Council of Technological and Scientific Development (CNPq) Research Directory and immortalized as holder of Seat # 44 at the São Paulo Academy of Law.

The symbol that represents Humanistic Capitalism was developed by Luciano de Abreu Tavares, artist and designer with a PhD in History of Sciences by the Pontifical Catholic University of São Paulo (PUC-SP).

It was inspired by the Star of Bethlehem, the astrological guide of the Gospels, and a combination of the Alpha (A) and Omega (Ω) from the Greek alphabet, which represent Christian culturalism in regards to Jesus Christ's proposal of eternity and universality. The color, maroon, recalls the blood of Christ that is drunk in communion among men and quenches our spiritual thirst.

Alpha and Omega are structured in harmony, creating a star that indicates the cardinal directions (north, south, east, and west.) It is a symbol of universalism that unites, at the same time, Capitalism and Anthropophilic Humanism to embrace Humanity and the Planet.

The contrast seen between the Greek letters that form the symbol outlines the path towards where opposites will meet, due to its gravitational curve, in the infinite universe and, consequently, represents the dialectic synthesis between Capitalism and Anthropophilic Humanism. They also converge upon deliberation and lead to studies in Economic Law, combined with Human Rights, to result in the legal-economic theory used by Humanistic Capitalism.

By overlaying Alpha with Omega—Alpha's top points to the irradiation angle of Omega—we intended to show that the concept of Human Rights is found within the intertextuality of Positive Law, thus showing the fate that must be sought with an efficient positivation in regards to fulfilling the dignity of Humans and the Planet in order to reveal Normative Legal Humanism.

WITHOUT LOVE[1]

Intelligence without love makes you vicious;
Justice without love makes you merciless;
Diplomacy without love makes you a hypocrite;
Success without love makes you arrogant;
Wealth without love makes you greedy;
Meekness without love makes you a minion;
Poverty without love restrains you;
Beauty without love makes you a narcissist;
Authority without love makes you a tyrant;
Work without love turns you into a slave;
Simplicity without love undermines you;
Praying without love makes you a fraud;
Law without love enslaves you;
Politics without love makes you an opportunist;
Faith without love makes you a fundamentalist;
Bearing a cross without love becomes torture;
Life without law... lacks any purpose.

---

1 Poem published at Jornal da Igreja de São Judas, São Paulo (SP), June 2008.
Unknown author.

Table of Contents

FOREWORD

The trajectory of human thought hints at certain historical facts that somehow have a decisive influence on the path ahead.

In fact, the French Revolution influenced modern thought in such a powerful way that we would all agree how, in the absence of that event, history would have evolved differently. Likewise, how the clear purposes of the Bolshevik Revolution failed at the threshold of the third millennium is something that imprinted in vivid colors a mandatory benchmark for social scientists.

Presently, in our absolute post-modern times, the notion and implications of a Risk Society have properly infiltrated social thought—albeit with a degree of perplexity and resistance.

They say the 21st century will be the century of a Risk Society.

They say Risk Society will fulfill its mission to modify concepts, labels, and how social stakeholders think and behave.

In an attempt to excite our conscience, Ulrich Beck cautioned that this new modernity will demand us to rethink concepts such as development, wellbeing, economic growth... In short, all thought categories must be revisited.

And such is the purpose of this book.

It starts with a seeming contraposition: Capitalism can be humanistic. It is worth mentioning that the act of generating wealth is not solely aimed at accumulating financial resources.

Therefore, the authors perused the large list of references that includes both classical and contemporary thinkers who, from different perspectives, sought to reflect upon the ethical implications that must subject Capitalism to the humanist's purposes for which Risk Society believes it is destined.

The propositions formulated here arise from the conception of integral humanism, a philosophy led by Maritain.

This book lays out its own scenarios and makes its own connections, which act as driving forces to guide readers toward a certain focus and, from that point, a chain of thought that will lead them to values that function as strategic rules to shape and restrict Capitalism. Without this clearly defined frame, Capitalism may not survive future shocks.

Opening a path through a line of thought that had been secondarily considered, at least in more recent times, this work hopes to guide a post-modern discussion and help us face the main challenges that, similarly to the severe global crisis in 2008, will be faced by Humanity ever so often, considering the characteristic features of a Risk Society.

The authors come from two different backgrounds—one social, the other economic—representing two sides of the same coin, thus suggesting that each has been properly explored.

As a matter of fact, both have achieved the highest academic degree in their respective areas of expertise.

Wagner Balera has had both a professional and academic career relating to social Human Rights; and his work has become a reference in this field. He is a Full Professor and Coordinator of the Human Rights Program at the School of Law at the Pontifical Catholic University of São Paulo.

In turn, Ricardo Sayeg has practiced Law and is a university professor in Economic Law, placing himself in the forefront of the movement, whose flagship is Humanistic Capitalism. He is an Associate Professor and Coordinator of Economic Law at the School of Law at the Pontifical Catholic University of São Paulo.

Both authors identify with the common purpose of understanding the spiritual intentions and contents that, from a Christian perspective, must be found in all normative structures, whether economic or social, in order to achieve fraternity for the better of each man and the whole man, as Maritain would say.

And thus is the challenge faced by Humanistic Capitalism!

The greatest share of responsibility that rests upon the shoulders of Law professionals—primarily Magistrates—is understanding and applying this ever so complex normative structure; always identifying this idealistic dignity of Man in each concrete moment of life, which is something that must be achieved first and foremost.

We highly recommend this book.

Let us wish that your reflections upon reading it may help us achieve this ideal to which we aspire.

São Paulo, June 2011.

APPEALS COURT JUDGE NELSON HENRIQUE CALANDRA
President of the Brazilian Magistrates Association (AMB)

Introduction

(**A**) The *Alpha*. Despite the global Capitalist crisis that caught fire violently in 2008, Neoliberalism still prevails in the worldwide economy and imposes a Capitalist economic globalization on the planet. In its original format, the process is supported by a legal structure whose anti-judicial, anthropocentric, individualist, and hedonistic conception is promoted by classical thinkers Adam Smith and David Ricardo.

Capitalist regime and market economy are indeed necessary, efficient, and commendable. However, we cannot overlook its main negative implications, which are consolidated by the depletion of planet resources and the exclusion of a substantial portion of society from the economic, political, social, and cultural scenario—to the critical point that said portion of society is relegated to hunger, poverty, and submission, all of which unacceptable conditions.

As a consequence, in order to shape Capitalism according to current demands in order to favor Mankind—that is, ALL men and women on the planet—we need to formulate a legal-humanistic judicial order for the economy and the market, which would not be repulsed by the latter and actually recommend it, thus proposing a structure for an inherent planetary law that would render sacred a rightful Humanistic Planet.

Notwithstanding the individual character of the powerful forces acting upon the market, we may then contemplate the multidimensional realization of Human Rights toward the universal achievement of dignity for all human beings, whose minimum concrete intent toward the planet is to meet the eight general objectives identified as

Goals for the Millennium: (1) ending extreme poverty and hunger; (2) achieving elementary education universally; (3) promoting equality of gender and the autonomy of women; (4) reducing infant mortality; (5) improving the health of mothers; (6) fighting HIV/AIDS, malaria, and other severe illnesses; (7) assuring environmental sustainability, and (8) fostering a worldwide partnership toward development.[1]

These reflections represent a legal proposal that, by applying the Law of Universal Fraternity within the Capitalist environment, will be able to lead humanity on a march toward democracy and peace through liberty and equality.

We believe that the foundation for this path is the proposal made by Jesus Christ, who taught us that, beyond being equal, we are all brothers connected by an element that is common to everybody and everything: The God Particle, identified by Quantum Physics and Cosmology in the Big Bang Theory and, in Biology, by the seed of life confirmed by the discovery of DNA.

Jeffrey Sachs confirms this planetary connection by assuring that "achieving the Millennium Development Goals will require a global partnership suitable for an interconnected world. The world truly shares a common fate."[2]

Therefore, with the realization of universal Human Rights in their three subjective dimensions—liberty, equality, and fraternity—our intention is to shed a new light over the economy, from a legal standpoint, thus elevating the market from its known mythical condition of a savage and heartless environment, so that it may become a humanistic market economy that will achieve the inherent goal of aligning universal rights to Human Dignity with democracy and peace. As Marques da Silva once said, "Dignity originates from human nature itself."[3]

All this will become effective from the perspective of an objective spirit of humanity, a synthesis of the cultural anthropophilic

---

1 United Nations Millennium Development Goals.

2 http://www.institutoatkwhh.org.br on 11/19/2009.

3 SILVA. *Cidadania e democracia: instrumentos para a efetivação da dignidade humana*, p. 227.

Thomism, turning the odds in favor of Mankind—all men, women, and the planet—based on a humanistic nature that will shape a legal-Humanistic normative that would render sacred a rightful Humanistic Planet.

According to his studies on Adeodato, Hartmann said that "all rights ascertained by laws and other judicial institutions must be subjected to the objective spirit and it will only be within the relationship advocated by it, as a live spirit, that law and court decisions will then be fair and just." Without the live spirit to serve as their roots, judicial norms do not find their counterpart in values and must then be considered unfair and unjust. Without it, they are but an expression of power that does not rest on rights; that is, it simply becomes an assumed power. Therefore, without it, decisions and the law are a mere expression of violence and those subjected to it are being violated."[4]

---

4 REALE. *Filosofia do direito*, p. 202.

I

FRATERNITY'S THEORETICAL FRAMEWORK

In order to judicially govern the economy and the market, we must start with a new theoretical framework, which is anthropologically supported by the love of *Jesus Christ, who united us and guides us towards God.* Through love, God has given life to Mankind and to the world: Jesus Christ, the path, the truth, and the life. We are brothers, connected to everything and everyone. Pope Benedict XVI says that "The love for God and the love for our neighbors are now truly together."[5] This is the Law of Universal Fraternity, which guides us with freedom and equality towards democracy and peace.

The document that summarizes this legal thought applied to Capitalism is unquestionably the Universal Declaration of Human Rights. It is rightfully so because, as stated by Senise Lisboa, "The Universal Declaration of Human Rights, passed by the General Assembly of the United Nations on 10/12/1948, set forth the inalienable rights of the individual as prerogatives that support Human Dignity."[6]

We can assure indeed that the proclamation of Human Rights Declaration is the cornerstone of a new era for rights and duties. Therefore, it initiates a path that imposes the redesign of the archaic structures of the State, of the international organizations and their respective legal theoretical frameworks, as well as, of course, a thorough reorganization of the structures that govern the globalized economy

---

5 *Deus Caritas Est*, item 14.
6 SENISE LISBOA. *Manual de Direito Civil*, v. I, p. 105.

RICARDO SAYEG AND WAGNER BALERA

and the very foundations upon which the market supports itself.

Moreover, the theoretical framework that distinguishes these contemplations is the product of a research conducted by the Economic Law and the Human Rights Departments with the Pontifical Catholic University of São Paulo. As Pope John Paul II stated in regards to catholic universities, they follow the parameter of "free search for the whole truth about nature, man and God"[7] and "By means of a kind of universal humanism a Catholic University is completely dedicated to the research of all aspects of truth in their essential connection with the supreme Truth, who is God. It does this without fear but rather with enthusiasm, dedicating itself to every path of knowledge, aware of being preceded by Him who is 'the Way, the Truth, and the Life,' the *Logos*, whose Spirit of intelligence and love enables the human person with his or her own intelligence to find the ultimate reality of which He is the source and end and who alone is capable of giving fully that Wisdom without which the future of the world would be in danger."[8]

Pope Benedict XVI clarifies that, "Throughout the 21st century, a belief has been developed that religion belongs in the subjective and private realms, to which it should be restricted. While being part of the subjective sphere, it could not be a determining force in the larger process of history and in decision-making. However, one of the consequences of the Council [Vatican II] should fairly be the following: emphasizing once again the fact that the faith of Christians encompasses their complete life, that its place is in the center of history and time, overcoming its importance in the merely subjective realm".[9]

In fact, Capitalism must benefit from a Christian Humanistic perspective, whose basic line of thinking ultimately reinforces Pope Paul VI's statement, in that "it is necessary to promote complete humanism. What is it in addition to the wholesome development of man and Mankind? A limited humanism could apparently triumph as restricted to the values of the Spirit and God, the source of true humanism. Mankind can organize the Earth without God, but 'without God,

---

7 *Ex Corde Ecclesiae*, item 4.

8 Idem.

9 BENTO XVI. *Introdução ao cristianismo*, p. 12.

Mankind can only organize itself against the Man. Excluding humanism is inhuman humanism.' Consequently, there is no true humanism but that which is open to the Absolute, recognizing a calling that expresses the exact idea of what human life is. Mankind, far from being the ultimate norm of values, can only fulfill itself when it overcomes itself. To quote Blaise Pascal: 'Man infinitely transcends man.'"[10]

We must therefore admit that Capitalism, which is the work of man, has been perverted into a neoliberal version that is savage and inhumane, which the main countries of the globalized economy have elevated to the *status* of economic policy for the world.

The main countries of Capitalism were instituted back in 1975 with the G7, that is, the seven most industrialized and economically developed sovereign nations in the world: the United States of America, the United Kingdom, Germany, France, Italy, Japan, and Canada. With the addition of Russia, the group is now known as G8. This is the globalization era.

Neoliberalism was instituted in 1989 with the Washington Consensus. Since then, as a universal practice, it has been imposing a certain legal and natural judicial structure that, while protected by the myth of non-intervention, has become concurrently impermeable to the legal positivism of national legal order, recognized by the general Positivation of the right to private property and free enterprise.

With a globalized economy and the strength of capital, which is mainly a consequence of its financial transactions and multilateral negotiations, nations at the core of Capitalism have imposed the neoliberal legal and economic agenda of the Consensus to the world, more specifically to the countries financed by the International Monetary Fund (IMF), practically all of them emerging and developing nations. Brazil, for example, as several other nations, borrowed IMF resources in the 1990s by committing to make State companies private and welcome the liberal Capitalist globalization, which has effectively taken place.

The planet has then migrated to a widely global market economy. It is about effectively implementing once again the classic liber-

---

10 *Populorum Progressio*, item 42.

RICARDO SAYEG AND WAGNER BALERA

al economic theories of Adam Smith and David Ricardo, under the premise that, if each member of the community acts in favor of their own individual interests, disregarding others, it will lead to a more efficient economy that ultimately will naturally benefit the interests of the collective.

According to this reasoning, the friction caused by the collective leads to an optimized economy that emphasizes efficiency, thus supporting the social role of anti-judicialism, individualism, and hedonism. Consequently, such aspects must be legally assured, because the effective application of such ideas, in their purely mathematical and monetary aspects and without regard for the Humanistic order, cannot take for granted the fact that it has the potential to achieve better economic results.

This state of affairs, without rhyme or reason and under the complacency of the law, represents the transposition of Darwin's biological law of natural selection into the economy: the savage and inhumane prevails in nature for the strongest to survive and the weakest to find its demise.

This way, exclusion at the economic, social, political, and culture level, as well as the depletion of the planet, are considered a natural occurrence,[11] all in the name of natural selection and an economic growth in which the wealthier become the wealthiest and the poorer become the poorest.

Likewise, upon democratizing poverty with an economic, political, social, and cultural lack of efficiency, since we can see that it has sunk in a global economic perspective, socialism was far from a sufficient alternative and it did not speak in favor of the poor and excluded, to which Eastern European countries can historically attest. With the fall of the Soviet Union and the Unification of Germany, the emblematic incorporation of Eastern Europe to the European Union was not by chance.

By imposing a strict plural symmetry of economic equality,

---

11 With the impressive allegory created in The Lugano Report, Susan George puts the spotlight on the economic Darwinism that has brought so many tragic consequences to the world.

thus suffocating hedonism and individualism by denying the right to private property and the consequential freedom of enterprise, socialism had mutilated human characteristics. In its disastrous aftermath were the lack of efficiency and the ruthless march toward economic failure, accompanied by insufficient social, political, and culture performance. In other words, socialism had lowered the bar for the civil society it had subjected.

Capitalizing on the bankruptcy of socialism, wealthy nations started to assure that there is no effective alternative to liberal Capitalism. Consequently, they wish to restore the human component to the economic environment, to the savage state of nature.

Ultimately, Neoliberalism believes that the State, through the so-called "invisible hand" coined by Adam Smith, must interfere the least to allow economy to follow its path at its own pace and rhythm. Upon frequently referring to creative destruction Alan Greenspan, former Chairman of the Federal Reserve, is one of the voices advocating for such view: the market causes destruction, but reinvents everything for the better, including man and the planet. This is market fundamentalism, whose faith in itself seemed to be able to absorb all evil.

However, such view is repulsive. Each man, and the whole man, cannot be destroyed and reinvented. Those who are destroyed are dead and excluded, afflicted by hunger and poverty. There are over a billion human beings and the market is not absorbing them. Provided that life is finite, they simply disappear from the Earth. In other words, for those who are excluded death is, as a rule, the only prospect of freedom. And such fate is unacceptable.

In turn, the 2008 global financial crisis, whose destruction of Capitalism reached the most fortunate ones, has definitely shown that Capitalism must be rescued from the hands of neoliberal Capitalists. They need an answer, and the best of all answers is humanizing the market economy to deontologically displace neoliberal Capitalism. It would go from its current essence, a savage and inhumane natural state, to what it may become with the multidimensional fulfillment of Human Rights through a universal elevation of the human being.

Such is the Humanistic philosophy of the Economic Law. Simply put, it is about bringing the Law of Universal Fraternity into the

Economic Law. This is what we propose here, for it would certainly constitute a new theoretical framework according to which we would analyze Capitalism from a judicial standpoint, whose objective within the economic field is to find solutions through fraternity and, while taking into consideration the three subjective dimensions of Human Rights, the dialectic tension between liberty and equality.

As construed by the Human Rights Catalog, Mankind is superior to national and international structures and overgrown by dignity to, after all, achieve a complete and universal citizenship that, beyond merely economic concepts of globalization, reveals broader and more ambitious purposes.

Therefore, fraternity is proposed as a solution to the tension that exists between liberty and equality, reviewing the body of ideas of the Age of Enlightenment from the 18th century and those of the movements that followed it. This is the focus promoted by Fernandez, for whom "all great revolutionary ideals, in a sense, were intended to recover the political freedom of the Republic from the Ancient World. That is why the revolutions of the late 18th century and early 19th century looked to both the future and the past. Their examples were the Athenian democracy for the left and the Roman republic for the right."[12] Moreover, "Robespierre's reaction to such an attempt is the cradle of fraternity as political ideology,"[13] since "in fact, fraternity represented the ideal of emancipation that became part of the political program created by Robespierre, author of the 'Liberty, Equality, Fraternity' motto who, during a speech made on December 5th, 1790 to advocate for the rights of men and citizens,"[14] uttered those legal categories of subjective dimension attributed to Human Rights "for the first time in the universal history of humanity,"[15] as aligned with the objective spirit of the peoples and the planet.

Inarguably, liberty, equality and fraternity are evoked in present times as part of a collective repertoire. In this scenario, this triad of

---

12 *Fraternidade: a "terceira" virtude ilustrada.*

13 Idem.

14 Ibidem.

15 Ibidem.

values configures the three dimensions of judicial universality within the Capitalist environment that cannot be parted from the subjective natural rights currently known as Human Rights. In a deeper, more balanced contemplation, it should influence the market to universally assure the dignity of human beings within the dimensions of democracy and peace.

As far as creating opportunities so that people can take care of themselves and make a positive impact in the world, development is the natural path capable of facilitating a peaceful and democratic transition from the rudimentary, egotistical formulas of Capitalism toward a superior stage of social harmony based on Human Rights.

It is up to the Humanistic philosophy of the Economic Law to provide the legal platform that will facilitate such development and, at the same time, assure a free market and planetary responsibilities of liberty, inclusion, sustainability, and conciliation.

As Amartya Sen states, cooperation and solidarity among members of society represent the changing gear from an economic growth based on selfishness, in which one destroys the other, toward an economic growth based on a more wholesome development. It is clear that such a path can only be traced when Humanistic values are applied. Among them, we must emphasize on a corporate ethical conduct supported by the supreme value of a fraternal society whose incorruptibility will lead to harmony between productive investments and speculations, and between full employment and automation, among other achievements.[16]

Sen's concepts allow us to paint a rough picture of a planetary reality that is true and more important when gauged by Human Development Index (HDI).

Therefore, the Humanistic philosophy of Economic Law understands that this developmental process must focus on the human element and the planet in order to address basic survival needs of all men and assure planet sustainability as a free result of the achievement of individual potential of each man and the whole man.

In conclusion, anthropophilic legal humanism is the essence

16 SEN. *Desenvolvimento como liberdade*, p. 33.

of the philosophy presented herein, according to the parameters that support the previously-mentioned theoretical framework. It aims at overcoming the deep-seated anthropocentric and positivist notions of Law to methodically arrange the most adequate judicial administration of a Capitalist economy through the evolution of theoretical concepts that will support the planetary reality that we currently known.

II

Premises

(1) Normative Legal Humanism

Throughout the legal contemplations indicated here in regards to Humanistic Capitalism, we can verify that even now, in the beginning of the third millennium, natural rights are once again being studied due to the unacceptable path of economic barbarism through which Capitalism has been led by the hands of a cold and scentless positivism personalized by the masters of money who (let's not be naive!) are the ones effectively guiding legislative and even constitutional decisions.

Under such a restrictively positivist perspective, Economic Law should not be conceived as something that is thoroughly applied. According to Becho, we must not forget that "when Radbruch (2004, p. 47) states that only what is just is right, he denies the Nazi System as being right; on the other hand, when Kelsen (1985, p. 4) ponders that only what is standardized is legal, it can be concluded that the Nazi System itself was right".[17]

Incidentally, the emblematic conversion of renowned German positivist Gustav Radbruch into a confirmed legal naturalist[18] represented a notorious transition toward accepting legal naturalism

---

17 BECHO. *Filosofia do direito tributário*, p. 232.
18 BOBBIO. *Locke e o direito natural*, p. 19.

among a significant part of the legal community upon assertion of Human Rights in response to the atrocities perpetrated by Hitler in the 20th century.

Even Kelsen himself, the Prince of Positivism, took refuge from the Third Reich's horrors in the United States and sympathized with values that were taken upon by legal naturalism, as stated in some of his works, such as *Peace Through Law* and *Das Problem der Gerechtigkeit*. In the former, Kelsen recognizes that we are "the men of a Christian civilization" and that "assuring world peace is our task."[19] Furthermore, he states, "Nevertheless, it is more likely that the doctrine of a social contract is not entirely false."[20]

Therefore, revisiting natural rights once again in regards to the legal systematization of Capitalism is a reaction to the fundamentalist positivation of the economic order, which does not intrinsically take into account the negative outside factors of economy in a private, public, and universal and sense that, albeit reciprocal, are unbalanced to the point that they will ruin Human Dignity and lead humanity to horrors and unacceptable borderline scenarios as those seen during Nazism, even under the economical aspect.

While facing the economic horrors of Postmodernism, we can see that the deepest offenses of Capitalism, such as the exclusion of human beings and the depletion of planet resources, will only be overcome once the dignity of human beings is restored as a metasynthesis of economy, politics, and law, which must lead to a fraternal society when brought together and properly aligned. It shall happen chiefly once we close the abyss created between the wealthy and the poor upon freeing ourselves from the stigma of social exclusion and planetary degradation.

By that token, the revisited natural rights have the Herculean task of reconciling the unrestrained, savage, and unethical economic freedom with the universalization of human and planetary dignity. As a result, a Rightfully Humanistic Planet will be established, which cannot be mistaken by an improper intervention into the economy, for

---

19 KELSEN.*La paz por medio del derecho*, pp. 35-36.
20 Idem, p. 42.

such realm must remain, preferably, in the hands of the private sector and under the dominance of the market. Nevertheless, in addition to assuring the market to the private sector, the Rightfully Humanistic Planet must have a legal order that is immanent, monist, planetary, and capable of undeniably and indissolubly recognizing the market economy while, at the same time, keeping a mutually dependent relationship with the multidimensional realization of Human Rights for the sake of man, Mankind, and the planet as well.

In fact, this revisited natural right corresponds to the post-modern notion of Human Rights. As Becho emphasizes, "the neo-legal naturalist construction paid the price estimated by D'Agostino (2000, p. 70), which consisted in changing the label to adopt the Human Rights terminology."[21] As far as the economy is concerned, in the multidimensional application of this notion, we would recover the significant influence of the Thomist legal-naturalism, which is a philosophical doctrine originated from Saint Thomas Aquinas' *Summa Theologica* and supported by the anthropological concept of the Absolute being: Jesus' God, whose anthropologically recognized good news came to include everyone, especially the poor and the destitute.

The Thomist influence acquires a noteworthy relevance in the historical affirmation of Human Rights. As we will see further in this book, Thomism perceives said rights as having anthropophilic humanism as a backdrop and being applied scientifically and theoretically to Capitalism. In fact, the Humanistic notion of rights, which is inherent to nature, breathed into life by the Creator, and symbolically identified by the objective foundation of the Law of Universal Fraternity, is the antidote against Capitalism savagely enforcing the law of natural selection on everything and everyone.

Unhesitatingly, this theoretical structural framework is applied to rights within the economic realm. Saint Thomas' philosophy foretells that, in its essence, Human Rights converge towards the Enlightenment of Locke, the philosopher of liberal Capitalism and rational Christianity.

Then, even though Ripert had understood that Capitalism

---

21 Idem, p. 164.

"contrasts the spirit of modern society with a society that would be guided by Christianity's great Law of Fraternity or by the principle of the Muslim religion that imposes begging,[22]" the opposite will actually take place: Upon being restructured through a Human Rights platform, even a Capitalist society must consider fraternity as a deepening factor that will solve the dialectic tension between liberty and equality in the economic field.

Ripert did not live to witness the exciting phenomenon of a unanimous acceptance of Human Rights and the revelation of the multidimensional facet of this modern version of natural rights, which furthers the three dimensions of our inherent rights: the Liberty that lays the foundation for Capitalism, the Equality, and the Fraternity.

We must look at Capitalism from the legal perspective of Human Rights. It is based on individual natural liberties that are inherent to men, specially the subjective natural right to property, which in turn corresponds to the negative liberties that are precisely those seen currently as first-dimension Human Rights. Consequently, Capitalism is subject to the multidimensional consolidation of Human Rights.

Even though Capitalists are well aware of this multidimensional nature, they do not implement it and have structured Capitalism as a one-dimensional system. Upon supporting it on negative liberties, under the exclusive perspective of "first dimension" Human Rights, they undoubtedly constitute a specific legal-natural power that acts in favor of said liberties, which subject the entire planet to a state positivation that must recognize this economic regime in order to assure its protection and reinforcement, as Comparato states.[23]

With this power, we can see that neoliberal Capitalism has imposed itself almost as a voracious monster that, despite legislation, governs legislative activities, causes offenses without regard for local sovereignty and manipulates State intervention, economic planning,[24]

---

22 RIPERT. *Aspectos jurídicos do Capitalismo moderno*, p. 352.

23 COMPARATO. *Ética*, p. 227.

24 By the way, we cannot forget the event involving Investigator George Soros who, in 1992, was able to bring down the British pound, breaking the

and even constitutional principles.

Ultimately, neoliberal Capitalism has conquered the planet by labeling a legal-natural power as the *spirit*, without any need for a supranational positivation and restricting itself to exclusively assuring free trade at all levels, for such is its indispensable vehicle for expansion and preservation, thus generating the economic globalization phenomenon we know today.

"The selfish spirit of commerce knows no country, and feels no passion of principle but that of gain,"[25] Thomas Jefferson once famously said. Such is the Capitalistic logic for a global economy that appears to be the same once implemented during ancient times, when Romans conquered the world by imposing themselves without positivation, keeping the danger of supranational ties at bay to avoid controversy and accountability. As Montesquieu once said, we cannot forget that "since Rome imposed no general laws, the various peoples had no dangerous ties among themselves. They constituted a body only by virtue of a common obedience, and, without being compatriots, they were all Romans."[26]

On the other hand, under the Humanistic philosophy perspective of the Economic Law, there is a monist legal order that is inherent to the rightful Humanistic Planet, which recognizes the predominance of Human Rights over national legal orders and furthers itself through Capitalism. Therefore, despite being liberal and permeating the entire world, Capitalism must also observe such fact and, upon doing so, it can be understood as a system structured in different dimensions of Human Rights, which are interdependent and must be considered as an indissociable amalgam.

It is inconceivable that, with Capitalism, we should only want to recognize the first dimension of these rights and exclude all others dedicated to equality and fraternity. We must consider Human Rights in their entirety, as interdependent and indissociable rights, thus cre-

---

Bank of England itself. Please refer to:

http://super.abril.com.br/superarquivo/2004/conteudo_354648.shtml

25 http://*www.frasesfamosas.com.br*, on 11/01/2009.

26 MONTESQUIEU. *Grandeza e decadência dos romanos*, p. 79.

ating a structure for Capitalism itself.

Once consolidated, the Humanistic structures for freedom, equality, and fraternity will be better equipped to support an exemplary form of Capitalism that acts in favor of humanity. In this way, Capitalism will be subjected to the legal apparatus of Human Rights, which is recognized universally and able to, at the same time, make it legitimate, restrain its inconveniences, and hold accountable those who violate its consolidated structure, whose liberty, equality, and fraternity are indissociable and interdependent.

Thus, as far as a Capitalism based on liberty is concerned, the Human Rights mission becomes clear: To reflect its multidimensional nature, from a consolidation perspective, in order to have it recognized and added to equality and fraternity. Seeking inspiration in the words of Aristotle, "it is important to render power dependent and not to accept that those in power act at their will, for the possibility of doing everything we want does not allow us to resist to the bad inclinations of human nature."[27]

In order to surround Capitalism in the wholesome multidimensional nature mentioned above, it is imperative that we comprehend it from this dimensional Human Rights perspective, which converges with positive law to resolve each concrete case, pursuant to legal realism. Then the theoretical structure, which determines the significant contents of modern natural rights consubstantial to Human Rights, identifies this Humanistic purpose according to legal realism, converging with the positivation of law to universally achieve the dignity of human beings.

From this point of view on Human Rights, converged with positivation and pursuant to the Humanistic legal realism, we must highlight Barros Carvalho's logical and semantic constructivism. Through such method and the undeniable promotion of Human Rights, it is feasible to have a pragmatic shift in the linguistic paradigm of philosophy as referred to by Santiago Guerra,[28] going from the linguistic integration of the accepted speculative natural rights, based on

---

27 ARISTÓTELES. *A política*, p. 24.
28 GUERRA FILHO. *Teoria da ciência jurídica*, p. 142 and following.

the nature of the universe, toward a positive law that breathes the Law of Fraternity into Capitalism.

As Barros Carvalho reminded us when he wrote a manifest titled *O ponto de vista científico do Círculo de Viena* ["The Scientific Point of View of the Vienna Circle"] in 1929, at the birth of the logical and semantic constructivism, epistemologist Rudolf Carnap, Hans Hahn, and Otto Neurath had announced that they would "take an absolutely Humanistic orientation."[29] In fact, upon applying it to law as a Humanistic episteme, this constructivism implies that the proposed law as a legal norm should be thoroughly stated textually, associated intrinsically with its metatext, permeated by the regenerating influx of Human Rights in its intratextuality, and capable of indicating the adequate path to apply all norms compatible with the *ordo iuris*.

According to the concrete reality, Human Rights indissolubly and accessibly permeate positive law in the full application of legal norms, so that multiple hermeneutic options must yield to such response attracted by humanistic intratextuality that is balanced by metatext, while adding the respective discursive, cultural, and Humanistic dimensions to legal positivism with the purpose of dignifying human beings.

Text is language. And language is alive and dynamic, an expression of human culture in the mental representation of the existence of the universe. Textual language is but a physical structure of legal norms and, on account of it, legal norms not only follow the nature of the text, but that of the language as well. It is not an inanimate object; by specificity, it is the live representation of the wishful thinking of each man and the whole man, which is in constant transformation.

Language is the living expression of a finite consciousness that defines representations of existence through codes that correspond to its discursive dimension, that is, the textual dimension, which is an inherently cultural attribute of each man and the whole man. It is particular to them and essentially consists of an effort to connect Men to themselves and to each other.

---

29 Idem, p. 23.

Ergo, legal norms are a connecting effort that legislators make through linguistic codes and the living representation of wishful thinking. They create modalities of conduct for each man and the whole man. They go through this intra and interhuman positivation process that makes the human element essential to the mental formulation of this universal representation, which comes from Men. It is a cultural reaction to the respective connecting efforts previously manifested by legislators with a relationship of cause and effect.

As a simple example, we can point to the fact that, in Brazil, the legislator who writes a legal norm must do so in the official language, pursuant to Article 13 of the Federal Constitution, which is careful to sanction Portuguese language as the official language of the country.

Considering that, the successful enforcement of a legal norm is not aprioristic, since it mutually depends on the cultural element, that is, the ability to codify and decode language when sending and receiving the linguistic codes that it is made of, when deciphering the living representation and dynamics of wishful thinking between humans and within ourselves. Since it emanates from Men toward the universe, as a final argument, the legal norm is at the service of each man's and the whole man's awareness of their own existence. It is upon understanding our own human essence that, anthropologically, we can perceive ourselves as created to the image and resemblance of God, that is, we carry the Divine Spark within ourselves. Or, if you prefer, we are the bearers of dignity. Therefore, legal language cannot deviate from human and universal dignity.

We must keep in mind the well-known principle of René Descartes: "I think, therefore I am." What is it, but the divine privilege of representing, through language that elaborates thoughts, our own existence in and of ourselves? It is through human existence that we understand our essence, which is celebrated legally as dignity.

If so, each man and the whole man must be taken into consideration, for in their dignity they are present in coding and decoding the legal norm: Human essence is in the diffuse medium of all things culturally represented in the process of organizing language between humans and within ourselves.

Due to their cultural repertoire, the legal norm sees Men as the interlaid element between their deontological character and their efficiency in the reality plane. As a linguistic representation, Law must assure human essence in its connection to Man, Mankind, and the planet, for the imposition of the Law of Universal Fraternity emerges from this connection, from the influx of normative intertextuality and according to reality, that is, the way universe is perceived by human eyes through the expression of the cultural repertoire of each man and the whole man.

Barros Carvalho has taught us that "the incidence of legal norms requires that Man, as the interlaid element, move the structures of Law, build upon general and abstract norms, other general and abstract norms, general and concrete norms, individual and abstract norms, or individual and concrete norms so that, in this way, positivity can be imprinted into the system, until it achieves the utmost motivation of consciousness and tries to move the axiological direction of intersubjective behaviors. It is within Man that we found the source of the legal message."[30] To further that thought, Man is not only the source, but the path and the destination, because we must consider each man and the whole man as being in the diffuse medium of all things.

Thus, the success of what is stated by legal norm comes as the result of integration to the literal text in the real-cultural dimension, which resides in the metatext, and in the simultaneously Humanistic dimension of its intratextuality, which assures a permanent active repercussion of the Human Dignity in Law, according to the reality of things.

Considering that, within a multidimensional flow whose purpose is to consolidate the legal norm in order to enforce it, between text and metatext, we shall not ignore the inherent dimension of language that exists in the intratext. Such was the Humanistic base stated in the Vienna Circle manifesto, which confers upon the Law the consciousness of human essence, that is, the value of each man and the whole man that awards dignity to everyone and to the planet.

---

30 Ibidem, p. 169.

In sum, there are three dimensions to language in the legal norm: (1) the discursive dimension, which exists within the text, (2) the real-cultural dimension in the metatext, and (3) the anthropophilic humanistic dimension in the intratext. The latter always leads the implemented Law toward the dignity of human beings and the planet. We must stress that the intrinsic Humanistic base is found in each and every legal norm, since Man is in the diffuse medium of all things and these things universally constitute the planet.

Therefore, normative legal humanism is positivist, despite progressing beyond Neopositivism such as that of Alexy, who in addition to the discursive dimension also identifies the ideal dimension within the legal norm, in a way that "an adequate concept of rights can only come forth when both sides are intertwined,"[31] which "represents a concept of positivist law."[32]

As we can see in this contemplation, philosophy of language goes beyond classic positivism and even the Neopositivism of Alexy and other authors, while it does not abandon the positivation process. Hence, we must consider the significant contents of integral legal norm as resulting from a synthesis of text, metatext, and intratext, while emphasizing that the latter comes from the Humanistic convergence with positivation.

Upon combining positivism, legal realism, and anthropophilic humanism, the normative legal Humanistic model that we are proposing here seeks to establish, with the support of Santiago Guerra, "a dialog from opposite theoretical positions to reach a possible agreement between them as a result of a fundamental determination to harmonize theory and practice."[33]

Consequently, the correct episteme of practitioners of Laws is that which overcomes the resistance to concrete application of Human Dignity and, as a result, recognizes Human Rights, which become part of the significant contents of natural and elementary essence within the process of positivation of rights that, from then on, go be-

---

31 ALEXY. *Constitucionalismo discursivo*, p. 20.

32 Idem, p. 19.

33 GUERRA FILHO. *Teoria da ciência jurídica*, p. 143-144.

yond the sterile position of classic positivism before Capitalism. Such is an unacceptable neutrality, for Human Dignity would otherwise be universally unattainable within Capitalism since, through the textual perspective, positivism is physical and Capitalism is the ontologically individualistic selfish spirit that must suffer the deontological impact of fraternity that imposes equality and solidarity in particular to itself. Max Weber's expression, as stated by Ripert, remarked that acknowledging that there is "a Capitalist spirit" is something universal.[34]

It is known that the physical does not reach the spirit, but the spirit interferes with the physical. Neutral positivation tries to generate controversy and accountability regarding the inconveniences of Capitalism; however, they are but feeble attempts, until we recognize, once and for all, the normative legal humanism that inherently fills the intertextuality of legal norms with humanism, thus reaching the spirit of Capitalism.

Under such terms, comparing the spirit of Capitalism with that of fraternity, it is imperative that Human Rights be converged with positivation through its intertextuality. Thereupon, the Humanistic dimension will be added to the discursive and cultural dimensions, aligned with Article 1st of the Universal Declaration of Human Rights, which expressly conjures the "spirit of fraternity."

It will be only through the effective legal Humanistic perspective within the intratext, exhibited herein, that the inconveniences of Capitalism will be controlled without our abandoning Capitalism itself, while keeping in mind that, let us admit it, such inconveniences are better corrected through the spirit of fraternity, which imposes the concretization of Human Rights in all its multiple dimensions for the universal fulfillment of Human Dignity.

This last truth conforms itself and imposes the permanent, undeniable affirmation of Human Rights through the enforcement of positive law; however, in order to come into effect, the legal text must be harmonized with the Humanistic principles of the Law of Universal Fraternity that, as mentioned above, converges toward Locke's Enlightenment and, then, to economic liberalism.

---

34 RIPERT. *Aspectos jurídicos do capitalismo moderno*, p. 341.

Normative legal humanism becomes relevant and must be applied if we consider that the thorough enforcement of legal norm can only take place through the synchronicity of the discursive, real-cultural, and Humanistic dimensions, under the penalty of it not being applied with complete efficiency, but only partially and waveringly.

This is the normative legal humanism, which assures proportionality between the spirits (Capitalism and fraternity) and acknowledges that Human Dignity is the purpose to be universally sought, even under a free-enterprise economic regime.

(2) Methodology

As Barros Carvalho ponders, "all works with more serious aspirations must lay out their methods in advance, so that the collective techniques used by the analyst to define the object can be fully understood, placing it as the main subject to, only then, dwell in its contents."[35] As such, the philosophical position shown here is a determining factor for the methodological determination, through which we hope to assure the scientific quality of the reflections expressed herein.

In this manner, upon addressing the Humanistic philosophy of the Economic Law, we acknowledge that the law "presents itself before our eyes as a cultural object in nature, shaped into a language that, perforce, bears axiological contents."[36]

Resorting to the semiotics of law, the reflections herein decipher and draw inspiration from lexical meanings found in the governing rule of positive law within the economic order, as set forth in Article 170 of the Federal Constitution in Brazil. As Barros Carvalho states, "Taking positive law as a system of objectification, the Theory of Signs divides it methodologically, of course, into the three lev-

---

35 CARVALHO. *Direito tributário, linguagem e método.*, p. 200.
36 Idem, p. 181.

els of semiotics analysis: syntactic, semantic, and pragmatic. It goes through the prescriptive discourse from top to bottom in an enviable effort to decompose it."[37] Moreover, Barros Carvalho also states that, "The literal and logical methods are at the syntactic level, while the historical and teleological ones have influence over both the semantic and the pragmatic levels. The systematic interpretation criteria involve the three levels and, for that very same reason, is exhaustive in the language of the law. Only the last one (systematic) acts in isolation, precisely because it presupposes the foregoing ones."[38]

Nevertheless, following the effort to decompose the object, the study goes beyond: It investigates the subatomic, quantum normative level to extract the intratext, according to the spirit of fraternity, from the governing rule of positive law within the economic order in Brazil, which is set forth in Article 170 of the Federal Constitution. As a path to achieve the supreme value of a fraternal society, as proclaimed in the preamble of the Brazilian Constitution, this perspective identifies Human Rights in the intratext.

Human Dignity is confirmed by the jurisprudence of the Supreme Federal Court (STF, "Supremo Tribunal Federal") as a structural legal category within the current global and local legal system. According to a study performed on September 13, 2010, the STF makes reference to Human Dignity in 141 judgments. In this scenario, among other jurisprudential manifestations of that Court, Judge Ricardo Lewandowski expressly mentions in sentence HC 93.782 the "structural vector of Human Dignity."

Therefore, the Economic Law is not restricted to the text confirmed by the Constitution or the legislation, because it takes into consideration the intralanguage, emphasized in the legal category that structures Human Dignity, at the quantum level of the legal norm itself, which is metaconstitutional and travels the entire planet.

It means that, according to the thoughts shared by Telles Jr., "legal order is universal order itself. It is the universal order in the

---

37 Ibidem, p. 191.
38 Ibidem, p. 201.

uman sector,"[39] according to what the author refers to as "systems of effectively invigorating references."[40] At the quantum level, where the intratext comes from, it is verified that the referential system for the Economic Law in Capitalism is composed of Human Rights in their multiple dimensions. They are harmonically incidental, with the *status* of reflexive balance, and their purpose is to have the universal objective concretization of Human Dignity.

Since the synthesis of human knowledge is expressed legally and, therefore, becomes a cultural object, Law is authorized to be related to other areas of knowledge, especially Anthropology, Biology, Philosophy, and Physics. The Golden Rule created by Jesus is present in these areas of wisdoms, for it is the universal rule of fraternity according to which we are not only equal, but brothers, and shall love our neighbors as we love ourselves. Based on this thought, the concretization of Law must be considered.

In fact, as Laubier demonstrates, fraternity is an expression of utmost kindness and the realization of Christ's proposal to Man: "The importance of realizing God's project, as outlined in the story of the end of time, does not arise of the joy of men reconciled and picking the fruits of their labor, nor is it the preparation that this period may represent for ulterior tests; foremost and, above all else, it arises of realizing a project desired by God, who created everything that is perfectly good, which the rebellion of creatures has partially curtailed."[41]

Mindful of the analysis from a legal standpoint, through the methodology of the reflections herein, we aim at having quantum intralanguage emerge from the system of references to Human Rights that, as penned by Barros Carvalho[42] and Santiago Guerra, resorts to interdisciplinarity, chiefly Economy, Anthropology, Sociology, and Philosophy, among others, in order to "add to traditional fields of Law studies those results originated from research in empirical evidence,

---

39 TELLES JUNIOR. *O direito quântico*, p. 286.

40 Idem, p. 285.

41 LAUBIER. *As três cidades*, p. 275.

42 CARVALHO. *Direito tributário, linguagem e método*, pp. 194-196.

formal sciences, and philosophical speculation."[43]

Then, under the integral humanism approach of Maritain, who rescues Thomism, the method used by our approach is, from the Human Rights perspective, recognizing and analyzing the contents and implications of the Law of Universal Fraternity within the economic realm and Capitalism itself.

Here, we will show that, through anthropophilic humanism, the Law of Universal Fraternity will ultimately structure Capitalism by considering the multidimensions of Human Rights. With this set of instruments, the reader will be able to capture, within the economic order, the legal incidence of these rights as an intralinguistic structuring system of natural rights, which is universally accepted and converges with positive law, according to legal realism.

Finally, with this method, Human Rights are revealed in all their dimensions, according to the Humanistic philosophy to be exhibited here, and become the most acceptable path of application for the Economic Law and the judicial discipline of Capitalism.

(3) Liberalism, Democracy, And Peace

The clash between liberalism and democracy is well known in political, economic, social, and cultural aspects. Calling upon the prevalence of natural rights to freedom, unlike a democracy that is based on material perspectives, thus calling upon the prevalence of natural rights to equality, the foundation of liberalism is the formal perspective of rights.

As an inherent right that structures Human Dignity, liberty originally confers certain prevalence to liberalism in its first subjective dimension. However, Justice Carlos Ayres Brito cautions that "The new humanism orbits around more paradigmatically democratic values."[44]

---

43 Idem, p. 104.
44 BRITTO. *O humanismo como categoria constitucional*, p. 87.

Back in his time, Ripert had realized that "The might of Capitalism collides today with the power of democracy. The power of money or the power of numbers: From this encounter, a new Law shall be born, be it conquered or granted."[45]

As Bobbio emphasizes, "The relationship between liberalism and democracy has always been difficult: *nec cum te nec sine te.* Today, when liberalism floats once more anchored in the theory of Minimal State, besides being consistent with its best tradition, this relationship has become more difficult than ever."[46] Dwelling in this difficult relationship, the philosopher makes the following statement: "For those who examine this constant dialectic between liberalism and democracy from a general political theory perspective, it is clear that this continuous contrast that definitely will never be resolved (to the contrary, it is always destined to reach higher levels) between the demands made by liberals, for whom the State must govern the least possible, and the demands made by democrats, for whom the State must have a government that is increasingly in the hands of its citizens, reflects the contrast between two ways to perceive liberty, routinely referred to as negative and positive liberty."[47]

Still about this dialectics, but now in the post-modern world, we can see the remarkable features of the historical materialism of Marx, even though it is not emphatically and restrictively between Capitalists and the proletariat, but between the interests of the business community and all other inhabitants of this planet.

It is not by chance that Bobbio, the respected protagonist of the "Neither with Marx, neither against Marx" slogan, ultimately concluded that "liberalism and democracy have necessarily evolved from enemy brothers into allies."[48] This is the alliance that the Democratic State of Law tried to implement in Brazil in the introduction to Article 1st of the Federal Constitution.

Santiago Guerra explains that "Rule of Law and Democra-

---

45 RIPERT. *Aspectos jurídicos do capitalismo moderno*, p. 14.

46 BOBBIO. *Liberalismo e democracia*, p. 92.

47 Idem, p. 97.

48 Ibidem.

cy are [...] synthesizing expressions for (sub)series of principles and values of which these principles are the positive and objective manifestation. Therefore, one could say that such form represents, above all, the intention to reconcile, in the best possible way in the present and even more in the future, those principles and values that, once united in joint application, increase their reach and strengthen themselves, while at the same time they impose limitations to one another in order to prevent an exaggerated emphasis on one or some of them, which would lead to their misrepresentation."[49]

The synthesis required by this dialectic tension entrusts fraternity with the task of resolving the compromise reached between liberalism and democracy, infiltrating it with a reflexive balance used as a parameter of proportionality that contemplates the legal Humanistic conscience of Human Dignity. According to Aristotle, "virtue is the mean between two extremes," the "middle way" mentioned by Buddha, as long as this path leads to the fulfillment of Human Dignity.[50]

Building upon the significant contents of the Democratic State of Law, as known in the Brazilian Constitution in Article 1st, fraternity is the best facilitator between Capitalism and humanism. By creating an alliance between liberals and democrats, whose power of transformation goes beyond the States and reaches the planet itself (including and especially in the economic field, where it must achieve results for peace, emancipation, and complete inclusion), the inconvenient libertarians and egalitarians would be corrected as found in the existential legal situation of each man and the whole man, as well as that of the planet.

Liberal Democrats are not xenophobic; they cannot and must not be subject to a sovereignty that is located in a given territory. For these new men, the true mission consists of bringing peace to the world in every single aspect, especially politically, economically, socially, and culturally, with the emancipation and inclusion of everyone in a sustainable planet.

---

49 GUERRA FILHO. *Teoria da ciência jurídica*, p. 154.

50 Idem, p. 212.

Here is what is stated in item 8 of the Vienna Declaration and Program of Action adopted by the World Conference on Human Rights in 1993: "Democracy, development and respect for Human Rights and fundamental freedoms are interdependent and mutually reinforcing. Democracy is based on the freely expressed will of the people to determine their own political, economic, social and cultural systems and their full participation in all aspects of their lives. In the context of the above, the promotion and protection of Human Rights and fundamental freedoms at the national and international levels should be universal and conducted without conditions attached. The international community should support the strengthening and promoting of democracy, development and respect for Human Rights and fundamental freedoms in the entire world."

Such global awareness consubstantiates the objective spirit, which demands a planet of free, equal, and fraternal Men, as well as objectively peaceful, inclusive, and emancipating, structured by a monist legal order for Human Rights that prevails over any national legal order implemented internally.

In effect, in Brazil these significant contents have been recorded in Article 4th, item II of the Federal Constitution, which recognizes the prevalence of Human Rights in international relations. Such premise makes it clear that, as per the constitutional resolution, Brazil is part of the planet as a Humanistic country, positioning itself before the eyes of the world as a Humanistic State by decree.

The international treaties and conventions on Human Rights have such a strong presence in the Brazilian internal positive law that, pursuant to Article 5th, paragraph 3rd of the Federal Constitution, that those that are approved (in two turns, receiving three fifths of the votes from respective members) shall have the equivalent effect of constitutional amendments. Article 7 of the Constitutional Provisions Act also states that Brazil shall defend them at an international Human Rights court, to which it would evidently be subjected internally as well. The aforementioned Article confirms the prevalence of a monist planetary legal order on Human Rights over Brazilian sovereignty and makes it clear in its significant contents that we, the Brazilians, are subjected to it. Guimarães confirms the planetary monism of Human Rights.[51]

Within the economic realm, the teachings of the Second Vatican Ecumenical Council are being asserted, which follows in particular the lessons we have learned from Saint Thomas Aquinas: "God intended the earth with everything contained in it for the use of all human beings and peoples. Thus, under the leadership of justice and in the company of charity, created goods should be in abundance for all in like manner. Whatever the forms of property may be, as adapted to the legitimate institutions of peoples, according to diverse and changeable circumstances, attention must always be paid to this universal destination of earthly goods. In using them, therefore, man should regard the external things that he legitimately possesses not only as his own but also as common in the sense that they should be able to benefit not only him but also others."[52]

From the political, economic, social, and cultural perspective, each man and the whole man must be aware of their value; the planet, in favor of Man, loses its *status* as something that can be appropriated by Humanity, thus acquiring its own dignity.

Such awareness grants each man and the whole man a meridian dignity; if so, considering Man as the diffuse medium of all things, and the planet as the universality of all things, we must attribute to the latter the indispensable legal ownership for it to be granted peace, with the inclusion and emancipation of all, which is the meaning of democracy in its broadest sense.

Configured as the ownership entity of right to democracy and peace, the monist legal order for Human Rights emanates from the planet, notwithstanding a worldwide State. It can then be demanded, through an objective spirit, that each man and the whole man behave toward realizing said rights, since Man is in the diffuse medium of everything, that is, of all things and, consequently, of the planet itself.

---

51 GUIMARÃES. *Tratados internacionais*, pp. 123 cc. 129.

52 *Gaudium et Spes*, Pastoral Constitution on the Church in the Modern World, of December 7th, 1965, item 69, in *Vaticano II: mensagens. Discursos e documentos*. Translation by Francisco Catão. São Paulo: Paulinas, 1998.

That is what we can call "planetary dignity."[53] Since, as Yoshida stated, the planet is "strictly related to Human Dignity, a foundation of our Democratic State of Law."[54]

Therefore, at the present time, the demands for planetary dignity, which are attributed to acknowledging the value of the planet itself, imply that the Democratic State of Law shall be replaced by the rightful Humanistic Planet as the legal ownership entity and rightful recipient of democracy and peace itself, an instrument for the universal concretization of Human Rights in its subjective dimensions: liberty, equality, and fraternity.

(4) Federalism And Human Rights

In Brazil, due to its vast territory and as a paradigm for similar systems, we must consider Federalism in the concretization of Human Rights within the Capitalist environment through the lens of Human Dignity since, pursuant to Article 1st of the Federal Constitution, the nation corresponds to the indissoluble union of the States, Federal District and Municipalities.

There exists a plurality of legal orders within the Brazilian federal model, which implies a complete legal order and partial legal orders. The Federal Constitution divides authority by implicitly and expressly granting the powers enumerated therein, which is recognized in several cases taken to the Supreme Federal Court (STF), under the reporting of Dean of the Court Celso de Mello, as seen in Direct Unconstitutionality Actions (ADI, "Ação Direta de Inconstitucionalidade") numbers 2,995, 3,189, 3,293 and 3,148.

As we know, the Brazilian legal order is consummately guided by the vector of Human Dignity as the multidimensional concretization of Human Rights. That is why the Constitution expressly indicates both values, thus confirming this formal and positive statement

---

53 An expression used by Sodré in *Dignidade planetária*, p. 1174.
54 YOSHIDA. *Direitos fundamentais e meio ambiente*, p. 1131.

for its structuring purposes.

In regards to how Human Rights are treated internally, the federal authority in turn is implicitly evident, despite it not being explicit in the Brazilian Constitution. Such authority is not purely legislative, since Human Rights have a directly inherent and preexisting nature and come before the constitutional authority being granted. In fact, Human Rights do not need or presuppose positivation, which is an unessential measure, a merely formal reinforcement.

Since Brazil is a Humanistic country, and as far as Human Rights are concerned, legislators are systematically conferred the authority to ratify Human Rights in order to reveal them formally and positively, thus emphasizing on their concretization in order to assure Human Dignity. Regarding Human Rights, once they are inherent and precede the positive legal order, the authority over them is actually executive: their concretization must be considered in the organization of the State.

This constitutional and metaconstitutional system of ideas, of which Human Dignity is the substance, demands that the State take it into consideration in the norms to be edited or enforced in any of the different levels or spheres of action. Considering such premises, we are forced to conclude that there is a common authority among the Federal Government, the States, the Federal District, and the Municipalities even to legislate, but mainly to execute the concretization of Human Rights in all their dimensions. All members of the Federation must universally implement Human Dignity.

At long last, among every member of the Federation with all their individual attributions, there is a common authority in a constitutionally implicit manner that regards the power/ duty of realizing Human Rights and even legislates in favor of them, while giving prominence to the respective negative competence to offend them under any circumstances.

III
HISTORICAL APPEAL AND TRENDS

(1) Worldwide

Economy is a phenomenon of human activity and it has always been under the influence of men and legally governed since Ancient times. Paragraphs 241-277 of the well-known Hammurabi Code, the Babylonian law code dating back to the 18th century BC, has regulations on prices and wages.[55] In the Mosaic Law proclaimed by Moses circa 13th century BC and perpetuated by the Bible in Leviticus 19:34 and Deuteronomy 23:19 and 25:13-15, good faith and honesty are rules of commerce. Additionally, usury is prohibited for the people of Israel. Likewise, the Manu's Code of Law, an ancient Hindu law written between the 2nd century BC and the 2nd century AD, sets forth currency regulations in Articles 115-122, while Articles 396-399 limit economic activity. It also has norms on market reserve, fixing the price of goods, and fines for commerce fraud.

In Greece, due to the power of Hellenic democracy, general issues had priority over individual issues and equality and wealth relativity were predominant,[56] which also led to intense interventions into

---

55 BOUZON. *Código de Hammurabi*, p. 29.
56 HUGON. *História das doutrinas econômicas*, p. 32.

economic activity.[57] The age of Greek democracy did not create obstacles to commerce, as we can see from the records left by Aristotle[58] regarding Thales of Miletus, a philosopher who founded the Ionian school and monopolized the olive press and olive oil market in order to show how to become rich as a result of the knowledge he had.

Still in Greece, around 590 BC, Solon introduced currency and abolished slavery as a result of debt. This was a crucial step in the path of Humanity towards the dialectic solution between Human Dignity and economic property.

Likewise, the Law of Licinius of 367 BC was the result of the Tribune of Rome and equally abolished slavery due to debt. The Law of the Twelve Tables, completed in 450 BC and applied to plebeians and patricians, gave prestige to autonomy in the willingness to negotiate and respected the private property of its people. Justinian's *Corpus Juris Civilis*, dated 529 AD, addressed the legal framework that is still taken into consideration in our days, whose principles and structuring regulations are the foundation of Civil Law as far as property, obligations, and contracts are concerned.

However, the Romans and the nations they conquered had their history marked by the interventions of Rome into the economic activity, both within its national territory and dominated lands.[59] Rome did not impose general laws to the territories it conquered; it created casuistic laws as required in order to pillage their wealth.[60] Such is the symbolical Roman policy of "Bread and Circuses," especially that of Emperor Gaius Augustus, who governed Rome between 27 BC and 14 AD. With the pretext of having a social policy in place to distribute free food and make entertainment activities available, the people were alienated with demagoguery and ultimately the change of civil status from Roman Republic to Dictatorial Empire found popular support.

It is also worth mentioning Diocletian, Emperor between 284

---

57 MONTESQUIEU. *Grandeza e decadência dos romanos*, p. 34.
58 ARISTÓTELES. *A política*, p. 31.
59 HUGON, op. cit., p. 42 and following.
60 MONTESQUIEU, op. cit., pp. 76-77 and 79.

nd 305 AD, who legally intervened into economy by promoting the reform of the current currency as a measure to tackle inflation. In this edict, known as the "Edict on Maximum Prices," the Emperor fixed wages and prices of goods and services, regulating even the issue of currency and very strict punishment to transgressors.[61]

In High Middle Ages, between the 5th and 10th centuries AD, Europe isolated itself and became mostly rural through feudalism. This system was supported by self-sufficient agricultural activities intended mainly to consumption, with natural exchanges and land ownership distributed as a concession of benefits and a method to structure a military force, thus constituting the relationship between suzerain overlords and vassal servants.

It was in the Middle Ages, with Patristics, that the universal concept of the individual was consolidated to acknowledge the broad human nature.

Due to population growth, rural flight, technology development and the reopening of supply routes in the Mediterranean Sea in the aftermath of the Crusades, the markets in the Middle Ages were consolidated during the 11th century.[62] These markets were founded on the resurgence of cities, known as boroughs (*bourgs*), which branded as *bourgeoisie* the social class that controlled the means of production. In the 13th century, the term became synonymous with social prestige.

Known as the Late Middle Ages, the period initiated in the 13th century was extremely rich as far as the legal discipline of negotiations is concerned. In early 1215, the British barons limited the powers of their monarch with the *Magna Carta Libertatum*, assuring subjective vertical rights before the State and taking the first steps toward constitutionalism.

Under the influence of Scholasticism, the principle of moderation was developed to declare the right to private property, albeit not in the absolute sense, but addressing its respective social purpose. Within this context, the principle of balance in contracts, especial-

61 BARROW. *Los romanos*, p. 176 and following.
62 HUGON, op. cit., p. 46-47.

ly synallagmatic contracts, was then developed so that the price of goods could be set according to criteria of fairness and equality, thus the so-called "fair price."[63]

In the 15th and 16th centuries, European cities grew stronger, especially the ones in Italy, and they controlled commerce and the routes to the Mediterranean Sea with intense mercantile activity, a strong bourgeoisie, and urbanism, creating another economic category: artisans and their craft-based corporations, with the respective legal discipline regarding an economic activity founded on the common law. The Renaissance is then instituted, rescuing the classic anthropocentric humanism, in which Man is at the center of the universe, along with Rationalism, which criticized Medieval values with a school of thought that was in favor of the secularization of the State. This historical moment leads to Individualism, a value that would support the upcoming liberal economic thought both philosophically and legally.

Then came the Protestant Reform, followed by the Catholic Counter Reform. The bourgeoisie in northern Europe identified itself with the Lutheran ethics, which drove the development of Capitalism, since the doctrine accepted the accumulation of wealth and did not condemn usury, while Catholic Scholasticism insisted on social role, balance, and economic moderation.

Within this context, political centralization was solidified, originating the States we know today. A new economic system is born as a consequence of the modern States and the great discoveries, which is strictly connected to political absolutism: Mercantilism, which may be understood under the light of Machiavelli's and Hobbes' philosophy, was marked by an extremely strict State interventionism, whose purposes were the accumulation of wealth, thus applying several penalties to defend protectionism and the constitution of monopolies. Those who did not obey the economic order could even be punished with the death penalty.[64] The English Navigation Act of Oliver Crom-

---

63 Idem, p. 49 and following.
64 Ibidem, pp. 81-82.

well, establishing in 1651 that British products could only be transported by a British fleet, is an important historical example of those times.

However, Absolutism obstructed Capitalism in its early stages, since there was no opposition to the acts of the Prince through the recognition of subjective rights. Capitalism affirmed itself from then on, after several victorious bourgeoisie political movements during the institution of the Rule of Law in a historical period known as Enlightenment. The philosophical highlights of that time were John Locke and Thomas Jefferson, for whom Men had natural rights to liberty, property, and confrontation with tyrants who intended to infringe them.

The fruit of these Enlightenment movements are the historical events concerning the Glorious Revolution in England, the French Revolution, the Independence of the United States of America, the Liberal Revolution of 1820 in Portugal, and the Independence of Brazil and the Spanish-speaking American countries, thus severing the colonial pact, among others.

The declarations of rights emerge, assuring nations their sovereignty, life, liberty, and property. England proclaimed its Bill of Rights in 1689, the United States of America had the Declaration of Independence in 1776, and France had the Declaration of the Rights of Man and of the Citizen in 1789, inspired by Voltaire, Locke, and Rousseau. As mentioned above, Robespierre made his famous speech on December 5th, 1790, when his "liberty, equality, fraternity" motto was there for posterity. All these efforts, whose backdrop was the Enlightenment ideals that preached the disassociation of Man from Church and State,[65] laid the ground for the new political, legal, and economic philosophy of *laissez-faire* in the 18th and 19th centuries, under the protection of the Rule of Law that was being implemented unruly and without any counterbalance.

However, the Enlightenment that prevailed was of the so-called moderate nature, whose representatives were Rousseau, Locke, and Newton, the advocates for Rational Christianity.

---

65 FONSECA. *Cláusulas abusivas nos contratos*, p. 17.

It was then that Men were considered ethnically equal by the force of the Enlightenment school of thought from the 18th century, especially as a result of the predominating abolitionist movements of the 19th century, despite the unfortunate sparse reactions. The following events are worth mentioning: Chile abolished slavery in 1823 during the administration of President Ramón Freire; due to its political and economic relevance worldwide, the United Kingdom passed the *Slavery Abolition Act* in 1834 and, in 1845, prohibited the trade of slaves between Africa and America with the *Slave Trade Suppression Act*, also known as the *Aberdeen Act* (or *Bill Aberdeen* in Brazil,) and the United States, thanks to the determination of President Abraham Lincoln, who declared slavery abolished in 1863 and saw it come into effect amid the confrontation between the proslavery advocates of the south and the abolitionists of the north during the Civil War that ended in 1865. France abolished slavery in 1848; Portugal, in 1869; Spain, Cuba, and Puerto Rico did so in 1886, and Brazil, in 1888. The abolishment of slavery is then replaced by a confrontation that still drags on today: The former aristocrats of proslavery background state that work is contemptible, especially manual labor,[66] to the point that, in many cases, workers are dehumanized and reduced to a slave-like condition.

By assuring liberty and equality to humans in the 18th century, the legal order of the Rule of Law started to affirm full freedom of enterprise and right to private property. No restrictions were accepted, according to the principles of morality and civil rights, thus sanctioning *laissez-faire* based on the philosophy of Adam Smith and David Ricardo. Such was the proposal of a minimal State, which can be summarized by the notion that the market must be left in its wild natural state and coordinated by its own economic dynamics, the "invisible hand" that allows it to self-regulate with minimal State intervention only as critically needed.

Nevertheless, the Europe and the United States of the 19th century start to undermine the ability that the market would have

---

66 MANUS. *A dignidade da pessoa humana, o dano moral e o direito do trabalho*, p. 1312.

to regulate itself. Despite recognizing the liberties of the *laissez-faire* philosophy, the positive law in the economic order started to set forth some regulations and restrictions over business activities.[67] In the United Kingdom, norms of this nature date back to 1842, with the *Merchandise Marks Act,* in addition to the *Medical Act* of 1858. In the United States, the *Sherman Act* was proclaimed in 1890 to assure competition.[68]

The anti-human relations at the economic level reverberated in the world of work, which drove the encyclical *Rerum Novarum* issued by Pope Leo XIII in 1891. Regarding the fact that the previous century was governed by *laissez-faire*, the Pope states (item 3) "that working men have been surrendered, isolated and helpless, to the hardheartedness of employers and the greed of unchecked competition.

In opposition to *laissez-faire*, concurrently with World War I, the Russian Revolution took place and the liberal bourgeoisie was initially victorious in February 1917. A few months later, in October, they were overcome by the communists led by Lenin. With the dissolution of the Constituent Assembly and the nationalization of private property, the Union of Soviet Socialist Republics was then instituted. Authoritarian, mutilating the liberties of the Enlightenment, this nationalizing regime suppressed civil and political subjective rights.

Discussing the Soviet government, which was born out of fear, Lebret comments that "it is so unrelenting. It does not understand Man; it must then mistreat Man. It became present everywhere and cannot help but be oppressive. It is still so young; it contradicts itself. In annihilating God, it became a false god."[69]

Also in 1917, after a Civil War in the New World, Mexico proclaimed its first Constitution, which contemplated economic and social clauses, as well as the classic individual liberties and rights; it maintained the Capitalism, but started working on the first sketches

---

67 SAVAGE AND BRADGATE. *Business law*, p. 4.

68 BORK. *The antitrust paradox*, p. 15.

69 LEBRET. *Princípios para a ação*, p. 27.

of a Social Rule of Law.[70]

Two years later, in 1919, it was Germany's turn to proclaim the famous Weimar Constitution, bringing together economy and social issues in their highest set of norms. Weimar's country constitutionalized economy directly, but remained Capitalist, reaffirming the Social Rule of Law as a legal and institutional reality.

After World War I, following the New York stock market crash in 1929, Capitalism started to prevail worldwide in the schools of thought that addressed economy based on the rejection of market automation. On the other hand, said rejection was counterbalanced by the acknowledgement of subjective civil and political rights and, consequently, the reaction against collectivizing the means of production and investments, whose rationale authorized State intervention, under the banner of a welfare state, into the economic realm in order to solve negative external factors. In other words, State Capitalism was born.

The main spokesperson for the structuring thought of State Capitalism, John Maynard Keynes, published *The end of laissez-faire* in 1926.[71] The most remarkable historical example of that period was the *New Deal*, an economic interventionist planning program implemented in the 1930s by U.S. President Franklin Roosevelt.

In the aforementioned 1926, the Slavery Convention was signed in Geneva on September 25 and later amended by its subsequent Protocol open to signatures at the United Nations Headquarters in New York on December 7th, 1953. A Supplementary Convention was also signed on the Abolition of Slavery, the Slave Trade, and Institutions and Practices Similar to Slavery and adopted in Geneva on September 7, 1956 to "secure the abolition of slavery and of the slave trade" and "promote complete abolition of slavery in all its forms" at the universal level. In a nutshell, the Convention clarified that slavery is "the status or condition of a person over whom any or all of the powers attaching to the right of ownership are exercised"

---

70 URBINA. *La primera Constitución político-social del mundo.*

71 MAYNARD KEYNES. *The end of laissez-faire.* London: Hogarth Press, 1926.

and that "'Slave trade' means and includes all acts involved in the capture, acquisition or disposal of a person with intent to reduce him
to slavery; all acts involved in the acquisition of a slave with a view
to selling or exchanging him; all acts of disposal by sale or exchange
of a person acquired with a view to being sold or exchanged; and, in
general, every act of trade or transport in slaves by whatever means
of conveyance."

In 1931, starting a new chapter in the economy evolution, the
Encyclical of Pope Pius XI, entitled *Quadragesimmo Anno*, warned
that "capital hires workers, that is, the non-owning working class,
with a view to and under such terms that it directs business and even
the whole economic system according to its own will and advantage,
scorning the Human Dignity of the workers, the social character of
economic activity and social justice itself, and the common good."[72]

With stern criticism of economic despotism, the Pontifex
Maximus of the Catholic Church reproached that "This dictatorship is
being most forcibly exercised by those who, since they hold the money and completely control it, control credit also and rule the lending
of money. Hence they regulate the flow, so to speak, of the life-blood
whereby the entire economic system lives, and have so firmly in their
grasp the soul, as it were, of economic life that no one can breathe
against their will."[73]

In this manner, we can see two different movements transforming the economic scenario. In one corner, we have a greedy, irre-
sponsible Capitalism that is capable of everything to fulfill its purposes and, in the other corner, state interventionism and nationalization
in Communist countries and satellite states, which asphyxiates civil
and political rights, as well as free enterprise, and proved to be inefficient.

Throughout World War II, due to the efforts of combat, State
Capitalism and Communism were exacerbated by the countries par-
ticipating in the conflict.[74] In the 1930s, Hitler's Social Nationalism

---

72 Item 101.

73 Idem, item 106.

74 SAVAGE AND BRADGATE. op. cit., p. 6: *"By the 1920s it was apparent*

and Mussolini's Fascism erected radical State Capitalist economic regimes and affected deep interventions in the economic realm, to the
point of drastically suppressing subjective civil and political rights,
including the freedom and private property of certain groups, as it
happened with the Jews.

There emerges the figure of Father Louis-Joseph Lebret, who
conceived the *Économie et Humanisme* magazine, published until late
2007. He was engaged in a movement that sought to reflect the situation in which Humanity found itself back then, especially concerning the consequences of the Great Depression that had prostrated the
world as a result of what we now call "the first worldwide economic
crisis." The *Économie* magazine addressed economy as a system that
supported people and nations, exploring the close ties between economy and humanism.

A group of thinkers, among them Lebret, released in 1942 the
Pour une civilisation solidaire manifesto, the first study to "call attention to the state of the world and indicate a path away from the pre-
dicaments that humanity currently faces."[75]

Meanwhile, World War II was underway and, in this con-
juncture, the Bretton Woods Conference took place in July 1944 to
define the international financial architecture from then on. The purpose then was to reorganize the economy that would rise again amid
the debris left by the conflict. Henry Morgenthau, the U.S. Secretary
of Treasury at the time, advocated for a dynamic global economy in
which each nation would have a chance to realize its full potential in
peace while enjoying the biggest material progress there is: an Earth
that was blessed with infinite natural wealth.

As the fruits bore from this Conference, the International
Bank of Reconstruction and Development (IBRD), also known as the
World Bank, was formally established and implemented in December

---

*that the era of laissez-faire was coming to an end in favor of state intervention
in economic affairs"*; and on the following page: *"The two World Wars accelerated substantially the growth in government control and management of the
economy."*

75 LEBRET. *Manifesto por uma civilização solidária.*

1945, along with the International Monetary Fund (IMF), whose operations were initiated in March 1947.

The initial purpose of these organizations was clear: the World Bank would finance projects to recover the economy and leverage development, while the IMF would provide resources to countries with a trade deficit as a result of adverse conjectures in the international scenario. And so the distribution of power among the winners was established: the IMF would be presided by a European and an American would occupy the main position at the IBRD.

The U.S. dollar replaced the British pound as the international currency. The polarization of the world, led by the United States of America, placed many Western countries under the influence of Capitalism, while Eastern Europe started to suffer under the hegemonic authority of the Soviet Union.

As Prime Minister Winston Churchill declared, an iron curtain divided the world, because the Soviets did not agree to restore sovereignty to the Eastern European countries that were freed after the Nazi occupation. Such gesture provoked the reaction of the Capitalist world against Communism in 1947, as consolidated in the well-known Truman Doctrine. Harry Truman, the U.S. President at the time, made the following announcement on March 12, 1947: "It must be the policy of the United States to support free peoples who are resisting attempted subjugation by armed minorities or by outside pressures."[76]

On the other hand, even before the Cold War was declared, Humanity decided to leave the debris of World War II through the institutionalization of new international affair structures. In October 1945, the San Francisco Conference established the United Nations (UN) and released the so-called Charter of the United Nations, which initially had 50 signatory nations and declared its purpose to facilitate collaboration in terms of international law and security, economic development, social progress, Human Rights, and achievement of world peace.

From that moment on, the UN is characterized by an import-

---

76 GILBERT. *Enciclopédia das guerras*, p. 289.

ant division: one the one side, the Security Council is instituted as the highest decision-making body, where the Big Four from World War II—United States, Great Britain, France and Russia (the former Soviet Union)—, in addition to People's Republic of China, are assisted by ten countries with a temporary two-year term; on the other side, the Economic and Social Council has wide powers to make or initiate studies and reports with respect to international economic, social, cultural, educational, health, and related matters and may make recommendations with respect to any such matters to the General Assembly to the Members of the United Nations, and to the specialized agencies concerned, according to Chapter X of the Charter of the United Nations.

As a side note, it is also worth mentioning that, amid the debris of World War II, *démarches* were initiated within the framework of the UN for international trade to take its course. In 1948, a draft for an international negotiation model took shape in Havana and was signed by several countries. It became known as the General Agreement on Tariffs and Trade (GATT).

The conflict of interests, made known among the countries taken by selfishness, did not allow this multilateral instrument to become an effective institutional structure. However, the temporary GATT agreement fulfilled its historical mission of guiding international trade for almost fifty years.

Three main objectives governed said agreement: (a) restrictions to the use of customs fees, (b) the suppression of non-tariff barriers, and (c) the end of discriminatory double standards among the countries.

On December 10, 1948, the UN set forth the Universal Declaration of Human Rights with Resolution # 27, providing Humanity with a secure and effective list whose composition consolidated the objective spirit of the planet in regards to inherent rights of each man and the whole man.

However, in an ill-omened contraposition that contradicted the civilizing milestone seen in the second half of the 20th century, the Capitalist South Africa was influenced by the abominated, defeated ideals of Nazism and instituted the *apartheid* policy (in Afrikaans:

separation). The racial segregation regime openly appropriated the rights of the black population, even though racial equality had been achieved in the 19th century with the aforementioned abolitionist movements.

In order to neutralize the risk of a Communist takeover, Japan and Europe received financial aid; the latter was rescued by the Marshall Plan. And so the world would remain divided between Capitalists and Communists: on May 23rd, 1949, as a result of the Cold War, the Federal Republic of Germany was created. It corresponded to the western side of the country that was influenced by United States, Great Britain and France, the Capitalist winners that were allies during World War II. In October of the same year, East Germany was formed in the area dominated by the Soviets.

In the clash between Capitalism and Communism, both sides took extreme positions, committing severe violations to Human Rights both in the Capitalist World and in the Socialist Bloc. In 1949, China adhered to Communism when a group led by Mao Tsé-Tung took power through revolution. Ten years later, in 1959, it was Cuba's turn, by the hands of Fidel Castro's guerrilla. In both cases, the victorious rebels were supported by the Soviet Union.

On June 17th, 1953, one million East Germans protested against the regime and were repressed by the Communist State; several of them were fatally wounded. On the other hand, in the 1960s and 1970s, the United States of America provided political and financial support to the military coups and right-wing regimes in Latin America, when violations to Human Rights became commonplace. That was the case in Brazil, Argentina, Chile and Uruguay, among others.

In South Asia, Capitalism and Communism collided to large warlike proportions. The conflict in Korea, initiated in the 1950s, resulted in millions of deaths and disabled. To this date, the country is still divided between North and South at the 38th parallel north. As for the unfortunately well-known Vietnam War, initiated in 1965, an equally countless amount of victims was recorded. In both cases, the United States of America deployed troops to prevent an invasion of the South by the North and the unification of the countries under a Communist regime supported by the Soviet Union.

The friction between the Capitalist and Communist blocs was close to a nuclear war in 1962, an event known as the Cuban Missile Crisis. In response to the U.S. nuclear missiles installed in Turkey in 1961, the Soviet Union installed nuclear missiles in Cuban territory and pointed them to the United States.

The Berlin Wall was a symbol of that time: it was first erected on August 13, 1961, thus solidifying the border between the two sides of the city that was divided, as Germany itself, into one area under the influence of Capitalism and, the other, of Socialism. On October 22 of that year, Soviet and U.S. tanks were face to face in Berlin during sixteen hours.

During this serious moment in history, the glorious voice of John XXIII is heard. Encyclical *Pacem in Terris*, which already foresaw the close ties between peace and economy, reminded us that "The wealthier States, therefore, while providing various forms of assistance to the poorer, must have the highest possible respect for the latter's national characteristics and time-honored civil institutions. They must also repudiate any policy of domination." If they do so, the Pontifex adds, "a precious contribution will have been made to the formation of a world community, in which each individual nation, conscious of its rights and duties, can work on terms of equality with the rest for the attainment of universal prosperity."[77]

Following the argument of pacification through economy, United Nations Conference on Trade and Development (UNCTAD) was established in 1964 to promote the integration of developing countries over into the world economy. Considering the important role attributed to UNCTAD, it is possible to identify UN's inclination toward economic integration among countries and global development. We can also say that this was the first step that the UN took to become, at its own time, a competent authority to guide the world through globalization, which back then had not been put into future perspective.

However, we must acknowledge that, as it was the case with GATT, UNCTAD did not receive enough powers to act in favor of an

---

[77] Item 125.

effective humanization of trade.

The world scenario was correctly described by the *Gaudium et Spes* Pastoral Constitution of 1965, which stated that "Nations on the road to progress, like those recently made independent, desire to participate in the goods of modern civilization, not only in the political field but also economically, and to play their part freely on the world scene. Still they continually fall behind while very often their economic and other dependence on wealthier nations advances more rapidly. People hounded by hunger call upon those better off."[78]

In 1966, in an attempt to overcome the world division between Communists and Capitalists, two international covenants on Human Rights are written within the framework of the UN: one on Civil Rights and the other on Economic, Social, and Cultural Rights. Some countries only signed one of them, according to their Capitalist or Socialist convictions. Others, like Brazil, signed both.

Excited with the ideas of Father Lebret, textually quoted in the Encyclical, Pope Paul VI publishes the *Populorum Progressio* in 1967. In addition to suggesting feasible means to include the spirit of Humanism in the current economic ideas of that time, he thoroughly describes the Christian view of economy.

The core of the issue can be found on item 14 of the pontifical document: "The development We speak of here cannot be restricted to economic growth alone. To be authentic, it must be well rounded; it must foster the development of each man and of the whole man. As an eminent specialist on this question has rightly said: 'We cannot allow economics to be separated from human realities, nor development from the civilization in which it takes place. What counts for us is man—each individual man, each human group, and humanity as a whole." The expert quoted is Father Lebret himself, whose *Concrete Dynamics of Development* was transcribed *ipsis litteris* by the Supreme Pontiff.

With the 1970s, however, after the Vietnam War and the consequent mass mobilization for democracy and peace, the Welfare

---

78 Concílio Ecumênico Vaticano II. *Gaudium et Spes*, Pastoral Constitution on the Church in the Modern World, of December 7th, 1965.

State starts to be rejected and seen as unnecessary in those countries where, upon the structural and conjectural reestablishment of economic health, social demands were met once again by the natural order of economy dynamics, through the creation of wealth, employment and tax revenues, in addition to the positive liberties previously addressed.

We need to mention that, in those days, the world was awakening to the finitude of natural resources in the planet, which led to the UN Conference on the Human Environment that took place in Stockholm in 1972 and acknowledged that "The natural resources of the earth, including the air, water, land, flora and fauna and especially representative samples of natural ecosystems, must be safeguarded for the benefit of present and future generations through careful planning or management, as appropriate." Thus the institutionalization of a universal awareness of planet sustainability was established.

The return to economic liberalism resulted in the creation of the Group of Seven (G7) in 1975, which included Germany, the United Kingdom, France, Italy, Japan, Canada and the United States of America (it is currently known as Group of Eight, or G8, after the inclusion of Russia,) that initiated and now leads the current economic globalization phenomenon.

In 1980, Pope John Paul II warned that, "It is obvious that a fundamental defect, or rather a series of defects, indeed a defective machinery is at the root of contemporary economics and materialistic civilization, which does not allow the human family to break free from such radically unjust situations."[79] In fact, these defects in how contemporary economics works were explained by the increase of wealth in wealthy nations and poverty in poor countries, an evidence of what we could call "social market failure."

In turn, we saw two important events in 1986.

On the one hand, the Uruguay Round was conducted within the framework of the GATT, spanning from 1986 to 1994 and resulting in the Final Act that would create the World Trade Organization (WTO). Upon embracing all the agreements and understandings cre-

---

79 *Dives in Misericordia*, item 11.

ated within the GATT scope since 1947, the WTO set a new foundation to validate what henceforth would be known as the GATT/1994. Within the new framework of negotiations for a global society, a diversified set of subjects would become the object of these understandings, thus sanctioning a neoliberal economic globalization. They included agriculture, health and phytosanitary measures, textiles and fabrics, technical obstacles to trade, trade-related investment measures, antidumping, customs valuation, pre-shipment inspection, origin rules, procedures related to importing licenses, safeguards, subsidies and compensation measures. In this neoliberal hindrance, due to the importance given to the services sector, GATT/1994 also comprised the General Agreement on Trade in Services (GATS) frame agreement, as well as the Agreement on Trade-Related Aspects of Intellectual Property Rights (TRIPS).[80]

On the other hand, also with the Uruguay Round in 1986, the UN established a new paradigm upon proclaiming the *Declaration on the Right to Development* as a catalog of Human Rights in the third dimension, bringing the macroeconomics issue to the table once and for all when discussing the effectiveness of Human Rights.

Nevertheless, we must not lose track of the unrelenting resistance. Pope John Paul II made sure to remind us of them upon celebrating the 20th anniversary of the *Populorum Progressio*, quoted in the Encyclical *Sollicitudo Rei Socialis*, published in 1987, upon writing the following warning: "Surmounting every type of imperialism and determination to preserve their own hegemony, the stronger and richer nations must have a sense of moral responsibility for the other nations, so that a real international system may be established which will rest on the foundation of the equality of all peoples and on the necessary respect for their legitimate differences. The economically weaker countries, or those still at subsistence level, must be enabled, with the assistance of other peoples and of the international community, to make a contribution of their own to the common good with

---

80 LAMPREIA. *Resultados da Rodada Uruguai: uma tentativa de síntese*, in: http://www.scielo.br/scielo.php?pid=S0103-40141995000100016&script=sci_arttext.

their treasures of humanity and culture, which otherwise would be lost for ever."[81]

On those very same days, there were rising attacks to the Welfare State, construed as inefficient and burdensome. From then on, the behavior of international financing organizations was very clear, chiefly the IMF, in their attempt to impose their unfailing neoliberal agenda to developing countries.

In fact, without not even vouchsafing to assume the fatherhood of this initiative, several economists associated with the IMF, the World Bank, and the U.S. Department of Treasury decided to establish the Washington Consensus in 1989, which consolidated the neoliberal agenda that, since then, has been imposed worldwide.

Within this new context of neoliberal global imposition, Socialism crumbled down due to its own lack of efficiency. In 1989, Hungary opens its borders with Austria and hundreds of eastern Germans flee the Communist regime. On November 9, 1989, East Germany authorizes individuals to cross the border to the West side of the country. The Berlin Wall comes down, and so does the Iron Curtain. On October 3, 1990, after 45 years of separation, Germany is unified once again. Finally, in December 1991, under the administration of Mikhail Gorbachev, the Soviet Union was dissolved and Socialism as a worldwide doctrine was declared defunct. At the same time, the former Communist nations started to adhere to the global Capitalism, especially after the right to private property was recognized in courts in China, even though strict restrictions over political liberties remained.

Structured by the fundamentalism of external negative liberties, in which property is a subjective natural right, the world has since then acquired predominantly neoliberal characteristics, notwithstanding the fact that the 1993 UN World Conference on Human Rights had adopted the Vienna Declaration and Programme of Action, which reasserted the solemn commitment made by Humanity to promote universal respect and observe Human Rights, without deviating from the focus of subduing neoliberalism.

---

81 Item 39.

Next, neoliberal economic globalization was sanctioned when the World Trade Organization (WTO) officially commenced in 1995 as a result of the Uruguay Round. With features borrowed from solidarism, it was shy to adopt the special treatment principle to developing countries, as established in Article 28 and Item 4 of the GATT/1994. According to said principle, developing countries would have tariff benefits and enjoy more favorable measures as applied by the developed nations. However, among the many mechanisms created within the modern WTO structure, perhaps the most important one is the so-called Dispute Settlement System. As per this mechanism, the safety and predictability of the multilateral trade system, which was patiently engineered by WTO regulations, started to find pertinent instances to deliberate over dispute settlement upon seeking a consensus among the arbiters of a Panel created within the framework of the Dispute Settlement Organization and, eventually, the Appeals Body that started to remarkably establish neoliberal jurisprudence.

For neoliberals, international intervention in view of free trade is restricted to seeking a consensus of this nature. Although laborious and oftentimes sluggish, it could bring about the aspiring peace in world economy relations, according to the neoliberal philosophy and the experience that such an institutional channel could provide.[82]

Concomitantly, to the relief of Human Rights advocates, South Africa put an end to *apartheid* in 1994 with multiracial democratic elections. The African National Congress led by Nelson Mandela prevailed, after he had spent 27 years in prison while fighting against this cruelty and ultimately received the Nobel Peace Prize in 1993.

On September 6-8, 2000, the Millennium Summit took place in New York. This unprecedented meeting was attended by 100 heads of state, 47 heads of government, three crown princes, five vice pres-

---

82 For a more encompassing analysis of the issue, please refer to Luiz Olavo Baptista *et alli*, *Dez anos de OMC – uma análise do sistema de solução de controvérsias e perspectivas*. São Paulo: Aduaneiras, 2007.

idents, three prime ministers and 8,000 delegates. It resulted in the UN Millennium Declaration, implementing the aforementioned eight general objectives known as Millennium Development Goals: (1) ending extreme poverty and hunger; (2) achieving elementary education universally; (3) promoting equality of gender and the autonomy of women; (4) reducing infant mortality; (5) improving the health of mothers; (6) fighting HIV/AIDS, malaria, and other severe illnesses; (7) assuring environmental sustainability, and (8) fostering a worldwide partnership toward development.

In 2007, 50 years after its inception, the European Union ratified the Lisbon Treaty, which entered into force in December 2009. The two most important decisions made in this historic document, from the perspective of a Humanistic Capitalism, was the proclamation of the bloc as a "social market economy,"[83] thus attesting to the irreversible inclusion of the social component into the economy, and the implementation of the Charter of Fundamental Rights of the European Union, a formal and solemn commitment to affirming and advocating for Human Rights.

Meanwhile, in 2008, on the other side of the Atlantic, a very severe financial crisis was taking shape in the United States of America. It was an unprecedented event for neoliberalism, and there was a risk of concrete economic collapse in the leading nation of global Capitalism, which would extend the resulting negative effects to the

---

83 Article 3, # 3, Lisbon Treaty. "The Union shall establish an internal market. It shall work for the sustainable development of Europe based on balanced economic growth and price stability, a highly competitive social market economy, aiming at full employment and social progress, and a high level of protection and improvement of the quality of the environment. It shall promote scientific and technological advance. It shall combat social exclusion and discrimination, and shall promote social justice and protection, equality between women and men, solidarity between generations and protection of the rights of the child. It shall promote economic, social and territorial cohesion, and solidarity among Member States. It shall respect its rich cultural and linguistic diversity, and shall ensure that Europe's cultural heritage is safeguarded and enhanced."

worldwide economy.

Due to this crisis, core Capitalist countries shifted to an economic government activism, thus redefining its role in global Capitalism. Upon being the supposedly protagonists of this economic coordination, they performed an intense intervention into the financial system and the market.

The U.S. government, for example, disregarded the neoliberal philosophy completely and disbursed an enormous amount of public funds to rescue its financial system and companies considered to be "too big to fail." They have even nationalized some companies, whether they were financial businesses or not, with the declared purpose of preventing their bankruptcy. It would protect the collapse of the financial system and the U.S. economy, in addition to avoiding mass unemployment and the loss of several savings and private insurance accounts, among other damages to the population. It would also refinance, secure, and take over a significant amount of defaulted mortgage payments.

When the crisis peaked Nicolas Sarkozy, who was then the President of France, remarked that "self-regulation as a way to resolve all problems has come to an end. *Laissez-faire* is over. The almighty market that knows it all is over."[84] Likewise, Germany's Minister of Finance asserted: "We need to civilize the financial markets, not only with moral arguments against excesses and speculation. Self-regulation is not enough anymore."[85]

Therefore, hastened by the global crisis of 2008, the current economic trend burned violently down to a global advent required by a social market economy that would season the subjective natural right to property with a social balance that would take liberties into account: a social market Capitalism.

With this crisis, one group was on the spotlight: Brazil, Russia, India, and China, or BRIC, are the four countries projected as the future world economic powers. On June 16, 2009 their first sum-

---

84 *Folha de S. Paulo*, 26.09.08, *Dinheiro* section, by the Correspondent in Geneva, p. B6.

85 Idem.

mit took place in Yekaterinburg, Russia. The declaration that resulted from this meeting pleaded to a multipolar world order.

The G8 lost significant terrain to G20, which brings together the Ministers of Finance and the chiefs of Central Banks from the main nineteen economies of the world (South Africa, Argentina, Brazil, Mexico, Canada, United States, China, Japan, South Korea, India, Indonesia, Saudi Arabia, Turkey, France, Germany, Italy, Russia, United Kingdom and Australia,) in addition to the European Union.

The opening of the final declaration of the G20 summit in Toronto, which took place with the presence of the G8 on June 27, 2010, already self-recognizes the group as the main international forum for economic cooperation.

In the aforementioned declaration, the G20 observes that, by building upon its accomplishments concerning the economic crisis, the countries that are part of the group agree that their next steps must be to assure the complete return to development, with quality employment, in order to reform and strengthen the financial system and promote a strong, sustainable, and egalitarian global growth.

In this manner, considering the G20 commitment of which Brazil is a member, we would walk toward a social market economy moving forward.

Notwithstanding the fact that the worldwide community is facing the aforementioned crisis and its effects with sobriety, the threat of a new problematic episode is looming, chiefly because the bill of the recent state interventionism has not been paid yet after promoting the economic salvation of the international financial system. For this bill to be paid, it is necessary to implement "a new Humanistic synthesis," according to the teachings of Benedict XVI,[86] that is capable of overcoming even the market social economy through the complete realization of multidimensional Human Rights, aimed at achieving overall Human Dignity through a required path for the healthy victory of a Capitalism that relies on a fraternal society.[87]

---

86 *Caritas in Veritate*, item 21.

87 FELICE. *L´economia sociale di mercato*, p. 74, verbis: *"piuttosto nel campo dela filosofia sociale quanto di meglio ci hanno potuto tramandare ter milleni*

In a 2010 General Assembly Resolution, the UN includes access to drinking water and basic sanitation to the universal catalog of Human Rights, which clearly shows its concern with the bare necessities required by human beings.

On our part, we hope that market Capitalism evolve to be driven by humanism and committed to the concretization of Human Rights in all their dimensions, willing to acknowledge the objective inherent right to dignity for Man, Mankind, and the Planet.

Therefore, we hope that the Humanistic Capitalism be the sign of the times for the third millennium of the Christian civilization, which draws upon the supreme values that synthesize a fraternal universal society to consecrate a rightful Humanistic Planet.

(2) Within Brazil

In regards to Brazil, the following events of the Colonial Period must be emphasized: inexistence of political autonomy, Portugal's trade monopoly, Minas Gerais Conspiracy ("Inconfidência Mineira," a movement that superseded the national Enlightenment independence and was contemporary to the French Revolution,) and the opening of ports in 1808, when the Portuguese kingdom was transferred to Brazil with the proclamation of the December 16th Law of 1815, signed by John VI, which elevated the country to the status of member of the United Kingdom of Portugal, Brazil and the Algarves.

Brazil proclaimed its independence in September 7th, 1822, thus becoming a monarchy. In 1824, the first Constitution takes effect. Placing himself at the center of the political scene, Emperor Pedro I exercised Reserve Powers, which according to Article 98 of said Constitution was the key to all political organization within the Empire and granted him authority to assure the maintenance of inde-

---

del pensiero occidentale, l´idea di umanità, il diritto di natura, la cultura della persona e il senso dell´universalita."

pendence and the balance and harmony of all other political powers.

Nevertheless, Article 179 of that Constitution recognized the sanctity of the civil and political rights of Brazilian citizens, based on liberty, individual safety, and property. Right to property was fully warranted in Section 22, while Section 24 ensured the practice of any occupation, culture, industry, or trade inasmuch as the activity did not disturb public behavior, safety, and the health of citizens.

In this manner, a liberal-aristocratic economic regime managed Brazilian economy, which at the time was essentially based on agriculture and exports, with economic relations being governed by the Trade Code of 1850.

Back then, the European civilizing process had started to oppose slavery. Commercial interests in Brazil and abroad, chiefly those of Great Britain, indicated the need for the Brazilian domestic market to develop into a market based on free labor, with liberties assured to every race. This was certainly one of the ideological sources of the abolitionist movement that achieved liberty and racial equality for all Brazilians. Consequently, the national legislation granted all citizens a title to the subject inherent rights of the human condition.

Following this new reality, on September 4, 1850 the Eusébio de Queirós Law (# 581) was passed to prohibit the international traffic of slaves to Brazil, making it a crime; on September 28th, 1871 the Freedom of the Wombs Law ("Lei do Ventre Livre" # 2,040) freed all children born to slave parents; on September 28, 1885 the Saraiva-Cotegipe Law, known as the "Sexagenarian Law" (# 3,270), set forth the gradual extinction of servitude, and finally, in May 13, 1888 the Golden Law ("Lei Áurea" # 3,353)[88] abolished slavery once and

---

88 The complete text, published in the *Diário Oficial do Império*, deserves to be transcribed here: "*Slavery is hereby declared abolished in Brazil: The Regent Princess Imperial, in the name of His Majesty the Emperor, Dom Pedro II, brings to the attention of all subjects of the Monarchy that the General Assembly has proclaimed the following decree, which she has sanctioned into law: Article 1st: Slavery is hereby declared abolished in Brazil from the date this law comes into effect. Article 2: All provisions contrary to it are hereby revoked. Therefore, it is ordered that all authorities, to whom the knowledge*

for all.

On November 15th, 1889, under the political positivism ideal, the Republic was proclaimed in the country and the first Republican Constitution was adopted in 1891. In Article 72, it assured the sacred rights to individual liberty and safety to all Brazilians and foreigners living in the country. In Paragraph 17, it assured full and warranted rights to property and, in Paragraph 24, the free exercise of any moral, intellectual, and industrial activity. In the same Article, pursuant to the principles exhibited in Paragraph 22, *habeas corpus* was instituted as a more extensive right than currently, inasmuch as an individual were the victim or believed to be in imminent risk of suffering violence or coercion due to unlawful act or abuse of power. It was very close to the Last Resort Constitutional Appeal found in the Spanish Legislation.

The liberal-aristocratic nature of Brazilian economy did not find continuity with the advent of the Republic. Within such a scenario, the Civil Code of 1916 would be written with clear Enlightened and individualistic bias.

After the Revolution of 1930,[89] industrialization flourished. With the Constitutionalist Revolution of 1932, the State of São Paulo signed its surrender. Brazil, however, adopted the Constitution of 1934 with clear influences of Weimar's social constitutionalism.[90] Al-

---

and execution of the aforementioned law is attributed, shall enforce and assure the enforcement of this law on the matters contained therein. The Secretary of State for Agricultural Affairs, Commerce, and Public Works and Provisional Secretary of Foreign Affairs, Mr. Rodrigo Augusto da Silva, a Counsel for His Majesty the Emperor, shall print, publish, and distribute it. Signed at the Rio de Janeiro Palace, May 13, 1888, the 67th Year of our Independence and Monarchy. The Regent Princess Imperial Rodrigo Augusto da Silva. Letter of Law, in which Her Imperial Highness orders for the execution of the General Assembly Decree, sanctioned by her, declaring that slavery was thereby abolished in Brazil."

89 FURTADO. *Formação econômica do Brasil*, p. 199.

90 PERI GUEDES. *Estado e ordem econômica e social – A experiência constitucional da república de Weimar e a Constituição brasileira de 1934.*

though Article 113 assured sacred rights to liberty, subsistence, individual safety, and property to Brazilians and foreigners living in the country, it was the end of the economic liberalism in Brazil, since Item # 13 set forth that individuals were free to seek any occupation, inasmuch as the conditions provided by Law and dictated by public interests were observed. Item # 17 assured the right to property. However, it could not be exercised against the social or collective interest, according to the applicable law. This Constitution actually records, for the very first time, the Economic and Social Order that, pursuant to Article 115, provides for an organized economic order that complies with the principles of justice and the needs of national living in order to make a dignified existence something achievable for all.

Such a model would be reinforced by the Constitution of 1937 due to the totalitarian political regime established then and known as The New State ("Estado Novo.") Article 136 imposed a legitimate economic statism with a market central command. It expressly indicated that, "The national wealth and prosperity finds its foundations in the self-initiative and the individual power for creation, organization, and invention exercised within the limitations of commonweal. State intervention can only be legitimate in the economic realm when self-initiative is lacking and when it coordinates the factors of production in order to avoid and resolve conflicts or introduce the inception of national interest in the game of individual competitions. The intervention in the economic realm may be direct or indirect, supporting the form of control, stimulus, or direct management."

The main character of those times was President Getúlio Vargas, who intervened intensely in matters of economy. For example, the Vargas Era included the direct management of the National Iron Smelting Company, the Consolidation of Labor Laws (Law Decree # 5,452 of 1943), the Usury Law (Decree # 22, 626 of 1933), the Oil Law (Law Decree # 395 of 38) and the Law of Crimes Against the People's Economy (Law Decree # 869 of 1938), the first Brazilian law with antitrust features. Law Decree # 7,666 of 1945, known as the "Malayan Law," was the first specific norm to suppress the abuse of economic power. The United States of America considered it an instrument of economic nationalism in the hands of the federal government,[91] even though the U.S. had passed a law of the same nature fifty years earlier. Not even the forests were left behind: the Vargas Era also addressed the first Forest Code of Brazil, instituted with Decree # 23,793 of 1934.

Until October 31st, 1942 the Brazilian currency was the *milréis*, later replaced by *cruzeiro* (represented by Cr$) with Law Decree # 4,791 of 1942.[92]

In response to the totalitarian New State, the Federal Constitution of 1946 was adopted after Getúlio Vargas was removed from government. Article 145 set forth that "The economic order must be organized according to the principles of social justice, reconciling free enterprise and the valorization of human labor." As seen here, even though it translated into a reaction against the previous political regime, as far as the economic order was concerned the new Constitution preserved the centralized command of Capitalism and maintained the commonweal State, thus preserving the social rights acquired before.[93] Law # 1,521 of 1951 on the Crimes Against the People's Economy and Law # 1,522 of 1951, which authorized the federal government to intervene in the economic realm in order to assure the free distribution of products necessary to the consumption of the nation, also dated from this time.

Another outstanding moment in Brazilian history was the JK Era, whose main character was Juscelino Kubitschek. In 1956 he triggered an important developmental surge to replace imports with a State economic planning focused on social welfare. Known as the Goals Program ("Programa de Metas,") the slogan "Fifty years of progress in five" translated the ideal accelerated growth that JK wished that Brazil would experience. The program had thirty goals, among them the implementation of an automobile industry in national territory at a time when the so-called "auto society" was globally evident.

The JK administration was successful in leading the nation toward an average 8% annual growth, but the country had to face an

---

91 FORGIONI. *Os fundamentos do antitruste*, p. 111.

92 NEGRÃO AND GOUVÊA. *Código civil*, p. 1394.

93 NAZAR. *Direito econômico*, p. 59.

unstable currency that doubled the annual inflation from 20% to 40%, something that the President had done deliberately.

During this developmental leap, the Antitrust Law (Law # 4,137 of 1962) was edited.

In 1964, a military coup took down João Goulart, who was then the President of Brazil. A totalitarian political regime was implemented and a substantially interventionist State was instituted with the Constitution of 1967 and the Constitutional Amendment # 1 of 1969. The new set of governing principles maintained the constitutionalization of the economic order in Article 160, which was subordinated to state interests and preserved the centralized command of Capitalism.

Those days, state interventionism was unrestrictedly imposed upon the financial system with Law # 4,595 of 1964, which instituted the normative power of the National Monetary Council in order to "formulate currency and credit policies."[94]

The new order had two other initial acts: The new Forest Code, with Law # 4,771 dated September 15, 1965, and the replacement of the national currency, whose name was changed from *cruzeiro* to *cruzeiro novo* (represented by NCr$)[95], pursuant to Decree # 60,190 dated February 8th, 1967.

In regards to its authoritarian profile, the military government issued Decree # 58,563 of 1966, which ratified the decision of the National Congress to approve "with Legislative Decree # 66 of 1965, the Slavery Convention that was signed in Geneva on September 25, 1926 and later amended by its subsequent Protocol open to signatures at the United Nations Headquarters in New York on December 7th, 1953, as well as the Supplementary Convention on the Abolition of Slavery, the Slave Trade, and Institutions and Practices Similar to Slavery, adopted in Geneva on September 7th, 1956."

Consumer and market protection was exercised through institutional mechanisms of direct control, namely the Interministerial

---

94 Article 2.

95 NEGRÃO AND GOUVÊA. Op. and p. cits.

Council for Prices (CIP), implemented by Decree # 63,196 of 1968[96] and validated by Law Decree # 808 of 1968,[97] whose legal attribution was to set prices and enforce the domestic market price policy in order to harmonize it with global economic and financial policies. In fact, the Brazilian government would mandatorily lead the financial system, the market and, thereby, the universality of economic segments.

It is worth mentioning the unfortunately well-known Institutional Act # 5 of 1968 that seized the fundamental rights of Brazilians, banning the universal remedy of *habeas corpus* for both political crimes and those against the economic and social order and the people's economy.[98]

Facilitating industrial development and corporate concentration was a trademark of the military era in 1971, especially with plans to foster the national economy, as those implemented by the National Development Plan I approved with Law # 5,727 of 1971. The plan aimed at "injecting life into the private sector, originated from a new corporate concept, leaning toward mergers and modern production and trade structures," [99]which once again encouraged an uncontrolled inflation.

In 1974, the National Development Plan II emphasized basic

---

96 Decree # 63,196 of 1968, Article 1st. – "The Interministerial Council for Prices (CIP) is hereby created with the purpose of setting prices and enforcing measures intended to implement a system that will regulate prices, as provided in this Decree, while observing the general orientation of the Federal Government's economic policy."

97 Law Decree # 808 of 1968, Article 1st. – "The Interministerial Council for Prices (CIP), implemented by Decree # 63,196 of August 29, 1968, is the organization through which the Federal Goverment shall set prices and enforce the domestic market price policy in order to harmonize it with global economic and financial policies."

98 AI 5 – Article 10 – "The writ of habeas corpus is hereby suspended in cases of political crimes and crimes commited against national security, the economic and social order, and the People's economy."

99 BULGARELLI. *O direito dos grupos e a concentração de empresas*, p. 39.

consumption goods, infrastructure, and energy resources as the foundation for economic growth in Brazil. As a result, the national economy in that period was intertwined with an intense State Capitalism.

Law # 6,938 of 1981 is equally worth noting, for it provided for a National Environmental Policy, its purposes and formation and application mechanisms.

On August 15, 1984 Law # 7,214 brought back the *cruzeiro* and its former symbol (Cr$) as the national currency.[100]

With the end of the military regime, the Cruzado Plan was implemented according to the terms of Law Decree # 2,283 of February 27, 1986, when José Sarney was the President of the Republic. The goal was to create a price table and freeze wages to fight inflation. *Cruzeiro* was replaced with *cruzado* (represented by Cz$) and a series of monetary shocks took place in the country.

By the end of the 1980s, still during the Sarney Administration, the country was redemocratized with the proclamation of the current Federal Constitution in October 5th, 1998. Under the aegis of a so-called "Citizen Constitution," State interventionism diminished and the principle of Subsidiarity was acknowledged in State Intervention with Article 174 of the Federal Constitution of 1988.

However, with Article 1st, Paragraph 4, and Article 170, the new Constitution did not overlook the social values of labor and free enterprise as fundamental precepts of an economic order, thus assuring a dignified existence to everyone pursuant to the principles of social justice. Consequently, the following principles must be observed: national sovereignty, private property, social role of ownership, consumer protection, environmental protection, free competition, closing the gap of social and regional inequalities, full employment, assistance to small domestic businesses, and suppression of abuse of economic power.

Moreover, Article 6 of the 1988 Constitution also implemented a series of social rights that included "education, health, work, leisure, safety, social security, maternity and childhood protection, and assistance to the destitute." With Article 225, it recognizes that "every-

---

100 NEGRÃO AND GOUVÊA. Op. and p. cits.

one has the right to an ecologically balanced environment, a property of common use that is essential to a healthy quality of life, which the Public Authorities and the collective must protect and preserve for present and future generations."

On January 15th, 1989 the national currency was replaced once more: *Cruzado* gave room to *cruzado novo* (represented by NCz$), pursuant to the terms of Provisional Measure # 32.

As a result of the new Constitutional Regime, the traditional economy intervention was moved from the centralized power of the State to the natural forces of the market. In fact, in the early 1990s, the administration of President Fernando Collor dissolved the Welfare State and led the country toward a market economy, so much so that a National Privatization Program was implemented with Law # 8,031 of 1990, whose fundamental purpose was to organize the State's strategic position within the economy, transferring it to the private enterprise. Companies that were directly or indirectly controlled by the State had their ownership transferred, even though the State and the market continued to share control over corporate resolutions and jointly elect members of the Board in certain sectors.

The new president inaugurated his administration with an economic shock known as The Collor Plan, with Provisional Measure # 168 dated March 15th, 1990. Once again the national currency would be called *cruzeiro*, represented by the original symbol (Cr$). This Plan also confiscated the financial assets of individuals through the Central Bank, which ultimately was rejected by the Judiciary Branch to assure the right to property.[101]

It was only with the Real Plan, implemented by the Itamar Franco Administration in April 28th, 1994 through Provisional Measure # 482, that the country achieved monetary stability and was able to keep inflation to an acceptable level. *Cruzado novo* was then replaced by *real* (represented by R$).

Until then, considering the severe inflation rate, monetary correction was extensively legislated by Law # 5,670 of 1971, which governed inflation calculations and, more prominently, supervised

---

101 NEGRÃO AND GOUVÊA. Op. cit., pp. 1375-1376.

economic plans in order to keep the national currency stable amid the continuous substitutions and replacements.

The Fernando Henrique Cardoso Administration (1995-2000) kept the National Privatization Program, but implemented changes through Law # 9,491 of 1997 to better coordinate a strategic position for the State within the economy, transferring it to private enterprise by restructuring the public sector in regards to activities that had not been properly explored, especially concerning the modernization of infrastructure and the national industrial complex. The purpose was to extend competition and strengthen corporate capacity in different economic sectors, including through credit extensions. Once economic policies were changed, the Brazilian State became better adjusted to the social market economy.

By the end of the Fernando Henrique Cardoso Administration, with Constitutional Amendment # 26 of 2000, housing was added to the list of social rights set forth in Article 6 of the Federal Constitution.

Another effort made by the Fernando Henrique Cardoso Administration with Constitutional Amendment # 31, of 2000, whose Article 1st changed the Temporary Constitutional Provisions Act to implement a Fund to Fight and Eradicate Poverty within the framework of the Federal Executive Branch, Article 79. With the purpose of giving every Brazilian access to dignified levels of subsistence, Fund resources would be applied to supplementary efforts in support of nutrition, housing, education, health, and household income, among other programs of relevant social interest aimed at improving quality of life.

Still during the Fernando Henrique Administration, a new Civil Code was sanctioned in 2002 to reinforce the inclusion of Brazil in the social market economy. It granted features of sociality and ethics to private judicial relations, thus instituting legal instruments as the center of interests around which the community shall move.

President Luis Inácio da Silva, known as "Lula," was inaugurated on January 1st, 2003 and, despite leaning toward nationalization, his administration kept Brazil within the social market economy. It removed the Piauí and Santa Catarina State Banks from the

National Privatization Program through Decrees # 6,380 of 2007 and 6,502 of 2008, respectively. However, Companhia Energética do Amazonas was added to the program through Decree # 6,026 of 2007.

During his administration, Lula rendered market economy important, strengthened the middle class, and emphatically fought poverty. Within the framework of the Presidency of the Republic, the Family Allowance Program ("Bolsa Família") was implemented with Law # 10,836 of January 9th, 2004 and received the praises of the United Nations. Intended to provide direct financial aid to those living on or below the poverty line, this program was implemented with the purpose to consolidate how the Federal Government manages and performs cash transfers, especially through the National Minimum Income Program associated with the Education Department, known as School Assistance ("Bolsa Escola") and implemented with Law # 10,219 of April 11th, 2001; the National Food Access Program (PNAA, "Programa Nacional de Acesso à Alimentação") created by Law # 10,689 of June 13th, 2003; the National Minimum Income Program associated with the Health Department, known as Food Assistance ("Bolsa Alimentação") and implemented with Provisional Measure # 2,206-1 of September 6th, 2001; the Gas Assistance Program, implemented with Decree # 4,102 of January 24th, 2002, and the sole registration with the Federal Government, instituted by Decree # 3,877 of July 24th, 2001.

The Family Allowance Program consisted of financial benefits through direct cash transfers to beneficiaries, namely (i) basic benefits for households in extreme poverty and (ii) viable benefits for households living on or below the poverty line and that included expectant or nursing mothers, children from zero to twelve years of age, or teenagers of thirteen to fifteen years of age.

With Constitutional Amendment # 64 of 2010, the Lula Administration added nourishment to the list of social rights in Article 6 of the Federal Constitution.

Facilitated by the National Monetary Council and the Brazilian Central Bank, whose authority remains as granted by Law # 4,595 of 1964, the domestic financial system was kept uninterruptedly under the stern hand of the Federal Government, more emphatically after the 1960s as a trace of the totalitarian regime of that era.

In order to offset the lack of direct public government throughout the neoliberal period between the Collor and the Lula administrations, the Brazilian State issued specific norms in an attempt to legally correct all distortions created by the free market in several economic segments. One of them was Law 8,078 of 1990, known as the Consumer Protection Code (CDC), which was updated by the following laws: # 8,656 of 1993, # 8,703 of 1993, # 8,884 of 1994, # 9,008 of 1995, # 9,298 of 1996, # 9,870 of 1999, # 11,785 of 2008, # 11,800 of 2008, # 11,989 of 2009 and # 12,039 of 2009. Another example is Law # 8,137 of 1990, which defines Crimes Against the Economic Order and Consumer Relations and was updated by the following laws: # 8,176 of 1991, # 8,383 of 1991, # 8,884 of 1994 and # 9,080 of 1995. It is also worth mentioning Law # 8,176 of 1991, which defines other Crimes Against the Economic Order, and Law # 8,884 of 1994, with provisions to Prevent and Restrain Violations to the Economic Order, updated by Laws # 9,021 of 1995, # 9,069 of 1995, # 9,470 of 1997, # 9,873 of 1999, # 10,149 of 2000, # 10,843 of 2004 and # 11,482 of 2007, in addition to Law # 9,018 of 1995 that set forth the commercial defense of the Brazilian Industry within the framework of international trade by enforcing the rights provided by agreements on antidumping and subsidies and compensatory rights.

Plenty of environmental laws were also written after the Federal Constitution of 1988. Here are the most important ones: Law # 7,653 of 1988 updated the contents of Articles 18, 27, 33 and 34 of Law # 5,197 of 1967, which addressed animal life protection; Law # 7,661 of 1988 implemented the National Coastal Management Plan; Law # 7,754 of 1989 set forth measures to protect existing forests in the source of rivers; Law # 7,802 of 1989 addressed pesticides, their components and other related subjects, including research, trials, production, packaging, storage, labeling, transportation, commercialization, advertising, use, importing, exporting, disposal of waste and containers, registration, classification, control, inspection, and supervision; Law # 7,803 of 1989 updated the contents of Law # 4,771 of 1965 and revoked Laws # 6,535 of 1978 and # 7,511 of 1986; Law # 8,005 of 1990 addressed the collection of and updates to credits held by the

Brazilian Institute of Environment and Renewable Natural Resources (IBAMA); Law # 8,974 of 1995 regulated Sections 2 and 5, 1st Paragraph, Article 225 of the Federal Constitution, setting forth norms for the use of genetic engineering techniques and release of genetically-modified organisms to the environment, authorizing the Executive Branch to create a National Biosafety Technical Commission within the framework of the Presidency of the Republic; Law # 9,433 of 1997 implemented the National Policy on Water Resources, creating the National Water Resources Management System that regulates Section 19, Article 21 of the Federal Constitution and updates Article 1st, Law # 8,001 of 1990, which in turn had modified Law # 7,990 of 1989; Law # 9,605 of 1998, known as the "Environmental Crimes Act," addressed criminal and administrative sanctions resulting from conducts and activities detrimental to the environment; Law # 9,795 of 1999, the Environmental Education Law, addressed environmental education and created a National Policy on Environmental Education; Law # 9,966 of 2000 addressed the prevention, control, and supervision of pollution caused by oil and other harmful substances being poured into waters within national jurisdiction; Law # 9,984 of 2000 addressed the creation of the National Water Agency (ANA), a federal entity that would enforce the National Policy on Water Resources and coordinate the National Water Resources Management System; Law # 9,985 of 2000 regulated Article 225, Paragraph 1st, Items 1, 2, 3 and 7 of the Federal Constitution, creating the National System of National Preservation Units; Law # 10,165 of 2000 updated Law # 6,938 of 1981 that provided for a National Environmental Policy, its purposes and formation and application mechanisms; Law # 10,650 of 2003 addressed the public access to data and information stored by the organizations and associations that are part of the National Environmental System (SISNAMA); Law # 11,284 of 2006 addressed the management of public forests and sustainable production, in addition to creating the Brazilian Forest Services (SFB) and the National Fund for Forest Development (FNDF) and updating Laws # 10,683 of 2003, # 5,868 of 1972, # 9,605 of 1998, # 4,771 of 1965, # 6,938 of 1981 and # 6,015 of 1973; Law # 11,428 of 2006 addressed the use and protection of the native vegetation in the Atlantic Forest Biome, and

Law # 12,305 of 2010, created the National Policy on Solid Waste and updated Law # 9,605 of 1998.[102]

Within this context, since those privatizations took place, the Fernando Henrique Cardoso Administration structured Brazil as a standardized State that regulates economic activity and environmental sustainability, which President Lula reaffirmed until the end of this term. Leaning toward a nationalizing philosophy, Lula had important programs under his command, such as the Growth Acceleration Program (PAC, "Programa de Aceleração do Crescimento") and management proposals for the oil found in the pre-salt layer in Brazil. However, acting directly into the capital market through Petrobras, in 2010 his administration was responsible for the largest financial funding within the open market in the history of the country in order to explore the pre-salt layer.

Therefore, upon emphasizing the idea of social market economy while being aware of the dynamics of the market itself, the Lula Administration did not abandon economic coordination: They kept, at the same time, intense monitoring and regulation until the end of the term.

According to the December 2010 CNI/ IBOPE survey, Lula ended his two consecutive four-year terms as president with an 87% approval rate from the Brazilian population. Still in 2010, Marina Silva was a candidate for the Presidency and received approximately 20% of the votes due to her environmental sustainability platform.

Within the current historical moment and due to the Global Capitalist Crisis, economic neoliberalism has been deeply affected, which will certainly worsen the human and planetary social deficit. Such reality, however, does not support any hypothesis that would lead to a change in gears by the Dilma Rousseff Administration toward Socialism.

On the contrary, the Dilma Administration has been giving continuity and implementing the economic and social policies of her predecessor. On her inauguration speech, she stated that fighting extreme poverty is her most fundamental goal and, with her social

---

102 Source: http://www.conama.gov.br.

accomplishments, she has already created the No Poverty in Brazil Plan ("Plano Brasil sem Miséria") to identify families who are living below the poverty line and provide assistance to them through social programs.

In fact, Brazil needs to become more aware of Capitalism and we hope that this book will contribute to it. Under the current political and institutional circumstances, as mentioned earlier[103] and while keeping in mind the undoubtful reach of Human Rights on account of the economic order and considering the fact that the introduction to Article 170 of the Constitution is aimed at assuring a dignified existence to every one according to the principles of social justice,[104] we must acknowledge that Brazil contemplates a Humanistic Capitalism market within its constitutional positivation, to which the planetary dignity scope must certainly be incorporated as well.

---

103 SAYEG. *O Capitalismo humanista no Brasil*, pp. 1250-1264.

104 This is also Matsushita's philosophy, as stated in *Análise reflexiva da regra matriz da ordem econômica.*

IV
INTEGRAL HUMANISM

(1) Definition Of Integral Humanism

"Certainly, the origins of Humanism can be traced to classical Greek civilization,"[105] represented by the myth of Antigone, in view of the "attribution of universal rights engineered by a natural cosmic law," [106] Wolkmer reports.

The anthropocentric principle that "man is the measure of all things" is attributed to Protagoras.[107] However, "in Ancient times, men were valued by their possessions, qualities, and heroic feats; thereby the poor, women, and slaves were not included in such concept."[108] This perspective, which carried Humanistic characteristics, referred to "man as citizen,"[109] as Aristotle once corrected, disassociating the concept of Man from human gender, and especially from those less materially fortunate ones.

Jesus Christ goes beyond with his message of universal fraternity, creating an anthropophilic humanism in view of the human race,

---

105 *Fundamentos do humanismo jurídico no ocidente*, p. 12.

106 Idem, p. 13.

107 LALANDE. *Vocabulário técnico e crítico da filosofia*, p. 479.

108 WOLKMER. *Fundamentos do humanismo jurídico no ocidente*, p. 16.

109 Idem, p. 201.

which is deciphered into Law in the natural rights concept through the Aristotelian teachings of Saint Thomas Aquinas. "This new cosmovision presented by Christianity proclaims that Human Dignity encompasses equal relationship among all Men, since they are not only equal, but brothers, and they are all sons of the same celestial God; therefore, fraternity is considered an absolute value, an essential element to Christian Humanism," Wolkmer highlights.[110]

Reale emphasizes that "with the advent of Christianity, a fundamental and definite distinction has been made between Politics and Religion, between the sphere of the State and Man's field of action, since he is not only worthy as a citizen, but as a man."[111] He continues to state that "it is well known that the idea of a Natural Law, as strongly stated in Socratic and Aristotelian thoughts, in Stoicism, as well as the works of Cicero and Roman jurisconsults, acquires a different meaning in the Christian culture coordinates, not only upon becoming a conscience law, an interior law, but also considered to be inscribed by God in the heart of Men."[112]

However, this theocentric thought from Christian Humanism (God created Man and the Universe, thus He is at the center of everyone and everything[113]) gave room to regrettable extremist interpretations in the Middle Ages, which were sectarian and excluded non-Christians, as shown by the historical example of the Inquisition[114] that spanned three centuries and progressed to this day, with Christian Nazis like Carl Schmitt, who unfortunately distorted the Catholic doctrine of love that is clearly pronounced in Encyclical *Deus Caritas Est* by Pope Benedict XVI.

Just as it happened with Nazism, historian Francisco Bethencourt wrote that "the inquisitions also participated actively in the process of excluding social groups, thus contributing strongly to the

---

110 Ibidem, p. 16.

111 VILLEY. *Filosofia do direito*, p. 636.

112 Idem, p. 637.

113 The expression "everything," in this context, refers to "all things," considering that "everything" is the work of God as the creator of the Universe.

114 BETHENCOURT. *História das inquisições*, p. 405.

consolidation of prejudice based on cleanliness of blood."[115]

Enlightenment, both in its radical (e.g. Spinoza) and moderate (e.g. Locke, Newton, and Voltaire) positions, built another vision of humanism: individualistic, bourgeois, anthropocentric, and secular. As a reaction to Fundamentalism, Enlightenment placed Man at the center of things, in an independent position in regards to the Church and the State and consequently assuring religious, political, and economic liberty through private property, as well as formal equality among Men. Consequently, it allowed economic liberalism to flourish.

Evidence of that are Locke's *Letters on Toleration*, which supported the natural right to religious liberty and private property, in addition to opposing a despotic State as an oppressor of said liberties, as indicated further below.

Taking into account different expressions of Humanism, Lalande warns us about "the ambiguity of the term, even when reduced to its principal meanings."[116] Assuming an anthropocentric position, Lalande defines Humanism as "a reflected anthropocentrism that, starting with Man's conscience, is aimed at attributing value to Man; an exclusion made of that which alienates Man from himself, whether it subjects Man to superhuman truths and powers, or disfigures him due to any subhuman utilization."[117]

Other philosophers do not accept a Humanism founded in theological issues either, even though they do not denounce the Christian sources of Western Humanism. However, the Christian philosophy of universal Fraternity was a pioneer in assuring the value of life and dignity to each individual, encompassing all human races.

Maritain explicitly refutes said definitions of Humanism as individualistic, bourgeois, anthropocentric, and secular upon asserting that "we must be warned against defining Humanism by excluding all reference to the superhuman and by foreswearing all transcen-

---

115 Idem, p. 407.
116 Ibidem, p. 482.
117 Ibidem, p. 481.

dence."[118] Following the same train of thought and quoting Maritain, Pope Paul VI demands that Integral Humanism be assured "to promote the good of every man and of the whole man,"[119] meaning that it is all-encompassing and reaches both human existence and its essence, that is, dignity (which in a Secular State is a legal secularization of the human soul) in the name of all Humankind and the Planet. Said perspective is a contraposition to the pessimistic, selfish, and individualistic existentialism of Sartre, Nietzsche, and Schopenhauer.

Without returning to Medieval times, Maritain defines Integral Humanism as "This new humanism, which has in it nothing in common with bourgeois humanism, and is all the more human since it does not worship man, but has a real and effective respect for Human Dignity, and for the rights of human personality, I see as directed towards a socio-temporal realization of that evangelical concern for humanity which ought not to exist only in the spiritual order, but to become incarnate; and towards the ideal of a true brotherhood among men."[120] Incidentally, it is important to remember that the supreme value of a Fraternal Society is included as synthesis of the mission stated in the preamble of the Brazilian Federal Constitution of 1988.

This Humanism that fulfills Human Dignity brings with it the idea of Fraternity as the center of gravity, the gravitational element that consolidates Liberty, Equality, and itself. According to the Houaiss dictionary, Fraternity is "kinship between brothers, brotherhood," "unity, affection from brother to brother," or "altruism." Considering the current meaning, it is the core value of Christianity that identifies everyone as brothers united in love.

Jesus Christ has taught us that, beyond equal, we are brothers. Inspired by him, Pope Benedict XIV states that "Union with Christ is also union with all those to whom he gives himself."[121] Therefore, there is "unbreakable bond between love of God and love of neigh-

---

118 MARITAIN. *Humanismo integral*, p. 2.

119 *Populorum Progressio*, item 42.

120 MARITAIN. Op. cit., p. 6.

121 POPE BENEDICT XVI. Encyclical *Deus Caritas Est*, item 14.

bor,"[122] for said love "comes from God and unites us to God; through this unifying process it makes us a 'we' which transcends our divisions and makes us one."[123]

According to Kant, "human actions, like every other natural event, are determined by universal laws."[124] Consequently, in Fraternity, we are all at the same time originators and recipients of the Law of Universal Fraternity consecrated by Integral Humanism and culturally applicable to everyone and everything.

Nobody, in their right mind, could deny the universal value of Fraternity. It is not without reason that fraternity is celebrated in the French Revolution's historical and glorious motto. It is a precursor to the Rule of Law and is also in Article 1st of the Universal Declaration of Human Rights that is widely confirmed by the peoples of the planet.

According to Canotilho, rights and liberties are "rights fundamentally associated to the assurance of one's own political liberty and to the pursuit of solidarity and fraternity ideals."[125] Within this scope, Integral Humanism as an expression of the Law of Universal Fraternity is the map that deciphers the Natural Law of Fraternity in favor of the whole each man and the whole man, as well as of the Planet.

As a constitutional category, imprinted in Article 3, Section 1 of the Federal Constitution, Fraternity in Brazil is indisputably ascertained in the principle that sets the objective of a solidarity society. It is also qualified in Section 3 of the aforementioned Article, which also sets the objective of eradicating poverty and marginalization, as well as social and regional inequalities.

The precedents set by the Supreme Federal Court, Direct Unconstitutionality Actions # 2,649, and Ordinary Writ of Mandamus # 26,071 proclaim a fraternal society as the supreme value of the legal

---

122 Idem, item 16.

123 Ibidem, item 18.

124 KANT. *Ideia de uma história universal de um ponto de vista cosmopolita*, p. 4.

125 CANOTILHO. *O círculo e a linha – da liberdade dos antigos à liberdade dos modernos na teoria republicana dos direitos fundamentais*, p. 190.

constitutional category, as indicated in the preamble of the Constitution: "We, representatives of the Brazilian People, convened at the National Constitutional Assembly to institute a Democratic State that is destined to assure the exercise of social and individual rights, liberty, safety, wellbeing, development, equality, and justice as the supreme values of a fraternal society that is pluralistic and free of prejudice, founded on social harmony and committed, nationally and internationally, to the peaceful solution of controversies, hereby promulgate, under the protection of God, the following Constitution of the Federal Republic of Brazil."

Awareness of Humanism as a legal category permeates the work of the Supreme Federal Court. Evidence of that is a particular thesis written by Justice Carlos Ayres Brito regarding Humanism as a constitutional category. After all, according to Dworkin's thoughts, everything is a matter of principles and it is possible to achieve a concrete answer.[126] With the reflections written herein, we will see that the answer is to permanently seek the concretization of Human Rights in their multiple dimensions, thus fulfilling an individual dignity that is supported by Anthropophilic Humanism. Thereby, according to Maritain, "it is absurd to expect, however, that a city could make all men good and brotherly toward one another when they are taken as individuals; it is possible and it should be demanded that that the city have social structures, institutions, and good laws inspired in the spirit of fraternal friendship, which is something entirely different."[127]

Maritain's demand regarding the spirit of fraternal friendship, that is, a fraternal society, is achieved when Man loves others as he loves himself. In legal terms, such is accomplished with the broad realization of Human Rights. *Id est*, a fraternal society is that which, without reservations, attributes tangibility and feasibility to Human Rights, thus universally achieving Human Dignity.

Fraternity removes Man from the center of things to their diffuse medium. The assertion made by Nicolaus Copernicus in 1520 must be applied to the Law once and for all: neither Earth nor Man

---

126 DWORKIN. *Uma questão de princípio*, p. 175 and following.
127 Idem, p. 196.

is the center of the universe. Since Man is in the diffuse medium of things, Anthropophilic Humanism accepts everything that comes from the "God Particle," the common element that created the universe, as believed by Big Bang theorists, notwithstanding a theocentric view.

Regarding the Big Bang, theoretical physicist and Nobel laureate Steven Weinberg explains that, "In the beginning there was an explosion. Not an explosion like those familiar on earth, starting from a definite center and spreading out to engulf more and more of the circumambient air, but an explosion which occurred simultaneously everywhere, filling all space from the beginning, with every particle of matter rushing apart from every other particle."[128] Said particles, in Weinberg's account, are the "elemental particles,"[129] the purpose of a "theory of elemental particles"[130] associated to the aforementioned theory for the beginning of the universe, a phenomenon that "may have begun 10,000 to 20,000 million years ago."[131]

From these elemental particles, the Earth was formed with everything that exists in it, as though confirming the universal connection among everyone and everything as preached by Jesus Christ upon professing that, beyond being equal, we are all brothers.

Furthermore, as confirmed by recent DNA and evolutionary biology studies, Darwin indicated in his Theory of Evolution that there is a tree of life,[132] with one single trunk. Thereby, each and every species shares a common seed, as though it reaffirmed the universal connection of life and the condition of Men as brothers. For that reason, as Watson cautions, Humanity "cannot continue to believe that Man is the result of an isolated act of creation."[133]

---

128 WEINBERG. *Os três primeiros minutos – uma análise moderna da origem do universo*, p. 18.

129 Idem, p. 19.

130 Ibidem, p. 11.

131 Ibidem, p. 59.

132 FUTUYMA. *Biologia evolutiva*, p. 301. It scientifically confirms existence in modern times and clearly illustrates the tree of life.

133 DARWIN. *A origem do Homem,* p. 536.

James Watson, recipient of the Nobel Prize in Physiology or Medicine, implemented the Human Genome Project in the United States and emphasizes that "all humans alive today, even those who do not share similar features, had a common ancestor."[134] This connection between everyone and everything, which encompasses the Universe, the Planet, Life and Man, shows that Anthropophilic Humanism gives purpose and meaning to human nature and the planet, so that Man can rationally love everyone and everything as he loves himself.

Watson says that Saint Paul, the Apostle, "clearly revealed the essence of our Humanity: Love, this impelling force that makes us care for others, is what has allowed us to survive and thrive in the planet." In conclusion, he says that "love is so essential to human nature that I am certain that the ability to love is in our DNA."[135]

According to this concept, which is also present in Article 1st of the Universal Declaration of Human Rights, Fraternity for human families demands that Man respect and be respected, pursuant to the Human Rights in all their dimensions. Everyone must act toward others with the spirit of fraternity.

Moreover, Maritain makes a clear reference to the core element of practicing love in Jesus Christ[136] and, consequently of Integral Humanist, when addressing "good" structures, institutions, and laws. Thereby, compassion comes to the stage as the state of mind that implements Fraternity, primarily in the face of a request for help, aid, or assistance. Jesus Christ, who was absolute, spread compassion when He walked the Earth.

Hannah Arendt remarks that, "Kindness, in its absolute sense and in contraposition to the usefulness or excellence attributed to it during Greco-Roman antiquity, became known to our civilization

---

134 WATSON; BERRY. *DNA – O segredo da vida*, p. 260 and following.

135 Idem, p. 433-434.

136 Saint Alphonsus Maria de Liguori states: *"that is, obliges, and, as it were, forces us to love Him."* And he recalls the teachings of Paul the Apostle: "The love of Christ compels us..." (2 Cor. 5:14). Cf. LIGÓRIO. *A prática do amor a Jesus Cristo*, p. 18.

only after the advent of Christianity."[137] She adds that, "The only action that Jesus has taught us through words and behavior was the action of kindness."[138]

The current meaning of compassions, as recorded by Houaiss, is as follows: "Definitions: female noun, the pious feeling of empathy for someone's personal tragedy, followed by the desire to appease it; a spiritual participation in the unhappiness of others that drives an altruistic impulse of affection for those who suffer. Etymology: Latin, *compassìo, ónis* 'common suffering, community of feelings, common opinions, empathy'; [...] Synonyms: charity and commiseration; Antonyms: refer to equivalents of malevolence." Language is, undoubtedly, the utmost expression of culture in a country. Upon recording the meaning of the word *compassion* as a "spiritual participation," synonym to "charity" and antonym of "malevolence," Houaiss shows that the message of Christianity is reflected in culture and how the term is currently construed, being seen by Law as the subjective meaning of mercy.

(2) Significant Subjects In Integral Humanism

Pure Positivism, devoid of any ties with Fraternity, let alone without compassion, tends to become Draconian Law. Ripert ponders that "this pure Positivism is not of the most dangerous kind, for it only leaves legislators with their own powers and does not prevent that rivaling forces arise against the State with enough force to offset them. Such concept is so clear that it frightens most jurists. They loathe stating that legislators are the masters of edifying Law at their own will."[139] This unacceptable danger derives from a thought that, in trying to abstract from the axiological deliberations of Law, places everyone and everything at the mercy of legislators.

---

137 ARENDT. *A condição humana*, p. 84.

138 Idem.

139 RIPERT. *O regime democrático e o direito civil moderno*, p. 61.

Law can be an instrument of oppression and violence. As Vera Cruz Pinto would say, "the formalist-positivist radicalism of legal Kelsenianism"[140] is abominable, as demonstrated by the chronological horrors of Hitler's Third Reich. On September 13th, 1935, Adolf Hitler proclaimed the so-called Nuremberg Laws to protect the honor and blood of Germans. On November 14th, the first decree of the National Law of Citizenship is published to define the term "Jew" as the status of *Mischling*, that is, "of impure blood." With this norm, Aryan origins become a critical status for individuals to receive official nominations and the union of Jews and *Mischlinge in matrimony is banned.* In the Spring of 1937, Jewish businessmen lost their companies without any legal justification. On July 12th, Reinhard Heydrich, known as "The Hangman," gave the secret order to hold in protective custody those who offended the Aryan race, even after they had already served their time in jail, thus placing them in asylums and similar institutions. On March 26th, 1938, a decree was published to set forth the mandatory disclosure of information pertaining to all property and assets held by Jews whose value was estimated to be above five thousand marks. On July 14th, the third decree of the Reich Citizenship Law set forth the registration of all companies owned by Jews into public records. On August 17th, the second decree of the Law on the Alteration of Family and Personal Names ordered Jews to add "Sarah" and "Israel" to their first names. In late 1938, upon imposing a solidarity and collective fine of 125 million marks against the Jews, decrees were published regarding their elimination from German economy, as well as an order to aryanize all Jewish companies and confiscate all properties and assets owned by Jews. On November 9th and 10th, over twenty thousand Jews were incarcerated and, on the 15th, Jewish children were expelled from their schools. In 1940, Jews started to be deported. On March 7th, 1941, German Jews started to be subjected to forced labor. On July 31st, Hermann Göring, who founded Gestapo and promoted concentration camps, authorized Heydrich to evacuate all European Jews from German-occupied territories. On September 1st, new limitations to the freedom of movement were set forth and it was man-

---

140 PINTO. *Os tribunais militares e o estado democrático de direito*, p. 65.

datory that all Jews had a yellow Star of David sewn to their clothes. On September 17th, the general deportation of German Jews was initiated. On April 24th, 1942, Jews were banned from public transportation. In June, the mass extermination of Jews in gas chambers was initiated in Auschwitz. On September 18th, food rations given to Jews were drastically reduced. On September 30th, Hitler publicly declared that the annihilation of all European Jews would come as the result of World War II.[141] Fortunately, in 1945, the Third Reich was defeated and Adolf Hitler committed suicide in Berlin.

This exhaustive chronology reveals the normative framework on which the Holocaust was structured. Those led by Hitler did not start to kill people overnight; there was intense legal normative activity geared toward the dehumanization of a group and the appropriation of their wealth to support what the Nazis called their "economic miracle."

Those days, through the radical and hate-filled disregard for the most fundamental Human Rights of millions of people and the pillage of their property, Germans faced disastrous consequences with the 1929 global economic crisis and the Treaty of Versailles, which ended World War I and had Germany pay heavy reparations to the victorious nations.

It is clear that, with Positive Law, Nazi Germany disregarded human essence by regulating the Aryan and Jewish races and their miscegenation, which was outlawed and seen as racial corruption. People had their given names altered and they were branded with the yellow star. Nazis took inventory of properties, assets, and companies and then confiscated them. A gigantic collective fine was applied to Jews. Their freedom of movement was restricted, and so was their access to public transportation. Jews were incarcerated and victims of genocide.

Despite the inhumanity, the country still had judges and courts. As Grunberger observes, the Ministry of Justice under the Third Reich conferred the power to administer justice upon the spokesperson

---

141 Chronology indicated by Grunberger. *Historia social del tercer reich*, pp. 489-491.

for the SS, the paramilitary unit associated to the Nazi Party. Justices as Herr Bumcke, President of the Leipzig Supreme Court of Justice, used to wear the SS uniform. Courts would pronounce judgments without evidence. Draconian forms of punishment were applied. The verdict was agreed upon in advance between government officials and magistrates.[142]

In a Germany where, according to Ian Kershaw, nine out of ten Germans supported Hitler at the height of his popularity,[143] not even a political democracy consubstantiated by the expression of the majority will was able to prevent the horrors of Nazism. This is a historical example of a Positive Law system applied with the consent of most of the population, structured with a legal normative foundation and, nevertheless, marked by the hate-filled intolerance of others and economically supported by legalized pillage.

As a matter of fact, the German abuse founded in a legal, normative, and popular basis was not limited to a group in particular based on their religion; it reached other minorities and peoples, such as homosexuals and gypsies. Within this spectrum, Grunberger cites the following, among other examples: the Law Against Homosexuality was revised to become more severe; Communists accused of homicide were sentenced to 133 years in prison without any evidence being presented in court, and divorces were granted, upon the request of the husband, if the wife was believed to come from a family with bad reputation (a sister with a criminal background.)[144] Oliver Thomson highlights that "In 1939, Germans killed twenty thousand Poles in Bydgoszcz and, later, nine thousand Serbian Yugoslavians in Ravna Cora. These are only two examples of mini-genocides against non-Jews."[145]

It is no wonder that in 1945, during the Nuremberg Trials held for the prosecution of Nazis who committed crimes against Humanity, the Defense alleged that the defendants were only following

---

142 Idem, pp. 130-141.

143 KERSHAW. *El mito de Hitler*, p. 15.

144 Ibidem.

145 THOMSON. *A assustadora história da maldade*, p. 508.

orders given by their superiors, thus complying strictly with the laws of a mechanism institutionally established by the Nazi legal regime.

With these dreary examples, we must acknowledge the rectitude of Saint Thomas Aquinas' words regarding the fact that "Law and Justice are not one and the same." As for the Law, "We call things proceeding from the human will 'positive things.' But nothing is just simply because it proceeds from a human will; otherwise, the will of a human being could not be unjust."[146]

In order to avoid absurdities of this nature, human intelligence must apply the unwritten norm to the core of the fundamental essence in Positive Law, so as to assure that good shall be done and evil shall be prevented. This precept, which has been written in the heart of Humans since the beginning of times, is the supreme Law of Universal Fraternity, the universal realization of Human Rights in all their dimensions to fulfill the dignity of Humans. His authoritative logic is that the Planet will be better the larger and more encompassing the concrete realization of multidimensional rights become, having said dignity respected as well, but without resorting to paternalism or demagoguery.

Therefore, transfused with this Christian inspiration, Human Rights correspond in modern times to the natural rights accepted by the peoples of the planet, becoming part of the universal awareness that reaffirms them and has no doubt about their existence and legitimacy. From this perspective, inhuman law has no mandatory enforcement. Saint Thomas states that, "The human will can, by common agreement, make something just in the cases of things intrinsically compatible with natural justice." That is why the Philosopher says, in *Ethics V*, that "Legally just is that which, in principle, does not demand that things be this way or another; however, once a way is established, things must be that way indeed. And, if something in and of itself is opposed to Natural Rights, it cannot become just through human will. As, for example, if stealing or adultery were established as licit acts. That is why Isaías 10:1 exclaims: 'Woe unto them that decree unrighteous decrees.'"[147]

As Dante Alighieri said, positive laws that contest natural rights, and Human Rights under the same perspective, "are laws only in name; in reality, they cannot be laws."[148]

Therefore, being universally applied, inspired by Thomism and expressive of Integral Humanism, life of law transversely encompasses Human Rights and is not restricted to positivistic aspects. Thus, the realization of Human Rights through Anthropophilic Humanism is justified to permeate universal awareness and, then, the objective spirit of the world. As Maritain emphasizes, "I understand that, to some, an authentic humanism can by definition only be one that is anti-religious. I hold the contrary opinion."[149]

For Maritain, we must accept that, "said Humanism is capable of exalt Man in communion."[150] According to Christian conduct, even if someone is not a Christian they will still act in the name of Fraternity, an essential legal category that is expressed in the Federal Constitution of Brazil in both its mission elucidated in the preamble and in its objectives, being the best way to also address humanitarian deficit and the sustainability of the planet in present times.

Through Fraternity as the contents of this Anthropophilic Humanism, Jesus Christ, in all his compassion, fostered in Humanity the value of human life in an unprecedented and absolute way, since "prior to the coming of Jesus and the influence of Christianity, human life was extremely undervalued."[151] Jesus breathes in this ever-encompassing Humanism into Human Rights; a Humanism that understands and resolves the dialectics between Liberty and Equality.

Addressing the collective unconscious with scientific precision, Jung[152] states that "Certainly, Christianity has shown us the

147 Idem.

148 ALIGHIERI. *Da monarquia*, p. 67.

149 MARITAIN.Op. cit., p. 4.

150 Idem, p. 7.

151 KENNEDY; NEWCOMBE. *E se Jesus não tivesse nascido?*, p. 23.

152 On a sidenote, regarding Jung's quotes found in the reflections herein, there is a Research Group at the School of Law at the Paraná Federal Uni-

way"[153] to avoid evil, a path that we travel objectively within society through Integral Humanism. The fraternal proposal made by Jesus Christ has promoted a true humanistic revolution in favor of each man and the whole man, revealing to Law, through love, the integral and universal concept of what it is now known as Human Rights.

That is what Nalini states when highlighting that "Christianity has had a preponderant role in the inherent concept of rational beings. Whether or not we accept it, the fact is that the Church's doctrine has contributed to universal thought as it acknowledges Equality among Men."[154] The same philosopher indicates that this Equality among brothers represented "madness and scandal in the sophisticated Hellenistic thought, for which slavery was an institution modeled by the intrinsic inequality of the species. In the Gospels, 'Love thy neighbor' is the consubstantiation of this new order," [155]without forgetting to include himself.

We must acknowledge this new order: Fraternity. As Adeodato also confirms, "the initial revolutionary idea is Christian; it comes from the Evangels who refer to Jesus and from Paul the Apostle. The notion of Human Rights as a subjective right inherent to the human condition is the new concept they created. Greek predecessors, as Sophocles and Aristotle, saw indeed the existence of natural rights above positive rights; however their extension to all human beings (radical equality) seems to be a Christian concept."[156]

In fact, we can see a clear difference between the fraternal proposal made by Jesus Christ, who provides the contents of Integral Humanism, and the philosophical thought of Aristotle, for whom, for example, "Hence wherever there are two classes of persons, and the one are as far inferior to the other as the body to the soul or a beast to

---

versity called "Law and Psychoanalysis Studies" and led by Jacinto Nelson de Miranda Coutinho, which has been properly enrolled with the National Counsel of Technological and Scientific Development (CNPq).

153 JUNG. *Os arquétipos e o inconsciente coletivo*, p. 247.

154 NALINI. *Duração razoável do processo e a dignidade humana*, p. 192.

155 Idem.

156 ADEODATO. *A retórica constitucional*, p. 125.

a man—these persons are natural slaves and for them as truly as for the body or for beasts a life of slavish subjection is advantageous. For the natural slave is one who is qualified to be and therefore in fact is the property of another, or who is only so far a rational being as to understand reason without himself possessing it."[157] While Jesus said, "I am the way, truth, and life," Aristotle stated that "Happiness seems to be perfect in and of itself, thus becoming the end purpose of all actions."[158]

Incidental, the logic of the universe seems to confirm the teachings of Jesus Christ, since according to physicist Stephen Hawking, "The universe is expanding."[159] Upon expanding, it follows a path and, if it moves forward, we can conclude that it moves toward evolution. Hawking also explains that "the situation is very similar to that of a balloon being inflated;"[160] consequently, the universe expands as a whole, without leaving anything behind, in a way that this evolution takes place in an all-encompassing and inclusive tone. The purpose of the universe is not happiness, but evolution. Upon preaching the path towards the Father, Jesus Christ is aligned with the universe.

Thus is the mission of Man and the Universe: following the path. Therefore, Jesus preaches the attitude of Man by proposing a new commandment, according to which everyone should be treated as brothers. This Fraternity encompasses everyone and everything, converging toward the physical explanation of universal connection and eternal expansion.

Hence, the Integral Humanism that is presented in the reflections herein is not theocentric; nor is it a regression to Medieval Christian Fundamentalism. It should not be construed as accepting an anthropocentric individualistic and bourgeois Humanism either. It is indeed Anthropophilic Humanism with a clear proposal for universal relationships that encompasses and includes all Men, among everything and everyone, realized through fraternal love.

---

157 ARISTÓTELES. Op. cit, p. 19.

158 ARISTÓTELES. A ética – textos selecionados, p. 36.

159 HAWKING; MLODINOW. Uma nova história do tempo, p. 66.

160 Idem, p. 70.

Hannah Arendt states that loving our neighbors starts with the premise that "love loves itself as well as the object"[161], thus materializing said connection. And, if it is so, it is due to this universal connection that affection (loving others as you love yourself) comes natural do Mankind. It is the source of fraternity among everyone and everything. According to Pope Benedict XIV, "Anyone who needs me, and whom I can help, is my neighbor. The concept of 'neighbor' is now universalized, yet it remains concrete."[162]

Beyond equals, in the words of Jesus Christ, we are all brothers. Or, in Voltaire's words, "to regard all men as brothers"[163] and, at the same time, care for ourselves: That is the key to Anthropophilic Humanism, which legitimizes adequate rights and does good instead of evil.

Francis Bacon once said that "in charity there is no excess,"[164] and charity may and should evolve toward the infinite. This belief will elevate each man and the whole man, since, according to Montaigne, "Confidence in another man's virtue is no light evidence of a man's own."[165] Everyone should place themselves in the position of their neighbors (brothers) and make an attempt to treat them with Fraternity, as they would expect to be treated themselves. Our neighbors should also engage in this fraternal treatment with reciprocity, so that we can achieve true and rational solidarity and proportionality among everyone and everything in order to fulfill the dignity of our one human family.

Pope Benedict XVI points to the need for reciprocity in loving and being loves upon stating that "man cannot live by oblative, descending love alone. He cannot always give, he must also receive. Anyone who wishes to give love must also receive love as a gift."[166]

The same reasoning is explained by Dworkin upon asserting

---

161 ARENDT. *O conceito de amor de Santo Agostinho*, p. 115.

162 POPE BENEDICT XIV. Op. cit., Item 15.

163 VOLTAIRE. *Tratado sobre a tolerância*, p. 121.

164 pt.wikiquote.org, on 11/01/2009.

165 Idem.

166 POPE BENEDICT XIV. Op. cit., Item 7.

that "Every individual is responsible for choices flowing from his own convictions, preferences, and personality"[167], in order counterweigh the "principle of equal importance,"[168] which means, in regards to individuals, that "it is important [...] that human lives be successful rather than wasted, and this is equally important [...] for each human life."[169] Along the same lines, there is the "principle of special responsibility,"[170] according to which "though we must all recognize the equal objective importance of the success of a human life, one person has a special and final responsibility for that success—the person whose life it is."[171] According to the principle of equal importance, we must consider our neighbors with the fraternal treatment he wishes to have, while the principle of special responsibility states that each one of us must love ourselves and also demand said fraternal treatment of our neighbors.

At the same time, Dworkin stresses that each one of us must take responsibility for our own good, as well as for the good of our neighbors and, ultimately, for the good of the planet. It is not a matter of individualism or collectivism; it is a matter of dignity for humans and the planet, from whom and to whom Fraternity should be directed. We must not give up our responsibility for our own good in favor of responsibility for the good of others; nevertheless, we must not give up our responsibility toward others and toward everything in favor of responsibility for our own good.

In sum, as Lugon explicates, "a first approach to Ethics brings the notions of good and evil to the surface in its first legal naturalist concept. Even if we disregard the obsolete Manichean perspective, which divides men between good and evil; even if we abandon any metaphysical forays and restrict ourselves exclusively to the field of philosophy, we would still have man and his free will, looking for

---

167 DWORKIN. *A igualdade importa?*, pp. 250-252.

168 Idem.

169 Ibidem.

170 Ibidem.

171 Ibidem.

a compass to guide him toward personal fulfillment."[172] He adds, "Notwithstanding such substantiation, 'De lege' is construed as leading to an idea of good in the sense of spiritual uplifting. Whether it is based on faith or has philosophical or sociological grounds, a positive guidance is imposed to contain some solidarity and mercy, a healthy inspiration that inhabits the relational nexus between Man as an individual being and the society to which he belongs."[173]

This game of balancing and counterbalancing leads to the necessary application of the Law of Universal Fraternity and, through it, good keeps evil at bay without dishonoring anyone's respective rights and interests, which legally happens when Human Rights are put into effect. Obviously, such fact must objectively take place in a fraternal society that is understood as such due to a satisfactory level of multidimensional realization of Human Rights, both vertically and horizontally.

The move evolved each man and the whole man are, thus civilized, loving their neighbors as they love themselves, the more concrete Human Rights will be in all their dimensions and the more fraternal Humanity and the Planet will thoroughly be.

As we can see, there is no relativism in the reflections herein as far as good and evil are concerned. Such concepts have meaningful contents, since they are intertwined in the evolutionary scale that measures milestones of civilization in the planet according to the level of Human Rights realization, which is measured today by the United Nations Development Plan by means of an annual Human Development Index (HDI) survey conducted in each country using Fraternity as a benchmark.

Consequently, in each concrete scenario, good will be legally determined through its acknowledgement and respective realization, while evil will be legally determined according to its suppression in the face of Human Rights for each man and the whole man, inasmuch as they are realized in their multiple dimensions for the fulfillment of Human Dignity. Therefore, Manichaeism and Relativism have no

---

172 LUGON. *Ética, direitos humanos e princípios constitucionais*, p. 8.
173 Idem. pp. 8-9.

place in the discourse.

(3) Integral Humanism And Anthropophilia

Integral Humanism does not intend to impose fraternity to people by means of a religious conviction. As Maritain states, "The end of political society is not to lead the human person to his spiritual perfection."[174] Focused on Jesus Christ's proposal, the power of fraternity and compassion, it is a Christian Humanism that permeates Law and, ultimately, acts as a legal category that supports Human Rights in all their dimensions.

Still according to Maritain, Integral Humanism acknowledges that Fraternity and its development into compassion are not exclusive virtues of Christians since, objectively, the French philosopher expounded that "being a man who is purely and simply good and virtuous, firmly constituted in a state of moral rectitude, supposes in fact the gifts of grace and charity; these infused virtues rightfully deserve to be called 'Christian virtues,' because they come from Christ and lead to Him even when, as a consequence of some obstacle for which Man is not responsible, the individual who possesses said virtues ignores or does not know Christian religion."[175]

In his theocentric Integral Humanism, in which "God is the center of man,"[176] Maritain accepts a Secular State, even though he acknowledges tolerance for other creeds. However, we must go beyond the concepts of the aforementioned philosopher. This tolerance does not suffice, for it could translate ecclesiastical liberty and characterize a hierarchy of religions. Porto Oliveira is right when he states that "a Democratic Capitalist State does not obey faith, nor it is associated to any religion."[177]

---

174 MARITAIN. Op. cit., p. 129.

175 Idem, p. 162.

176 Ibidem, p. 27.

177 OLIVEIRA. *O Estado, a ordem econômica e a dignidade da pessoa humana,*

Ecclesiastical liberty is of a metaphysical and theological order; when improperly transported to the political and legal arenas, it consists of an institutionalized tolerance for other creeds while being based in one of them, which potentially encourages fundamentalism toward the dominating creed and poses a serious risk of leading to intolerance. Lepenies, a sociologist, warns us that "Nazi ideology is the most flagrant example that obsession with purity leads to intolerance."[178]

Living in harmony, free of a hierarchy of creeds, realizes the right to complete religious liberty. According to Mendes Machado, "In this sense, there is a clear contradiction between the exclusivist discourse of ecclesiastical liberty and the inclusive discourse of Constitutional Law."[179]

Notwithstanding the fact that we are Catholics, with personal and unconditional belief in Jesus Christ, we understand that, regarding legal thought, Mendes Machado is correct upon pondering that "it is possible to reveal the existence of a fundamental difference between the concept of a political community as a moral community with a confessional source built upon the particular concept of objective truth, or as an inclusive constitutional community that is based on the assurance of subjective rights of equal liberty to all citizens and the respect for the principle of separation of religious confessions and the State."[180]

Rule of Law must be secular and democratic, while the freedom of belief is a fundamental assurance, just as it is expressly assured in the Brazilian Constitution, for example. If so, we must not admit any regress in this realm, or we would go back to the Middle Ages. This secularization that characterizes law is a claim that has been echoing consistently and firmly since the Lower Middle Ages, emphasized by the thoughts of Marsílio de Pádua, which were externalized in the

---

p. 77.

178 LEPENIES. *A intolerância – terrível virtude*, p. 116.

179 MACHADO. *Liberdade religiosa numa comunidade constitucional inclusiva*, p. 52.

180 Idem, p. 181.

14th century in *Defensor pacis*. Then, the Italian philosopher already advocated for the separation of Church and State for "civil peace to be assured," as Mezzaroba states.[181]

Therefore, the Rule of Law would be supported by ecclesiastical liberty instead of contemplating a theocentric doctrine. Ecclesiastic liberty is not of a legal institutional order. incidentally, Pope Paul VI clarifies that matter upon stating that "Founded to establish on Earth the Kingdom of Heaven and not to conquer any earthly power, the Church clearly states that the two realms are distinct, just as the two powers, ecclesiastical and civil, are supreme, each in its own domain."[182]

It is unworthy of believe that, in the Civil State, complete religious liberty should be reduced for the condition of ecclesiastical liberty, which would represent an inconceivable discrimination among creeds. Even if we consider that majority of the population is Christian, the result would be an "abuse of the masses," as coined by Benjamin Constant, who passionately defended religious liberty.[183] On the other hand, neither would an anthropocentric Humanism be acceptable without reservations, for placing Man at the center of all things is peculiar of an individualistic Enlightenment that leads to banality translated into Hedonism and Selfishness.

Due to this enlightened element, "monumental mistakes oppress, according to M. Villey, the concept of the Law: Individualism rests on the principle of elementary priority, which eliminates any idea of Men's natural sociability; it is accompanied by a rationalist faith, which ignores Law, *ars boni et aequi* and, through the reality of the experienced world, seeks solutions that are just."[184]

In fact, anthropocentrism disregards fraternal relations among Men when it emphasizes individualism and hedonism, which demand dogmatism of human sociability under the premise that the positivation of law is just, for the general will of the people becomes

---

181 MEZZAROBA. *Humanismo político*, p. 90.

182 PAULO VI. *Carta encíclica Populorum Progressio*, Item 13.

183 PISIER. *História das ideias políticas*, pp. 125 e ss.

184 GOYARD-FABRE. *Os fundamentos da ordem jurídica*, p. 206.

the law: It is all for the sake of having Law immune to other axiolog-ical reflections, except for the thorough obedience to the legislation.

As Maritain emphasizes, "The misfortune of classical human-ism did not consist in having been humanism, but in having been an-thropocentric."[185] Indeed, anthropocentrism leads selfish, hedonistic men to imagine themselves as part of a group of gods, such as the cru-el, unmerciful, and narcissistic gods of Greek and Roman mythology.

Pope Paul VI has taught us that "Far from being the ultimate norm of values, man does not realize himself except by transcending himself."[186] There is then another form of Humanism, a more ade-quate path, a fraternal Humanism that is inclusive, evolutionist, and emancipatory, that proclaims the multidimensional realization of Human Rights and is not theocentric, even though its proposal has Jesus Christ as a referential and, consequently, could not be anthro-pocentric: It is a Anthropophilic Humanism that is not theocentric, nor is it anthropocentric. It is anthropophilic because, from a cultur-al Christian perspective, men are more than equal; they are brothers who inhabit and are nourished by the Planet.

The Houaiss Dictionary defines Anthropophilia as a female noun: 1. quality or virtue of being anthropophilic; 2. affection for and interest in human beings; sociability. Thus is a Humanism of Frater-nity among everyone and everything: even though religion belongs to a group, culture belongs to everyone and, anthropologically, Christ is universal, concrete, and irrefutable; therefore, He is not subject to the relativism of faith and reaches the Law.

Guided by Legal Anthropology, this anthropophilic view acknowledges that the proposal made by Jesus has breathed the ob-jective spirit of Universal Fraternity into historical conscience, as addressed by Hegel.[187] Upon assuring and attributing value to Man, providing self-determination to him through free will and removing him from the center of all things to place him to their diffuse medi-

185 MARITAIN. Op. cit., p. 24.

186 PAULO VI. Op. cit., Item 42.

187 HEGEL. *Princípios de filosofia do direito*, p. 229. Please also refer to Miguel Reale, *Filosofia do direito*, p. 206.

um, this Humanistic Movement no longer considers Man absolute in his individualism, as Anthropocentric Humanism does, and thereby associates him to everyone and everything, through sociability, in the name of Christian Fraternity, as Anthropophilic Humanism does.

Eligio Resta has another perspective of Fraternal Law, based on the Greek *philia erotiké* (friendship through humanity).[188] He refers to "a law jointly declared by brothers, men and women, who make a pact and decide to share minimal rules of living in society,"[189] which is translated into a "shared intimacy free of sovereignty and enmity."[190]

Let us reflect that, instead of speculating about a joint declaration of Humanity, which is manifestly fictitious, it would be better to find support in historical conscience, which under Christian influence has built the objective spirit of a universal fraternity. Moreover, consonant with Giuseppe Savagnone, the ideal of Fraternity evolves *"from Greek philia to Christian Fraternity"*.[191]

In conclusion: Despite having in Jesus Christ its Master and Philosopher due to the cultural infusion of His proposal, which is synthesized in legislation within the Law of Universal Fraternity, the Integral Humanism embraced by the reflections herein is at the service of everyone and everything, notwithstanding creed. After all, said Humanism is based on anthropophilic principles that legitimize the Natural Law of Fraternity that constitutes Normative Legal Humanism.

As explained above, thus is the transposition of Thomism in Integral Humanism Laws, since according to Nicolas "Thomisms diversify themselves according to the issues that seem to be more current, at the core, and in agreement with modern philosophies through which we seek to understand substance in an original thought."[192]

---

188 RESTA. *O direito fraterno*, p. 74.

189 Idem, p. 133.

190 Ibidem.

191 SAVAGNONE. *El principio olvidado: la fraternidad*, p. 130.

192 NICOLAS. *Introdução à suma teológica*, p. 67.

(4) Judicial Culturalism

Aristotle and Saint Thomas Aquinas demonstrate the existence God with the premise of the First Motor, while Hegel explains that "God, as a pure being made of one substance, does not have shape and is taken in abstraction, for He could not externalize himself visually."[193] In turn, Victor Hugo states that "God is the invisible made evident."[194]

We, the authors of this book, have no doubt upon stating our belief in God. Nevertheless, notwithstanding our belief, Law is culture and, therefore, it is subject to universal consciousness in order to recognize the significant contents of archetypal models that "once revealed, become axiological invariables and act universally as inherent constants."[195]

According to Montoro, "The doctrine of culture or values is a modern formulation of philosophical and scientific matters. In the Judicial arena, it supports that Law, as Science, Arts, and other Social phenomena, belongs to the realm of culture, that is, to the world built by Man throughout history."[196]

From this perspective, legal culture must be construed, according to Reale, "as a concept of Law that is integrated into contemporary historicism and applies fundamental axiological principles upon studying the State and the Law; that is, it applies the theory of values in view of social evolution."[197] Reale recognizes that Culturalism "is fully adjusted to the idea of a Natural Law with conjectural basis."[198] This means that, as Adeodato observed, "Reale advocates for something beyond intradiscursive truth. He does not hide the assumption of having conjecture opening way for a knowledge that is

---

193 HEGEL. *O belo na arte*, p. 417.

194 pt.wikiquote.org, on 11/01/2009.

195 REALE. Op. cit., p. 214.

196 MONTORO. *Introdução à ciência do direito*, p. 280.

197 REALE. *Teoria do direito e do Estado*, p. 8.

198 Idem, p. 114.

firmer than the conjecture itself and moves toward the peculiar certainty of sciences."[199]

In turn, Santiago Guerra elucidates that, for Reale, the basis for the idea of truth and conjecture "is that it is possible to acquire knowledge on those realities beyond the experiences situated in the metaphysical realm. However, the nature of said knowledge is not scientific, for it is attributed to phenomenal reality, and the author understands that the former form of knowledge could be as rational as the latter if we acknowledge its limitations and potential."[200]

In fact, overcoming the concerns expressed by Adeodato and Santiago Guerra, anthropology surely elevates the Theory of Law, as culture, to the same level of science: It facilitates the respective ethnographical verification through which we can verify whether said conjectures are indeed "social (sociocultural) objects, so that we can take into consideration not only empirical sciences,"[201] thus complying with the epistemological requirements to which Lourival Vilanova refers.

Therefore, in Reale's words, "We reach a conclusion upon acknowledging value objectivity in the world of culture,"[202] since these values "refer to Man realized in History, to the *processus* of human experience in which we all participate, whether aware of unaware of its universal meaning."[203] Under the prism of Culturalism, "legal norms are, consequently, a type of ethical norm, just as the latter is a type of cultural law."[204]

If Law is culture and experience,[205] we cannot disregard two thousand years of irrefutable and relevant historical and anthropological evolution in shaping Christianity's universal conscience. No one could take for granted the influence that Christian culture has had in

---

199 ADEODATO. *Ética e retórica*, p. 290.

200 GUERRA FILHO. Op. cit, p. 84.

201 VILANOVA. *As estruturas lógicas e o sistema do direito positivo*, p. 2.

202 Idem, p. 208.

203 REALE. Op. cit., p. 209.

204 Idem, p. 253.

205 CARVALHO. *Direito tributário, linguagem e método*, pp. 201-204.

the current civilization, mainly the Western Civilization in which we live. The calendar of Human History is divided into a time before and after Jesus Christ.[206] Without detriment to all other important actors, He is the protagonist in building the universal conscience of Fraternity, which is the anthropological basis of Integral Humanism present in legal reflections.

Maritain himself expressly states that "Humanism is inseparable from civilization or culture, these two words being themselves taken as synonymous."[207] In fact, according to Morin, "human individuals are, in their own empowerment and at the same time, 100% biology and 100% culture."[208] In other words, Man is biocultural.

Montoro, in turn, has taught us that "The historicism and relativism of culturalists, who insist in the continuous variation of the Law, do not oppose the thoughts of masters of Natural Law. As Saint Thomas, they also state that Law and Social Institutions are constantly changing because, in concrete reality, the nature of humans is mutable."[209]

According to Bobbio, Thomism has a referential system in which "Natural Law is identified with the Ten Commandments and life principles preached by Christ."[210] Said proposal is globally known through the cultural representation of Fraternity and the resulting compassion of Jesus.

Through this method of Christian particular historical proposal[211], as Bourdieu states, the necessary elements are extracted to unveil and explain the Law of Universal Fraternity, as well as its reflections in compassion, as the natural imposition of Human Rights in their multiple dimensions, whose purpose is to fulfill Human Dignity. According to Garrido de Paula, this is due to the fact that "Human

---

206 Indeed, he speaks through John the Apostle: "*I am the Alpha and Omega, the Beginning and the End, the First and the Last*" (Apocalypse 22 12:13).

207 MARITAIN. Op. cit., p. 2.

208 MORIN. *O método 5, a humanidade da humanidade*, p. 53.

209 MONTORO. *Introdução à ciência do direito*, p. 275.

210 BOBBIO. *Locke e o direito natural*, p. 37.

211 BOURDIEU. *O poder simbólico*, p. 32.

Dignity is a value prescribed by Man, the product of his cultural development."[212]

In 312 a.D., Constantine I was the first Roman Emperor to profess Christ. He issued an Edict of Toleration to grant religious liberties to Christian and acknowledged Christianity as one of the religions of the Empire, which initiated the notorious expansion of Christian culture.

We cannot deny that Christian Fraternity represented a cultural revolution. Upon analyzing Hegel's philosophy, Losurdo highlights that "[he] also compares the Christian revolution to the French Revolution—the cross is the 'cockade' (Kokarde) that accompanies the struggle to overthrow a decrepit, intolerable order."[213] In fact, both the aforementioned Reale and Kelsen expressly talk about Christian culture and civilization. In spite of the fact that he was Jewish, Kelsen states in his texts that we are men of a Christian civilization.

Permeating Humanity and, consequently, people's culture, Jesus Christ's proposal started to inhabit the objective spirit of the world, according to Hegel, considering that "the fate of concrete ideas from people's Spirit reside in the concrete idea of absolute universality. Such is the World Spirit."[214]

We can safely assure that practically all human beings, from the East to the West, know Jesus. *Guia mundial de estatísticas*[215] [World Statistics Guide] records that Christianity has two billion and one hundred million followers, while atheism has one billion and one hundred million. Islam, the second largest global religion, has one and a half billion followers and also preaches Fraternity toward the less fortunate ones.

In fact, for Roccaro, "Catholicism is related to Islam in an exemplary manner."[216] Thus, since a cultural asset is under analysis here-

---

212 PAULA. *Criança e dignidade da pessoa humana*, p. 990.

213 LOSURDO. *Hegel, Marx e a tradição liberal*, p. 154.

214 HEGEL. *Princípios de filosofia do direito*, p. 312.

215 *Guia mundial de estatísticas*, p. 104.

216 ROCCARO. *Humanismo e Islã: Consummatio modernitatis e contemporaneidade. Nos traços de um ato ideológico*, p. 92.

in, both legally and from a premise of religious liberty, each one of us must meditate on the issue and select our own archetype of Fraternity.

For example, Barack Obama, currently the President of the United States, accepted Jesus Christ's proposal, as he has written on *Dreams of my Father*, mentioning his preacher's sermon: "At the foot of that cross, inside the thousands of churches across the city, I imagined the stories of ordinary black people merging with the stories of David and Goliath, Moses and Pharaoh, the Christians in the lion's den, Ezekiel's field of dry bones. Those stories—of survival, and freedom, and hope—became our story, my story; the blood that had spilled was our blood, the tears our tears."[217] Obama adds: "I also felt for the first time how that spirit carried within it, nascent, incomplete, the possibility of moving beyond our narrow dreams."[218] And he concludes: "Oh yes, Jesus, I thank you..."[219]

According to the figures shown in *Guia mundial*, 97% of the Brazilian population believes in God and 89% believes in Jesus Christ in some way. This trend seems to be constant, since a *Datafolha*[220] survey found that, among young Brazilians in the 16-25 age group, 85% believe in Jesus in their own way and 81% believe religion to be important.

And, if Positivists require the effective cultural and legal introduction of Jesus Christ, the issue would have been resolved with Law # 12,025 of 2009, proposed by the National Congress and signed by the President of the Republic, which sanctioned the "National March for Jesus Day, to take place annually on the first Saturday following sixty (60) days after Easter Sunday." Thereby, by Law, Jesus Christ is a cultural expression in Brazil.

Christian culture is also present within the Judicial Environment. Several courts throughout Brazil display a cross within their facilities and the Supreme Federal Court has an image with the Cru-

---

217 OBAMA. *A origem dos meus sonhos*, pp. 308-309.

218 Idem.

219 Ibidem.

220 Study published in the *Folha de S. Paulo* newspaper on 07/27/2008, Special Section.

cifixion of Jesus. The preamble to the Brazilian Federal Constitution of 1988 itself proclaims in text the expression "under the protection of God," which, despite not constituting a constitutional norm, is "in the political realm, reflecting the ideology of the constitution," as asserted by Carlos Velloso, President of the Supreme Federal Court, who supervised the ruling of Direct Unconstitutionality Action # 2,076-5 AC.[221]

Certainly, as Jung once confirmed, we are the "rightful heirs of Christian symbolism."[222] Due to His influence in the history of Humanity, especially in regards to Humanism, it is undoubtful that Jesus Christ's proposal carries, as Bourdieu put it, the symbolic power as "a power of constituting the given through utterances, of making people see and believe, of confirming or transforming the vision of the world and, thereby, action on the world and thus the world itself."[223]

According to anthropological studies, "Representations of private otherness, in the systems studied by ethnology, place the need for it at the very heart of individuality, at a stroke making it impossible to dissociate the question of collective identity from that of individual identity."[224] Said studies also assert that "any representation of the individual is also a representation of the social link consubstantial with him"[225] and concluded that "the social begins with the individual; and the individual is the object of ethnological scrutiny."[226]

Ergo, in addition to being a religious expression, we see Christianity as a cultural asset that accepts to be subjected to anthropological views, since the ethnographic method may be exercised "over any cultural product within a given society."[227] Moreover, the Gospels re-

---

221 Decision published in the Official Gazette on 08/08/2003, availble at the STF website.

222 JUNG. *Os arquétipos e o inconsciente coletivo*. Op. and p. cits.

223 BOURDIEU. *O poder simbólico*, p. 14.

224 AUGE. *Não-lugares – Introdução a uma antropologia da supramodernidade*, pp. 23-25.

225 Idem.

226 Ibidem.

227 LIMA; VARELLA. *Ensaios de antropologia e de direito*, p. 12.

sort to what anthropologists call "elaborated accounts,"[228] considering that "ethnographic reflection over texts also takes place on anthropological knowledge".[229]

According to Supiot, in his works on the anthropological function of the Law, the history of Human conception is part of the history of the Christian West.[230] If so, in a cultural, anthropological view, "the details of the dogma are not important, but the charity and morals that Christianity offers men,"[231] as Villey assures. He adds that "the reasoning to which Grotius has resorted will remain, above all, as that of Erasmus', a Christianized reasoning, the alliance between Christianity and the culture of Humanists."[232]

Ripert, supported by Charmont, acknowledges that "Grotius, a Protestant, had secularized Natural Law forever."[233] This is the reason why anthropological methods will be more fittingly limited to the cultural aspects of Christianity, not its religious dogmas, in order to support the Anthropophilic Humanism that legitimizes the Normative Legal Humanism that we address here.

Viewing Christianity as a cultural asset that builds a universal objective spirit is also supported by Jung, according to whom "Christianity remained because it matches the current archetypal model;"[234] therefore, it must be transported to the Law. For the reflections herein, as well as for Savagnone, "maybe it bears repeating that Fraternity was attributed value only with the advent of Christianity."[235]

Lima and Varella observe that "the world of culture is the world of values."[236] That is why it is possible to assure, through Christianity, that Fraternity is the value synthesis of our society. We can

---

228 Idem, p. 97.

229 Ibidem, p. 13.

230 SUPIOT. *Homo juridicus*, p. 48.

231 VILLEY. *A formação do pensamento jurídico moderno*, p. 638.

232 Idem, p. 648.

233 RIPERT. Op. cit, p. 58.

234 JUNG. Op. cit., p. 25.

235 SAVAGNONE. Op. and p. cits.

236 LIMA; VARELLA. Op. cit., p. 94.

unveil the objective spirit of the Law of Universal Fraternity, the fundamental basis of all Laws through constitutional and legislative intratextuality, as a Natural Law of which Human Rights arise, thus conforming the application of Positive Law to the elementary potentialization of Human Dignity pursuant to legal realism.

Therefore, based on Telles Jr.,[237] we go on to establish the contents of a referential system that, through Christianity, deciphers the Fraternal Natural Law and constitutes it as the elementary essence of Positive law, corresponding to Human Rights in all their dimensions. The aforementioned jurist explains that "said system could be the cognitive universe of an entire community. Originated from the same contingencies, it is only natural that the referential systems used by people within the same group are similar to one another. Said systems create a common cultural property."[238]

In conclusion, said cultural and philosophical foundations are anthropological because they allow, as Ripert would say, a "complete reconciliation between Saint Thomas' former concepts and the necessary evolution of modern societies."[239] These foundations allow Normative Legal Humanism to better apply Human Rights in their multiple dimensions in order to universally fulfill Human Dignity.

Inserted into the intertextuality of Positive Law and converging with it to produce Law, the Christian culture of fraternity must assert itself as the essential legal element that, concurrently, accommodates and conforms its effective application. Hence, it begins to produce the authentic conjectural law of nature that, being modern and universal, concentrates and accepts Human Rights in all their dimensions.

Therefore, the philosophical platform introduced herein acknowledges that the center of gravity in the legal order, as claimed by the objective spirit of the planet, corresponds to attainable multidimensional Human Rights as imposed by the Law of Universal Fraternity.

---

237 TELLES JUNIOR. *O direito quântico*. Op. and p. cits.

238 Idem, p. 177.

239 IPERT. Op. cit., p. 60.

(5) Human Rights And Their Quantum Application

The legal recognition of Human Rights is indisputable. They exist. They are real and concrete, notwithstanding positivation.

The Brazilian Constitution expressly refers to Human Rights in several occasions. Article 4, Section 2; Article 5, Paragraph 3; Article 108, Section 5-A and Paragraph 5, and Article 7 of the Temporary Constitutional Provisions Act.

Additionally, Multilateral International Acts are formally part of the national legal order, whose direct and indirect object is to address Human Rights. Among them, we may mention the following: Convention on Slavery, of 09/25/1926, Decree # 66/65; Convention on the Inter-American Indigenous Institute, of 02/24/1940, Decree # 36,098/54; Agreement on Issuing Travel Documents to Refugees under the Jurisdiction of an Intergovernmental Refugee Committee, of 10/15/1946, Decree # 38,018/55; Inter-American Convention on Granting Political Rights to Women, of 05/02/1948, Decree # 28,011/50 and Decree # 31,643/52; Convention to Prevent Crimes of Genocide, of 12/09/1948, Decree # 30,822/52; Convention to Improve the Fate of the Wounded and Ill among Deployed Army Troops, Convention to Improve the Fate of the Wounded, Ill, and Castaway among Naval Officers, Convention on the Treatment of Prisoners of War, and Convention on the Protection of Civilians during Times of War, all of them of 08/12/1949, Decree # 42,121/57; Convention Relating to the Status of Refugees, of 07/02/1951, Decree # 50,215/61; Convention on the Political Rights of Women, of 03/31/1953, Decree # 52,476/63; Convention on Slavery, signed in Geneva on September 25th, 1926 and amended by a Protocol open to signature or acceptance at the United Nations Headquarters, of 12/07/1953, Decree # 58,563/66; Supplementary Convention on the Abolition of Slavery, the Slave Trade, and Institutions and Practices Similar to Slavery, of 09/07/1956, Decree # 58,563/66; International Convention on the Elimination of All Forms of Racial Discrimination, of 03/07/1966, Decree # 65,810/69; International Covenant on Civil and Political Rights, of 12/19/1966, Decree # 592/92; International Covenant on Economic, Social and Cultural

Rights, of 12/19/1966, Decree # 591/92; Protocol Relating to the Status of Refugees, of 01/31/1967, Decree # 70,946/72; American Convention on Human Rights (Pact of San José), of 11/22/1969, Decree # 678/92; Convention on the Elimination of All Forms of Discrimination against Women , of 12/18/1979, Decree # 4,377/02; Convention against Torture and Other Cruel, Inhuman or Degrading Treatment or Punishment, of 12/10/1984, Decree # 40/91; Inter-American Convention to Prevent and Punish Torture, of 12/09/1985, Decree # 98,386/89; Additional Protocol to the American Convention on Human Rights in the Area of Economic, Social and Cultural Rights (Protocol of San Salvador), of 11/17/1988, Decree # 3,321/99; International Labor Organization (ILO) Convention 169 concerning Indigenous and Tribal Peoples, of 06/27/1989, Decree # 5,051/04; Convention on the Rights of the Child, of 11/20/1989, Decree # 99,710/90; Protocol to the American Convention on Human Rights to Abolish the Death Penalty, of 06/08/1990, Decree # 2,754/98; Agreement establishing the Fund for the Development of the Indigenous Peoples of Latin America and the Caribbean, of 07/24/1992, Decree # 3,108/99; Inter-American Convention on International Traffic in Minors, of 03/18/1994, Decree # 2,740/98; Inter-American Convention on the Prevention, Punishment, and Eradication of Violence against Women, de 09/06/1994, Decree # 1.973/96; Inter-American Convention on the Elimination of All Forms of Discrimination Against Persons with Disabilities, of 06/07/1999, Decree # 3,956/01; Optional Protocol to the Convention on the Elimination of All Forms of Discrimination Against Women, of 10/06/1999, Decree # 4,316/02; Declaration to Recognize the Mandatory Competence of the Inter-American Court of Human Rights, Decree # 4,463/02; Optional Declaration to the International Convention on the Elimination of all Forms of Racial Discrimination, Decree # 4,738/03; Optional Protocol to the Convention on the Rights of the Child on the Involvement of Children in Armed Conflict, of 05/25/2000, Decree # 5,006/04; Optional Protocol to the Convention on the Rights of the Child on the Sale of Children, Child Prostitution and Child Pornography, of 05/25/2000, Decree # 5,007/04; e Optional Protocol to the Convention Against Torture and Other Cruel, Inhuman or Degrading Treatment or Punishment, of

12/18/2002, Decree # 6,085/07.[240]

Likewise, the infra-constitutional legislation in Brazil acknowledges Human Rights in several legal texts, such as the Statute of the Brazilian Bar Association (OAB, "Ordem dos Advogados do Brasil").[241]

Legal order must take into account the sacred mission suggested by the Anthropophilic Humanism proposed herein: Encourage this acknowledgement of Human Rights and their respective realization, translated into the precept that the planet will be more peaceful, civilized, and sustainable the broader the realization of these rights are concerning universal Human Dignity. And so it is, as Afonso da Silva has taught us: "The individual is a center of legal accountability, because Law exists in the light of it and to facilitate its development."[242] Said development surely is the path to achieve a Fraternal Society as a manifestation of Fraternal Law.

As Ferreira da Cunha highlights, "Human Rights are the form of Fraternal Law."[243] Therefore, with more reason, we see Human Rights at the center of gravity of the complete legal humanistic order; an anthropophilic approach from subjective natural rights, that is, unavailable interests that are protected by law, intrinsic to the essence that constitutes the unbreakable core of biocultural Humanity, and whose relevance is insurmountable to Man, Mankind, and the Planet.[244]

Adeodato states that, "if, at first, subjective rights were debated only in the private law area, in the 21st century they have reached public law and, with the increasing constitutionalization and internationalization of Human Rights and the Law, they will gain their cur-

---

240 This list was excerpted from CNJ's website and highlights only part of the International Acts related to Human Rights.

241 "Article 44. The Brazilian Bar Association (OAB) is a federal public service formed as a corporate entity whose purpose is to: I – defend (...) Human Rights (...)".

242 *Comentário contextual à Constituição*, p. 37.

243 CUNHA. *Geografia constitucional*, p. 329.

244 Idem, p. 156.

| 123 |

rent dimensions."[245] Wherefore, they surpass Jhering's classic concept: The purpose of Human Rights is focused on the legal demand and assurance of the unceasing preservation of Human Dignity in all its dimensions, which is a broader concept than that of the traditional sphere from the 1800s, whose interest was merely individual and anthropocentric.

We then construe the purpose of subjective rights as a combination of interests and duties aimed at existential harmony, as Benacchio suggested in regards of what a legal situation is in modern times, for it "encompasses the legal position of an individual in a determined scenario (dispositive fact) conformed by the incidence of legal order, which thereby imposes rights and duties to that individual and, inclusively, could vary according to the individual associated to the legal scenario and other holders of rights, as well as the related collective."[246]

As Eloísa Arruda illustrates, "Man has dignity due to the simple fact that he exists as a human being; said dignity is inherent and inalienable."[247] In Gandra Martins' account, it arises of human conception.[248] Consequently, dignity is subject to the unceasing and variable evolutionary *status* of Man. Comparato asserts that "Human essence is evolutional, for the personality of each individual, that is, his own self, remains incomplete and unfinished throughout life, thus becoming a reality in transformation."[249]

In this case, notwithstanding its incorporation into the positive legal order, the Universal Declaration of Human Rights (1948), the Declaration on the Right to Development (1986), the Vienna Declaration and Program of Action adopted by the World Conference on Human Rights (1993), the Millennium Declaration (2000), and the Memorandum of Intent on the Mutual Agreement to Cooperate

245 ADEODATO. Op. cit., p. 118.

246 BENACCHIO. *Direito subjetivo — situação jurídica — relação jurídica*, p. 204.

247 ARRUDA. *O papel do ministério público na efetivação dos tratados internacionais de direitos humanos*, p. 362.

248 MARTINS. *A dignidade da pessoa humana desde a concepção*, pp. 143-150.

249 COMPARATO. *A afirmação histórica dos direitos humanos.*, p. 29.

in Developing and Implementing Broad Programs to Promote and Protect Human Rights in Brazil with the UN (2000), as well as other declarations previously proclaimed or yet to be proclaimed, for they address significant elements in the system of references on Human Dignity, they all express Human Rights as valid and efficient through the Law of Fraternity and interpenetrate Positive Law through its intertextuality.

Radbruch ponders that "There are, therefore, principles of law that are stronger than any statute, so that a law conflicting with these principles is devoid of validity. One calls these principles the natural law or the law of reason. To be sure, their details remain somewhat doubtful, but the work of centuries has established a solid core of them and they have come to enjoy such a far-reaching consensus in the declarations of human and civil rights that only the deliberate skeptic can still entertain doubts about some of them."[250]

This far-reaching acceptance of Human Rights is attested by Judge Lewandowski, who stated that "the mass vote in favor of the Universal Declaration, and the fact that no opposition to its passing was recorded during the vote, makes it a rare document that, to this day, still enjoys a unanimous consensus."[251] Consequently, Humans cannot be classified as things, for they are not an object of the potestative power of another.[252] Freedom is inhered to Man.[253] For Kant, it is not in human nature to subject ourselves to someone else's will and, as a result, we cannot be appropriable.

Freedom grants self-determination to Man, which implies awareness of self-worth within the formally legal equality enjoyed by all. As Kant states, "independence from being constrained by another's choice may as well constrain them."[254] Therefore, Man has no price; just the opposite: Man is aware of his own value, which confers

---

250 RADBRUCH. *Filosofia do direito*, p. 417.

251 LEWANDOWSKI. *A formação da doutrina dos direitos fundamentais*, p. 393.

252 KANT. *A metafísica dos costumes*, p. 53.

253 Idem.

254 Ibidem, p. 54.

dignity upon him. It is the legal secularization of the human soul. Incidentally, according to Senise Lisboa, "The idea of dignity was developed from the Biblical notion that Man was created in God's image."[255]

To such an extent, when referring to Kant, Comparato asserts that "As the philosopher indicated, thus was originated the idea that, unlike objects, all men have dignity, not a price."[256] Or, in the words of Justice Nancy Andrighi, "Objects have price; people have dignity."[257] Without contradicting the correct position of Siqueira Jr., who stated that "Man has self-worth and cannot be transformed into an object,"[258] we cannot alienate Human Dignity, which would transform Man into a thing. The attempt to set a price to each man and the whole man must be contrasted with the Law of Universal Fraternity and, consequently, with Jesus Christ's proposal, for both are sanctioned within the legal order by the inherent objective right to dignity conferred upon each man and the whole man, as well as upon the Planet.

With all due respect, it is precisely because of it that it would be unacceptable for someone to set a price to Human Dignity while claiming that it is a cost of rights.

We must conclude, then, that Human Rights naturally correspond to Human Dignity and, consequently, to the dignity of the planet, which is the synthesis of the innate subjective rights to Liberty, Equality, and Fraternity conferred upon each man and the whole man and, inherently, upon the planet. Such dignity is in force, effective, and independent from positivation, once "innate rights belong to all by nature."[259]

Kant identifies "Human Rights in our own self;"[260] Figueiredo

---

255 SENISE LISBOA. *Dignidade e solidariedade civil constitucional*, p. 35.

256 COMPARATO. Op. cit., p. 21.

257 ANDRIGHI. *A tutela jurídica do consumidor e o respeito à dignidade da pessoa humana*, p. 1138.

258 SIQUEIRA JR. *A dignidade da pessoa humana no contexto da pós-modernidade*, p. 252.

259 KANT. Op. cit., p. 53.

260 Idem, p. 56.

clarifies that "all human beings, regardless of their status or current situation, have the right to dignity."[261] And so it is precisely: Human Dignity is a right. However, as indicated above, it is indeed positivated in Article 1st, Section 3 of the Federal Constitution.

All Man's rights converge toward the specific natural objective right to Human Dignity and, consequently, toward the dignity of the planet. Thus, the realization of said dignity is also the best testimonial to the complete achievement of subjective natural rights. Hence, Human Rights are framed within legal realism and cannot be interpreted; they are realized. In other words, they are executed before real scenarios with the specific purpose of objectively and tangibly fulfilling the right to Human Dignity. For that reason, Human Dignity takes precedence over the legal order, as conciliated in the jurisprudence of the Supreme Federal Court, which demonstrates that such prominence is not an attribute of positivation, but an imperative consequence of the innate objective right of each man and the whole man.

We can affirm that there are three dimensions to human rights: innate Liberty, innate Equality, and the consubstantial value of each man and the whole man, which implies innate Fraternity. This triad shapes the structuring elements of one single core, a central beam that is indissociable and interdependent and constitutes Humanity as being intrinsic to each man and the whole man, thus objectively conferring upon the individual a value in and of itself (i.e. dignity.) There is a possibility that, in the future, new dimensions will be discovered, since the universe is unlimited, and so is the expression of each man and the whole man in the diffuse medium of all things. Therefore, violating Human Dignity is analogous to placing Man in an inhumane scenario. In other words, it would dishonor the existential biocultural human condition.

We would like to make it clear that these Human Rights dimensions do not ensue or replace one another. On the contrary, they further themselves. As Trindade explains, what takes place "is a phenomenon of non-succession, but rather expansion, accumulation, and strengthening of consecrated Human Rights upon revealing the

---

261 FIGUEIREDO. *O respeito à dignidade humana e a eutanásia*, p. 428.

complementing nature of all Human Rights."[262] As we can see, this multidimensional nature of Human Rights overcomes the classic dichotomy of public against private, since "a need to protect Human Beings arises of the inflexible distinction between Public Law and Private Law, and it is so with more strength amid the current diversification of sources of Human Rights violations. The inflexible distinction between public and private does not withstand the imperative Human Rights protection."[263]

We must admit that Human Rights, as subjective natural rights, are surrounded by a pretense that is assured by the legal order, thus being achievable. Such pretense consists of the spontaneous and objective exercise of Human Dignity. Therefore, Human Rights are not only ideals or values, much less programmatic principles voided of normativity. The Law of Universal Fraternity fits the category defined by Teller Jr., for whom "Law is not only the law that is effectively formulated by Man; so it is the unformulated law, that can be formulated by an abstract intelligence,"[264] thus emanating impositivity.

When analyzed from an anthropological perspective, the rights of Man are part of the good created by God. And, as Pope Pious XI once taught us, "All created good under God be considered as mere instruments to be used only in so far as they conduce to the attainment of the supreme end."[265] Integrated to human essence, these rights exist as an indissociable and interdependent beam endowed with an unbreakable legal universality; they can be realized within such universality, never removed from it. Human Rights cannot be trimmed or segregated from their legal universality. They are enforceable as a collective under the penalty of their inadmissible rupture, for the exclusion of one of their elements (dimensions) would lead to one of them prevailing over the others, thus leaving the collective unbalanced. It would impair the achievement of an objective right to dignity, since such a scenario would place Man in an inhuman situation.

262 TRINDADE. *Tratado internacional dos direitos humanos*, p. 43.
263 Idem, p. 42.
264 TELLES JR. Op. cit., p. 233.
265 *Quadragesimo Anno*, Item 135.

In fact, regarding the core of Human Rights, the dignity of an individual is indistinctively present with the consolidation of Liberty, Equality, and Fraternity, which objectively emerges from the respective reflective balance. We will explain: What good is it for someone to have dignity without Liberty? Without equality? Without Fraternity? Without Liberty, there will be a Tyranny of Equality. Without Equality, there will be a Tyranny of Liberty. And, without Fraternity, Liberty and Equality become incompatible.

As a matter of fact, since they are innate, Human Rights have not been granted by the State or by Civil Society. As Locke once demonstrated, social contracts cannot achieve a human essence that is naturally assured by the objective right to Dignity, which comes before the absolute title of each man and the whole man. Human Rights shape the complete legal order, being transversely applied to them and, consequently, applicable to all concrete legal cases.

In other words, Human Rights and their respective objective of conferring dignity to humans are not contingent upon a State sanction. As Souza Lima and Duek have construed, "It is not conferred upon humans, because it already belongs to them from birth."[266]

Once Human Dignity is proclaimed, its objective dimensions of democracy and peace stand out. Democracy is seen here in its universal sense, beyond being a political term alone, thus related to civil, economic, social, and cultural democracy. As for peace, evidently, it is the summit, the utmost objective of dignity to each man and the whole man, as well as to the planet.

In fact, achieving perpetual peace will only be possible when each man and the whole man are able to pride themselves in consubstantial dignity, creating concrete relations among themselves and implying the mutual fulfillment of their rights within the planet. As John XXIII once taught us, "All men are united by their common origin and fellowship, their redemption by Christ, and their supernatural destiny. They are called to form one Christian family."[267]

As we can see, Human Rights cannot be mistaken for Funda-

266 LIMA. *O princípio da humanidade das penas*, p. 437.
267 *Pacem in Terris*, item 121.

mental Rights. The latter are more restrict and represent the constitutional positivation of the former, among other values construed as fundamental and promulgated by the State in order to assure their realization. Human Rights come before them and are broader, for they are determined by the Natural Right. Hence, they are innate to each man and the whole man and cannot be mistaken for Fundamental Rights, whose list set forth in Article 5 of the Federal Constitution authorizes, for example, the citizen's arrest of an unfaithful depositary, which is a remedy that glaringly collides with Human Rights. The jurisprudence of the Supreme Federal Court, as recorded on Binding Abridgement # 25, intuitively realized Human Rights and suppressed the application of the command discussed herein.[268]

In sum, despite not being fully positivated, Human Rights are real, not merely ideals, thus shaping the complete positivation. As we have seen, they also include the constitutional positivation of fundamental rights through their intertextuality.

Aligned with the legal realism that arises of them, Human Rights find a path of respective realization in quantum method. Therefore, according to Tribe, Law professionals should learn about post-Newtonian physics.[269] By applying the quantum logic of the universe, which according to the "new physics"[270] has placed materialism "in crisis with contemporary science,"[271] it is possible to transpose Einstein's theory of relativity ($E=Mc^2$) to the legal order. Einstein taught us that "Classical physics introduced two substances: matter and energy. The first had weight, but the second was weightless. In classical physics we had two conservation laws: one for matter, the other for energy. We have already asked whether modern physics still holds this view of two substances and the two conservation laws. The answer is: No. According to the theory of relativity, there is no essential distinction between mass and energy. Energy has mass and mass

---

268 *"The citizen's arrest of an unfaithful depositary is an ilegal act, notwithstanding the nature of the deposit."*

269 TRIBE. *The invisible constitution,* p. 200.

270 PONTES DE MIRANDA. *O problema fundamental do conhecimento,* p. 315.

271 Idem.

represents energy. Instead of two conservation laws we have only one, that of mass-energy."[272] According to Bohr, this is "Einstein's fundamental law regarding equivalence."[273]

Once legal order is analyzed through this prism, we can see that matter and energy are two aspects of a single essential element, which varies according to density. We must then associate positive law with matter, human rights with energy, and realism with density. From this perspective, Telles Jr. states that "natural law is always positive law."[274] Consequently, quantum method confirms that the elementary composition of positivated legal norm is that of a sedimented natural right, while Human Rights constitute the natural law that is universally accepted.

Thus is formed a peculiar relationship of equivalence among positive law, Human Rights, and legal realism under the prism of matter (mass) and spirit (energy), which are adjusted by a vibrational density (movement/velocity) and arranged according to the following design:

- Positive Law = mass (matter);
- Human Rights = energy (spirit);
- Realism = density (movement/velocity);
- Result: Human Rights are consubstantial to positive law, according to legal realism.

Therefore, Human Rights are inserted into the intratext of positive law; while the latter is visible, the former becomes invisible. Or, as Oscar Wilde once said, "The true mystery of the world is the visible, not the invisible."[275] From this perspective, Human Rights present themselves and are enforceable whenever and wherever positive law is applied.

---

272 EINSTEIN; INFELD. *Evolução da física,* p. 166.

273 BOHR. *Física atômica e conhecimento humano,* p. 71.

274 Idem, p. 281.

275 frases.netsaber.com.br, on 11/01/2009.

Upon accepting, with Telles Jr., that "Essence is in fact the constant among all things of the same genus and species," it is possible to deduct that, according to legal realism, all positive legal norms are quantumly a Human Rights norm that, when applied, realizes Human Dignity—even those norms considered indifferent, despite remotely.

The Law of Universal Fraternity demands that, on resolving any case, Human Rights be realized on account of Human Dignity. Any other outcome would impose a legal vacuum, the absolute nothing, without the clear energy that is an elementary essence of matter and, consequently, does not exist.

In conclusion, according to legal realism, Human Rights operate under the essential elementary perspective of a sedimented positive law system. They are the essence that constitutes all legal norms and, for being based in legal realism, they assure dignity to Humans. Thus, all cases regulated by the law have a gravitational pull on Human Rights toward the respective subsumption, *id est*, Human Rights are transversely applicable throughout legal order and the Economic Law as well, shaping positivation even with the reduction or suppression of a constitutional text, as it intuitively happened in the aforementioned Binding Abridgement of the Supreme Federal Court in regards to the civil arrest of an unfaithful depositary.

We must accept that such is a monism before the supranational legal order of Human Rights. In fact, this predominance of legal-natural characteristics is expressly acknowledged in Brazil, according to the aforementioned Article 7 of the Constitutional Provisions Act, Federal Constitution, which accepts the impositivity of Human Rights over national legislations.

Ipso facto, international legislations on Human Rights are monist. There is a single legal order in the planet that, upon interfering with the inherent and elementary rights of Man, is fully compatible with sovereign national legal orders, thus becoming part of the legal legacy of a Human Family. The realization of such a mission for Human Rights, which is legitimized by anthropophilic humanism, can be therefore resolved through quantum efficiency. In plain words, it is resolved by the true applicability of multidimensional, vertical and horizontal Human Rights in each and every concrete case since, as Del Valle has taught us with accuracy, *"Los derechos del hombre son oponibles frente al gobierno del Estado, sus autoridades y todos los demás sujetos de derecho (individuos y personas morales de cualquier especie.)"*[276]

Notwithstanding the fact that the vertical application of Human Rights is conciliated in Brazilian legal doctrines, Resolution # 201819[277] by the Supreme Federal Court set a precedent in regards to the possibility that fundamental rights be applied horizontally. With more reason, Human Rights must be applied horizontally as well. In sum, we are aligned with Courtis, who said that "The idea that Human Rights are no applicable between private parties is exaggerated and wrong."[278]

There is relevance and truth in applying legal order to realize Human Rights, especially in the economic field, which transversely achieves vertical and horizontal efficiency. In order to do so, it suffices to bring to Law the principle of complementarity that Bohr identified in quantum physics. By right of this principle, "The evidence gathered from different experimental conditions cannot be contained within a single design; they must be considered complementary, for only the totality of phenomena depletes all possible information from the object."[279] In other words, "the data obtained from different experimental arrangements cannot be construed through usual molds; the need to take into consideration the conditions through which the experience is achieved imposes the mode of complementary description."[280]

---

276 VALLE. *Garantías del gobernado*, p. 10.

277 Here is an excerpt of the annotation: "Violations to Fundamental Rights do not occur only within the scope of a citizen-State relationship; it may also take place in relationships between individuals and private corporations. Therefore, the Fundamental Rights assured by the Constitution are binding not only to public authorities; they are also aimed at protecting individuals in the face of private powers."

278 COURTIS. *La eficacia de los derechos humanos en las relaciones entre particulares*, p. 406.

279 *Apud* STRATHERN. *Bohr e a teoria quântica*, p. 75.

280 BOHR. Op. cit., p. 3.

Such method was explained well by Strathern: "There cannot be a general scheme [...] we may use a set of complementing schemes to approach the same object."[281] Abdalla adds: "Since it is evident that there is a need for two complementing descriptions for the same phenomena,"[282] quantum method applies to the principle of complementarity. If we apply the range of efficiency from Positive Law (text) as a complement to the range of efficiency from Human Rights (intratext), with a crucial adaptation through a range of efficiency from Legal Realism (metatext), the point in which these three efficiency spheres intersect will indicate an adequate response to the concrete case, without parallels or overlaps, but with synchronicity and synergy.

If these ranges of efficiency converge, that of the Positive Law will prevail over the other two, as indicated explicitly by Natural Law (natural law of convergence) and adapted by Legal Realism. Such is the natural law of convergence. However, if they are divergent, the shaping effect of Human Rights (natural law of fraternal imperative) shall prevail in the application of Positive Law, which is also adapted by Legal Realism. Such is the natural law of fraternal imperative.

Finally, upon imposing the Law of Universal Fraternity, there is no legal solution that will contradict the objective right to Human Dignity within Legal Realism.

(6) A Humanistic Administration Of Justice

The task of a Judiciary Branch shaped by Anthropophilic Humanism is undeniably a relevant one. As Aristotle once asserted, "Justice is the basic structure of society. What is called 'judgment' is the application of what is just."[283] In Saint Thomas Aquinas' account, justice "must give each one what belongs to them, as it is due to them, in

281 STRATHERN. Op. and p. cit.

282 ABDALLA. *Bohr, o arquiteto do átomo*, p. 164.

283 ARISTÓTELES. Op. and p. cits.

equitable proportions."[284] Such proportionality is imposed by mercy, the true remedy against poverty, this unacceptable situation that, regardless of the circumstances, reduces Man to a glaringly subhuman condition according to what is advocated by Human Dignity.

In effect, with the Law of Universal Fraternity, the administration of justice has the role of promoting and assuring the fulfillment of Human Dignity to the people involved through the multidimensional realization of Human Rights.

Appeals Court Judge Rizzatto Nunes, with the São Paulo Court of Justice, ponders that "seeking justice must have its foundations in Human Beings. They are the ones intended to be satisfied and respected. Thus, it is fundamental that we understand the premise of all decisions and the purpose that it aims to achieve: Human Dignity."[285] This is the fraternal spirit that must encourage judges, for it is surrounded by the Anthropophilic Humanism proposed herein.

Saint Thomas Aquinas states that "some virtues, such as misery and freedom, among others, spring from Justice, which is a cardinal virtue. Therefore, helping the poor, even in an act of mercy and pity, as well as generous giving, which belongs to liberty, may be attributed to Justice as the principal virtue."[286]

Therefore, Anthropophilic Humanism wishes to promote and assure dignity to those who are subjected to the Judiciary Branch, thus applying mercy to fight poverty in judicial decisions, instead of being alien to or alienated from it. Mercy is proposed, so to speak, as a relevant instrument. According to Saint Thomas Aquinas, *"misericordia est Deo maxime attribuenda: tamen secundum effectum, non secundum pasionis effectum. Ad cuius evidentiam, considerandum est quod misericors dicitur aliquis quase habens miserum cors: quia scilicet afficitur ex miseria alterius per tristitiam, ac si esset eius propria miseria. Et ex hoc sequitur quod operetur ad depellendam miseriam alterius, sicut miseriam propriam: et hic est misericodiae effectus."*[287]

---

284 AQUINO. *Suma teológica.* Chapter 2, Article 11.

285 NUNES. *A dignidade da pessoa humana e o papel do julgador,* p. 421.

286 AQUINO. Op. cap. and art. cit.

287 AQUINO. Op. cit., part I, item 21, Article 3, translated issue by Editora

This foundation undoubtedly shows that mercy, in contraposition to poverty, refers to the earthly dimension of a manifestation of loving our neighbors as we love ourselves through fraternity. In other words: In the face of poverty, the mercy that effectively comes to the aid of the poor is the undeniable effect of Anthropophilic Humanism.

In sum, according to Dante Alighieri, "And since to live in peace is chief of man's blessings, as we said before, and since this is most fully and easily accomplished by Justice, charity will make Justice thrive greatly; with her strength will the other grow strong."[288] Mercy then becomes the legal expression of compassion, as clarified by Pope John Paul II, for whom the word "indicates a profound attitude of 'goodness.' When this is established between two individuals, they do not just wish each other well; they are also faithful to each other by virtue of an interior commitment, and therefore also *by virtue of a faithfulness to themselves.* [...] The fact that the commitment in question has not only a moral character but almost a juridical one makes no difference."[289]

Therefore, fraternal and merciful judges must guide their conduct according to the Anthropophilic Humanistic formula, that is, applying the undeniable respect for Human Rights to all cases, whether it is in his decisions, in how proceedings are conducted, or in dealing with all parties and the entire judicial family. Thus, judges must apply the Law of Universal Fraternity at all times throughout the exercise of their tasks, especially interpenetrating Positive Law in intertextuality with this supreme objective.

In view of Christian Culturalism, the anthropological meaning of Jesus Christ's cross displayed in courtroom is a symbol that

---

Loyola: "Mercy is especially to be attributed to God, as seen in its effect, but not as an affection of passion. In proof of which it must be considered that a person is said to be merciful, as being, so to speak, sorrowful at heart; being affected with sorrow at the misery of another as though it were his own. Hence it follows that he endeavors to dispel the misery of this other, as if it were his; and this is the effect of mercy."

288 ALIGHIERI. *Da monarquia*, p. 42.

289 *Dives in Misericordia*, item 29, note 52.

indicates said fraternity and mercy materialized into Human Dignity through the legal system. For Jung, "The symbolic process is an experience in images and of images."[290]

Comparato asserts that "Jesus of Nazareth was an ethical role model in history and made such behavior more accessible to men through imitation."[291] As a symbol, His cross calls for the practice of Anthropophilic Humanism with the effective application of the Law of Universal Fraternity in decisions that render humans important and remedy poverty, notwithstanding its location, with mercy. Therefore, regardless of the issue, an anthropophilic administration of justice is achieved when Human Rights are realized in all their dimensions in order to fulfill Human Dignity.

Judges must always make a decision upon demanding that both parties love each other as they love themselves, while concretely applying what objectively will be promoted by observing Human Rights, either vertically or horizontally. This is what we expect to accomplish by applying fraternity and mercy to the legal world. According to Trindade, it is through them that "we seek to correct the unbalance and disparity that affect Human Rights, instead of solely aiming for an abstract balance between the parties."[292]

We do not adopt strictly symmetrical measures towards our brothers. In order to achieve a fraternal relationship, brothers must collaborate with each other and then act jointly for the realization of Human Rights in general, not only towards others but towards themselves as well, thus not tolerating poverty. Justice among brothers is justice among equals; it is a fraternal and merciful justice, as shown in the parable of the prodigal son, who spent all his inheritance and, upon returning home as a poor man, asking to eat feed for pigs and be turned into a slave, was welcomed with open arms by his father and had his previous dignity restored.

The father did not accept the complaints of his virtuous son, who got upset and thought it was unfair that the prodigal son would

---

290 JUNG. Op. cit., p. 47.

291 COMPARATO. Op. cit., p. 17.

292 TRINDADE. *Tratado internacional dos direitos humanos*, p. 44.

be welcomed with a feast, and explained that either of them would be welcomed the same in that situation. It is evident that the prodigal son's thoughtless behavior is not endorsed; however, a son never loses dignity in the eyes of his father, who shall always dedicate fraternity and mercy to him. Likewise, a brother can never be thrown aside if symmetrical measures are balanced by an immersion into a sentiment of fraternity. And, if there is poverty, shall it be fought with mercy, even if the poor have incurred into their own misery.

Human Dignity is an inalienable right and, consequently, the bearer of a right cannot lose it, be it due to action or omission, notwithstanding a volunteer effort. There is an essential core in each man and the whole man that attributes value in and of itself and is expressed, in a legal sense, as an indissociable, interdependent, and multidimensional beam of Human Rights that, strictly speaking, must be observed, considered, respected, and realized by judges. Acting with fraternity and, in the face of poverty, with mercy as well is to precisely acknowledge said value that all Men carry within.

Popular wisdom indicates six steps, to be followed by acting judges in their administration of justice, in order to have the Law of Universal Fraternity implemented: (1) taking into consideration all parties involved, while keeping in mind that they are Humans who have Dignity; (2) perceiving their affliction when faced with a concrete issue; (3) listening attentively to the versions and reasons each party has stated; (4) putting yourself in their situation; (5) interacting with them, and (6) applying the most fraternal decision possible, that is, the one that will fulfill the dignity of all those involved, and showing mercy in the face of poverty.

As agents of the multidimensional realization of Human Rights, the spirit of magistrates must be fraternal and merciful. They are the ones responsible for fulfilling the natural objective law that corresponds to Human Dignity. While in conflict, society expects magistrates to do their work with said spirit in mind, thus weighing the legal remedy that is more aligned with the accepted Natural Law.

In Brazil, Section 8, Article 35 of the Organic Magistrate Law (Complementing Law # 35/79) demands that magistrates lead an impeccable public life, which includes the duty of maintaining a posture that realizes Human Rights in all their dimensions, at all times. Pursuant to Article 16 of the National Magistrates Code of Ethics, edited by the National Justice Council, judges must "be aware that the administration of justice imposes personal restrictions and demands that are different from those to whom the general population is subjected."

The Magistrates Code of Ethics sets forth in Article 3rd that "the administration of justice must be developed in order to guarantee and advance Human Dignity, thus assuring and promoting solidarity and justice towards people." This is the duty of a magistrate's work. We must make it clear that Anthropophilic Humanism does not preach for paternalism; it was also rejected by Maritain, as Pussoli emphasizes[293]. We would not expect it from magistrates.

Incidentally, HC # 36,067,[294] filed against a defendant accused of theft and subjected to the penalties set forth in Article 157 of the Brazilian Criminal Code, states the following: "Invoking the words spoken by Christ to a thief who was given the death penalty: 'Thou shalt be with Me in Paradise.'" In an unanimous decision on September 19th, 1958, the Supreme Federal Court responded by denying the order, on the grounds that, "As we can see, the patient, while living, seeks to receive from the Supreme Court a clemency that Christ can only grant him after death." Even though the verdict was correct, since Humanism is not Paternalism, the Court did not resort to the well-deserved and due fraternity towards the patient; the judge did not put himself in the defendant's place, nor did he strive to understand his affliction. We are not saying that the order should have been granted; however, the denial should be followed by fraternity and mercy in living, as opposed to the idea that Jesus Christ's compassion could only be applied after death. In such a situation, a magistrate cannot decline his duty of judging a defendant with fraternity; therefore, more concretely, within the strict limitations of *habeas corpus*, magistrates must verify whether constraints or procedural nullity had

---

293 PUSSOLI. *Humanismo de Jacques Maritain e o sistema jurídico brasileiro*, p. 235.

294 Decision available on the STF website.

taken place.

A magistrate cannot renounce aligning the administration of justice with the Natural Law of Fraternity that imposes Human Rights, which is very different from degrading legitimate rights and interests. Among other decisions, an exemplary judgment was made by Federal Judge Sebastião de Oliveira Lima on September 9th, 1981 against approximately three thousand leaseholders in São Paulo. In Case # 4197615, it was ordered that the property demanded by an organization with the Federal Administration be returned due to the fact that, according to the judge, "The law is openly in your favor. Owners have the right to see their property restored in case of expropriation." Throughout his ruling, Judge Lima displayed true and rational fraternity and mercy towards the land squatters, as we can see in the following excerpt: "Things are not that simple. Even though a judge must first and foremost enforce the law, he cannot be blind to social reality." At the end of his ruling, he proactively did what was within his power, albeit little, upon ordering the following: "I authorize the requested use of police force and recommend that law enforcement officers exercise utmost prudence and care." Thus, a fraternal and merciful decision, despite the fact that it was against destitute individuals.

The Law of Universal Fraternity is not stifled by cruel justice alone. An indifferent, alienated justice is equally unacceptable. In both cases, magistrates do not take human beings into account and do not fulfill the inherent objective right to Human Dignity, for it is disrespected inasmuch as Human Rights are not realized. In the administration of justice, it is imperative that Positive Law be applied in alignment with the natural right to Fraternity, which is deciphered according to the system of cultural references arising of Anthropophilic Humanism, under the penalty of characterizing an inhumane legal order that is corrupt, repulsive, and sordid.

Legal decisions that contradict Human Rights are a void in the law. They are equivalent to an administration of justice that, despite formally existent materially corresponds to the absolute nothing, which represents dark energy in the quantum perspective. Thus imposing a negative pressure, they create obstacles to the fulfillment of Human Dignity both privately and universally.

Among cases of non-existent sentences, Teresa Alvim Wambier includes "those lacking material grounds to have any effect."[295] Inhumane decisions belong to this category, for they violate Human Rights and obstruct the preservation of Human Dignity, an objective right of each man and the whole man.

Even after a judicial decision is made and becomes final, this preservation must comply with Human Rights. We must not forget Nery Junior's fundamental warning in regards to the fact that "the matter settled in court cannot be taken for granted."[296] However, not even matters settled in court can be considered absolute to the point that they are disassociated from the vertical and horizontal multi-dimensional achievement of Human Rights. In the event that such disassociation takes place, matters settled in court can also be considered legally non-existent. Moreover, inhumane decisions are more severe than matters that are considered unconstitutional, since Human Rights are responsible for shaping positivation, including that of constitutional nature. That is why said decisions achieve the status of being null, for those affected have the absolute right to see their Human Dignity assured both in the criminal and in the civil arenas.

In the criminal arena, inhumane orders can always be remediated by *Habeas Corpus*, since they could be considered a constraint related to the restricted freedom of movement. The right to a criminal review, in case of an inhumane criminal sentence against the defendant, can be exercised even *post mortem* in order to defend the affected party's dignity, which is eternal.

We must emphasize that, even in the civil arena, a matter settled in court may be considered null if affected parties have their Human Rights, that is, their absolute rights, violated. Additionally, still in the civil arena, *Habeas Corpus* can be resorted to against an inhuman decision that constrains a defendant's freedom of movement.

Therefore, upon being identified as an inhumane order, the matter settled in court can, at any time, become null even two years

---

295 WAMBIER. *Nulidades do processo e da sentença*, p. 470.
296 NERY JR. *Coisa julgada e o estado democrático de direito*, p. 1212.

after it became final, as set forth in procedural law, so that the case can be reopened. Human Rights never expire.

Let us imagine that a Brazilian judge authorizes the citizen's arrest of an unfaithful depositary, despite the Supreme Federal Court having ruled it unconstitutional. Under these circumstances, the affected party has the right to resist beyond the suit and the police can refuse to follow an order of this nature. Undoubtedly, pursuant to Article 475-L, Paragraph 1st of the Code of Civil Procedure, there are grounds for a refusal to execute an order considered inhumane, since the Supreme Federal Court has recurrently decided to assure and promote Human Dignity as a constitutional imperative. Still in regards to the Supreme Federal Court, Justice Marco Aurélio reminds us that, for Stuart Mill, protecting liberty is to "chiefly fight continuously against those who wish to restrict it,"[297] and, according to Justice Maurício Correa's HC # 73,454, "no one is forced to comply with or be subjected to an illegal order, despite it having come from a legal authority. Moreover, citizens have the duty to oppose illegal orders; otherwise, the Rule of Law is negated."

Inhumane legal decisions, such as death penalties or the citizen's arrest of an unfaithful depositary, authorize the broad right to procedural resistance, according to due legal process. Additionally, they authorize broad rights to resistance, not only in the procedural arena, albeit in the absence of violence or acts of atrocity. An example of inhumane decision is when the Chinese Government decided to keep University Professor Liu Xiaobo in a Jinzhou prison, without being able to communicate with anyone, after he took part in demonstrations at Tiananmen Square, Beijing, in 1989. He was sentenced to eleven years in prison for subscribing to *Charter 08*, a manifest from Chinese intellectuals who demanded the democratic opening of their country. In a clear and legitimate action of resistance beyond the suit and against the sentence, Liu was given the 2010 Nobel Peace Prize.

For Navy Pillay, United Nations High Commissioner for Human Rights, the prize awarded to the Chinese dissident acknowledged

---

297 MELLO. *Liberdade de expressão, dignidade humana e Estado democrático de direito*, p. 242.

the role of those to advocate for fundamental assurances in China: "Activists like him have much to contribute to the development of the country."[298] Obviously, the Chine Government reacted against the award.

In such cases, resistance beyond the suit translates into legitimate defense and, consequently, is exercised under the respective criteria. In Locke's account, acts of oppression and Human Rights violations are equivalent to piracy: They are acts without a judicial content, which correspond to the void, to the absolute judicial void. In the absence of a Law, there is nothing to authorize them to repeal resistance and, as a result, orders of this nature can be legitimately and concretely disputed.

Locke emphasizes that "Where-ever law ends, tyranny begins, if the law be transgressed to another's harm; and whosoever in authority exceeds the power given him by the law, and makes use of the force he has under his command, to compass that upon the subject, which the law allows not, ceases in that to be a magistrate; and, acting without authority, may be opposed, as any other man, who by force invades the right of another."[299]

As we can see, the triad of Natural Rights vaunted by Enlightenment philosophers, that is, internal and external liberties and the right to resist an oppressing State, are construed as pre-constituted rights opposable to all branches that constitute the State. They correspond to the essential elements of the Rule of Law, whose examples in history are the French Revolution, the Independence of the United States, and other Enlightenment movements that, ultimately, were universally victorious.

In regards to Human Rights, the legal contents of the right to resist are unquestionable and vested of the peaceful legitimacy that arises of, for example, the emotional event known worldwide as Tank Man. The conflicts that resulted in the arrest of Liu Xiaobo placed approximately one million dissidents face to face with the then despotic Chinese Government, according to journalist Débora Pinho, editor

---

298 http://www.onu-brasil.org.br on 10/11/2010
299 LOCKE. *Dois tratados sobre o governo*, p. 563.

of *Consultor Jurídico*. Among these dissidents was the "Tank Man." Débora narrates: "June 1989. A thin unarmed man stands alone in front of a tank convoy that the Chinese Army sent to Tiananmen Square, which in Mandarin means "Heavenly Peace." The first tank comes to a halt and, behind it, one by one, other tanks form a column."[300] It was not by chance that, before this legitimate and courageous manifestation of peaceful resistance, *Time* magazine "elected the character, who was never properly identified, as one of the 100 Most Important People of the Century,"[301] despite the fact that "Tank Man" was removed from in front of the convoy and his fate is still unknown.

Therefore, resistance without violence or acts of atrocity, especially civil disobedience before an inhumane legal order, must be accepted in any scenario as an immediate and proportional self-defense of each man and the whole man against transgressions of their Human Rights.

(7) Application Within The Economic Realm

Considering the unconquerable relevance of Human Rights to each man and the whole man, as well as that of the Planet, it is certain that Anthropophilic Humanism also applies to economic issues. Building upon Humanistic Capitalism, it penetrates the economic realm within the legal discipline to promote and assure that Human Rights will be realized in all their dimensions in order to fulfill Human Dignity.[302] As such, paraphrasing Ramos Tavares, property "will be aligned with the search for dignity,[303] since "Human Dignity or

300 PINHO. *O homem que parou o maior exército do mundo. In*: http://www.conjur.com.br, on 10/22/2009.

301 Idem.

302 SAYEG. *O Capitalismo humanista no Brasil,* pp. 1250-1264.

303 TAVARES. *Direito constitucional econômico brasileiro,* p. 156.

dignified existence certainly has economic implications."[304]

Upon applying the Law of Universal Fraternity to Human Rights in order to promote their multidimensional realization, they must also be realized in the economic realm without reserves. And it must be done mercifully, especially in the face of poverty. As James Kennedy once emphasized, "Jesus was a role model in assisting the poor and oppressed, as well as caring for those affected by poverty."[305]

However, due to its anthropophilic quality, such Humanism does not lead to Economic Socialism, far less to Communism. On the contrary, as Saint Thomas Aquinas acknowledged, private property is also a natural right.

Santiago Guerra tells us that, while arguing with Franciscans in the 14th century, Pope John XXII was inspired by Saint Thomas Aquinas, who back in his own time had coherently propagated ideas of contractual balance, social role and fair price, and pontificated "the notion that property is a natural right, as the most appropriate regime for human development in earthly existence."[306]

While addressing fair price in regards to commerce, despite proposing proportionality in the clash of interests, especially between the wealthy and the poor, Saint Thomas Aquinas acknowledged that there can be justice in profits that were obtained legally.[307]

However, Saint Thomas Aquinas incisively states that "as a natural right, all things that are superfluous to the wealthy shall be destined to provide for the poor."[308]

Therefore, it is safe to say that, according to Anthropophilic Humanism, Fraternity in the economic realm represents a proportional measure that implies the best possible realization of Human Rights in all their dimensions, which must be extended to everyone and everything, especially to fight poverty as a manifestation of mer-

---

304 Idem, p. 131.

305 KENNEDY; NEWCOMBE. Op. cit., p. 48.

306 GUERRA FILHO. *Filosofia, uma introdução*, p. 75.

307 AQUINO. Op. cit., Part II, IIa, Item 77: *Es lícito en el comercio vender algo más caro de lo que se compró?* in http://hjg.com.ar/sumat/c/c77.html.

308 Idem, Chapter 10, Article 7.

cy.

Before poverty, the subjective right to mercy is verified in the economic realm, thus emphatically demanding the vertical and horizontal application of the Law of Universal Fraternity that imposes the realization of Human Rights in all their dimensions. In Economy, as well, alienation is unacceptable on the part of each man and the whole man. Showing fraternity and mercy towards men and everything is to "wish for a solidary and inclusive society in which no citizens are left behind. It is to make a commitment to equality and believe that we have the duty to protect and care for the most vulnerable members of society,"[309] as well as the Planet itself.

As John Paul II once said, the right to private property is subordinated to the right to common use: "Property is acquired first of all through work in order that it may serve work. This concerns in a special way ownership of the means of production. Isolating these means as a separate property in order to set it up in the form of 'capital' in opposition to 'labour'—and even to practise exploitation of labour—is contrary to the very nature of these means and their possession. They cannot be possessed against labour, they cannot even be possessed for possession's sake, because the only legitimate title to their possession—whether in the form of private ownership or in the form of public or collective ownership—is that they should serve labour, and thus, by serving labour, that they should make possible the achievement of the first principle of this order, namely, the universal destination of goods and the right to common use of them."[310]

As Pope Paul VI once said, *it is unacceptable* that on these new conditions "These concepts present profit as the chief spur to economic progress, free competition as the guiding norm of economics, and private ownership of the means of production as an absolute right, having no limits nor concomitant social obligations. This unbridled liberalism paves the way for a particular type of tyranny, rightly condemned by Our predecessor Pius XI, for it results in the

---

309 GIDDENS. Op. cit., p. 23.
310 *Laborem Exercens,* item 14.

'international imperialism of money.'"[311]

The *Puebla Document* highlights that prioritizing wealth, as a result of an economicist view of the world, is the source of the tensions and injustices of our time.[312] Since it is the work of Man, even a neoliberal economy must respect Human Rights. Contradicting such a conclusion is irrational because it is offensive to self-preservation. As Pontes de Miranda has taught us, "Therefore, this reflection supposes respect for our neighbors; men stand together without fighting: in the economic arena, in sharing their prey."[313] According to the same author, it is so because "The human act of resolution or appropriation by force is beyond reflection or rational distribution, with respect (if not love) toward others. It is subhuman, a regressive animal instinct; it is Man extinguishing himself."[314] Economy must not be accepted as an instrument of force that subjugates everyone and everything and makes Human Nature superhuman or subhuman.

Maritain addresses the subject by assuring that "The remedy for abuses of individualism in the use of property must be sought not in abolishing private property; on the contrary, it lies in generalizing, popularizing projections in which it fortifies the individual.

---

311 PAULO VI. Op. cit., Item 26.

312 "Documento de Puebla" is the result of the 3rd Conference of Latin American Bishops, which took place in 1979 in the respective Mexican city. Here is the complete text of item 492: "The properties and riches of the world, due to their origins and nature and according to our Maker's will, will effectively serve their purpose and be enjoyed by all Men and Nations. That is why each one of us has a primary and fundamental right that is absolutely sacred: To use these properties with solidarity, as needed, in order to achieve Human Dignity. All other rights, including that of free enterprise and trade, are subordinated to it. As John Paul II once taught us: 'Private property carries a social mortgage.' A property compatible with such primordial right has, above all, a power to manage and administer that, despite not excluding sovereignty, is not absolute or limitless. It must be a source of liberty to everyone, not a domination without privileges. It is a great urgent duty to return it to its original purpose."

313 MIRANDA. *Garra, mão e dedo*, p. 144.

314 Idem, p. 145.

The issue lies in giving each human the real and concrete possibility to ascend."[315] Giddens shares the same thinking: "Or, by taking Amartya Sen's concept of 'social capability' as a starting point; equality and inequality don't just refer to the availability of social and material goods—individuals must have the capabilities to make effective use of them. Policies concerned with promoting equality should be focused upon developing people's capacities to pursue their well-being. Likewise, disadvantage must be defined as lack of capability—not only loss of resource, but loss of capability to achieve it."[316]

As Pope Paul VI indicates in Encyclical *Populorum Progressio*, we must accept Capitalism, but without forgetting that is the work of man; therefore, it shall not be inhumane. According to Maritain, Neoliberal Capitalism must not be considered the best model, since "It demands greatness and, at the same time, abundance and poverty."[317]

In other words, Neoliberal Capitalism is founded on disregard for Human and Planet Dignity, according to the natural selection that was transported to the social environment hosted by the Planet. This "tragic law, not of Human Nature but of Man's sin, makes the poverty of some generate the abundance of others; poverty in misery and slavery, abundance in concupiscence and pride. A law of sin that shall not be accepted, but contested."[318] Therefore, it is enough to accept and apply Fraternity to Capitalism.

Uelmen considers "Fraternity as a legal category" in *Business Law* and indicates precedents in which "Beyond an economic analysis, Fraternity is the secret heart of law; it is not only desired, but currently applied as well."[319] Hence, as Pope Paul VI once proclaimed, "Economy is at the service of man,"[320] not the opposite, under the

---

315 MARITAIN. Op. cit., p. 178.

316 GIDDENS. *A questão da desigualdade*, p. 255.

317 MARITAIN. Op. and p. cits.

318 Idem, p. 185.

319 UELMEN. *Fraternidade como categoria jurídica no direito empresarial*, p. 76.

320 PAULO VI. Op. and item cits.

penalty of it becoming inhumane, as Maritain would say.[321] Law has the mission to humanize economy through the multidimensional realization of Human Rights for the good of everyone and everything, thus instituting what we christened as "Humanistic Capitalism."

In conclusion, Anthropophilic Humanism believes that the economic order must be evolutionist, inclusive, and emancipating for everyone and everything. In sum, it must be fraternal and, especially, merciful when facing poverty. It does not dishonor, but edifies Human Rights in all their dimensions.

---

321 MARITAIN. Op. cit., p. 186.

V
HUMANISTIC CAPITALISM

(1) Locke's Capitalism And Legal Naturalism

There are several economic doctrines, each with its own regime: Capitalism, Socialism, etc. Some philosophers, among them Graham and Luke, even refer to Neo-feudalism as a new post-Capitalism doctrine.[322]

In general, economic regimes are divided into Capitalism or Socialism, founded on the presence or absence of legal recognition of the subjective natural right to property and, consequently, different levels of free enterprise. We have, in one end of the spectrum, a Liberal State that aspires to have right to property and freedom of enterprise as absolutes while, on the other end of the spectrum, we have a Communist State that aims at suppressing them completely. Therefore:

a. upon denying the subjective natural right to property and, consequently, of free enterprise, a regime is labeled as Communist;

b. upon treating as relative the denial of the subjective

---

322 *Militarizing the body politic: manifestations of neofeudal corporatism in political language about the war on Iraq.* Visited at http://www.philgraham. net on 08/13/2008.

natural right to property and, consequently, of free enterprise, a regime is labeled as Socialist;

    c. upon recognizing the subjective natural right to property and, consequently, of free enterprise with minimal State intervention, thus unleashing the natural forces of the market, a regime is labeled Liberal Market Capitalism;

    d. upon recognizing the subjective natural right to property and, consequently, of free enterprise, while having the State coordinate their universal exercise, a regime is labeled a Capitalist State or Autocratic;

    e. upon recognizing the subjective natural right to property and, consequently, of free enterprise, while calibrating the natural forces of the market with social balance, a regime is labeled Social Market Capitalism;

    f. upon recognizing the subjective natural right to property and, consequently, of free enterprise, but calibrating the natural forces of the market with the undeniable objective of realizing Human Rights in all their dimensions in order to universally fulfill Human Dignity, a regime is labeled Humanistic Market Capitalism.

Socialism, in the broad meaning of the word, and its more radical version, Communism, have been fatally wounded by post-modern individualism and hedonism, for both have disregarded the material well-being of all Humans. Capitalism does achieve it upon maximizing the best individual economic results, which implies overall prosperity in a cause-and-effect relationship.

In Giddens' words,[323] "The economic theory of Socialism was always inadequate, underestimating the capacity of Capitalism to innovate, adapt and generate increasing productivity." He adds, "As a system of economic management, Socialism is no more," because there came "the death of Socialism," for it sought "to confront the limitations of Capitalism to humanize it or to overthrow it altogether."[324]

Hobsbawm describes the end of socialism in detail, mention-

---

323 GIDDENS. *A terceira via e seus críticos*, p. 14.

324 Idem.

ing that "in the 1970s, it was clear that not only economic growth was lagging, but even the basic social indicators such as mortality were ceasing to improve. This undermined confidence in socialism perhaps more than anything else, since its ability to improve the lives of ordinary people through greater social justice did not depend primarily on its ability to generate greater wealth."[325] The radioactive accident that occurred in 1986 at a nuclear power plant in Chernobyl, Ukraine, proved that socialism was obsolete and had concrete negative effects for everyone and everything. Journalist César Tralli visited the "precarious facilities in Chernobyl" and reported that "TV is well acquainted with the power plant, in a certain way. First with the images of one of the nuclear reactors burning up in flames [...]. Then, with those dramatic scenes of workers walking through radiation clouds without any special protection. Men running left and right with shovels and bags of sand. A series of suicidal ideas and useless attempts to contain the radiation leak, which released two hundred more radioactivity to the environment than the Hiroshima and Nagasaki bombs combined."[326]

Greenspan, in turn, reports that the universal icons of Communism have entered Capitalism upon acknowledging the right to private property. In China, "in March 2007, the National People's Congress passed a more comprehensive right of ownership that grants the same legal protection of property that is granted to the State,"[327] while in Russia "Property rights have been extended in recent years"; Russian economy "is today best described as a market economy backed by a still-imperfect rule of law."[328] At long last, there is no longer a relevant socialist stronghold in the planet.

Capitalism did not prevail by chance; it was due to efficient private economic agents seeking their own interests, which are inherent to the individualistic and hedonistic human nature. On the other hand, the State was inefficient as an economic agent due to its natural

---

325 HOBSBAWM. *Era dos extremos*, p. 457.

326 TRALLI. *Olhar crônico*, p. 43.

327 GREENSPAN. *Era da turbulência*, p. 286.

328 Idem, 316.

inclination to aim for the collective interests.

The world is Capitalist and the global option for Capitalism necessarily implies the recognition of private property as corresponding to the subjective natural right to ownership, which drives it and is not contingent upon positivation. This behavior allows its imperialistic nature to be compared to that of Rome, which conquered the ancient world. Without establishing a worldwide unity, Capitalism has subjected all Capitalist men to the forces of the market. Incidentally, supranationality is a legal institution recognized by internationalists, including Finkelstein.[329]

The Constitution of the United States, global Capitalism leader, is a good example of this non-positivated natural right, since none of its precepts assures ownership directly and it only does so indirectly through a clause that addresses the due process of law. Historically, the U.S. forefathers refused to assure ownership directly by transferring it to the Positive Law in order to avoid diminishing such an important accomplishment of the Natural Law for all free men. Likewise, English addresses the right to private property in the same manner and they do not even have a written Constitution comprising of a single document.

The philosophical school of thought that considers private property to be a subjective natural right that is not contingent upon positivation can be found in John Locke's legal naturalist concepts that have been adopted by Capitalism. Pursuant to them, private property is acknowledged as an objective right corresponding to the subjective natural right to property.

According to Villey, "For Locke, before a contract and the creation of the State, there would have been social order in its inception: different pre-constituted rights in their natural state. Let us now change the expression to its plural form: The Natural Rights of Individuals. As a result of Hobbes' system combined with the Natural Law School, Locke adds to Hobbes' system an argument that was borrowed from Grotius, who dedicated himself to draw from Natural

---

329 FINKELSTEIN. *O processo de formação de mercados de bloco*, p. 47.

Law the existence of an individual's subjective natural rights."[330] This structural platform for the Capitalist phenomenon is consolidated in formulations developed by Locke, especially the one that men assembled to give origin to a State in order to defend pre-constituted rights, among which were the right to property (external liberties) and to religion (internal liberties).

Sengupta confirms that "The natural rights theorists, Hobbes (1588-1679), Locke (1612-1704) and Rousseau (1712-1778) were the principal proponents of this secular theory, which was best exemplified by Locke's claim during the English Revolution of 1688 and certain rights like the right to life, liberty, and property belonged to individuals as human beings because they existed in the state of nature before human beings entered civil society."[331] Summarizing Locke's concepts, Sengupta explains that, "Upon entering a civil society, those human beings surrendered through a social contract to the State only the right to enforce the natural rights, not the rights themselves. If the State failed to secure these rights, it violated the terms of the social contract and would be liable to be overthrown by a social revolution."[332]

Still in Sengupta's words, "A century after the English Revolution, the French Revolution of 1789 was supported by the natural rights theorists again in terms of action against the sovereign breaking the terms of the social contract and the French Declaration of the Rights of Men and Citizens asserted that the rights of liberty, property, security and resistance to oppression were "natural, inalienable and sacred."[333] It was through this legal naturalism that the revolutionary liberal French bourgeoisie of the 18th century proclaimed: *"Laissez faire, laissez aller, laissez passer"*.[334]

In view of the very same legal naturalism, Sengupta asserts that on the other side of the Atlantic, "among revolutionaries of the

---

330 VILLEY. *Filosofia do direito*, p. 147.

331 SENGUPTA. *O direito ao desenvolvimento como um direito humano*, p. 10.

332 Idem.

333 Ibidem..

334 "Let nature run its course."

18th century" in the Enlightenment period that marked America, "Thomas Jefferson claimed that it was not only permissible but morally required to overthrow tyrannies that violate these principles of 'natural equity and justice' that formed the basis of the legitimacy of the government."[335] In fact, as a mature development of such thought, the Declaration of Independence of the United States solemnly proclaimed on the 4th of July, 1776 that "We hold these truths to be self-evident, that all men are created equal, that they are endowed by their Creator with certain unalienable Rights, that among these are Life, Liberty and the pursuit of Happiness. That to secure these rights, Governments are instituted among Men, deriving their just powers from the consent of the governed; that whenever any Form of Government becomes destructive of these ends, it is the Right of the People to alter or to abolish it, and to institute new Government, laying its foundation on such principles and organizing its powers in such form, as to them shall seem most likely to affect their Safety and Happiness."[336]

Therefore, it is clear that the Capitalist economic regime is not part of Thomas Hobbes' perspective of predominance of the State, in which right to property is granted by the State. On the contrary, in the event that such right be threatened, as Locke had indicated, it is implied that the State would be confronted and, potentially, the respective government would be destroyed.

---

335 SENGUPTA. Op. cit.

336 In the original text: "*We hold these Truths to be self-evident, that all Men are created equal, that they are endowed by their Creator with certain unalienable Rights, that among these are Life, Liberty and the Pursuit of Happiness—That to secure these Rights, Governments are instituted among Men, deriving their just Powers from the Consent of the Governed, that whenever any Form of Government becomes destructive of these Ends, it is the Right of the People to alter or to abolish it, and to institute new Government, laying its Foundation on such Principles, and organizing its Powers in such Form, as to them shall seem most likely to effect their Safety and Happiness*". Please refer to the complete text available on the official U.S. Embassy website: http://www.embaixada-americana.org.br.

In other words, Hobbes construed that men, in their natural state, surrounded by savagery and in order to assure their self-preservation, had relinquished their natural rights to the State, including the right to property and its resulting external liberties; consequently, by the power vested in it, the State had the authority to recognize and control all rights and intersubjective property relationships among men.

Hobbes emphasized that "Where there is no state, there is no property."[337] He added, "[It] is annexed to the Sovereign, the whole power of prescribing the Rules, whereby every man may know, what Goods he may enjoy and what Actions he may do, without being molested by any of his fellow Subjects: And this is it men call Property."[338] He starts with the premise that "All people are unified by covenant of everyone with everyone (...): I authorize and give up my right to govern myself to this man or this assembly of men"[339] consequently "defined to be a multitude of men, united as one person" that he called State or, in Latin, *civitas*.[340]

Thus, there should be no resistance against the decisions of the State, in that Hobbes comes to the point of uphold that "a sovereign monarch, or a majority of a sovereign assembly, may order things to be done in pursuit of their passions and contrary to their own consciences; that would be a breach of trust and of the law of nature, but this fact isn't enough to authorize any subject to oppose his sovereign—to make war on him, to accuse him of injustice, or in any way to speak evil of him—because the subjects have authorized all his actions, and in giving him the sovereign power they have made his actions their own."[341]

If this is so, then all rights of Man would be those restrictively granted by the State, there would be no Natural Law and, as a result,

---

337 HOBBES. *Leviatã ou matéria, forma e poder de um estado eclesiástico e civil*, p. 86.
338 Idem, p. 110.
339 Ibidem, p. 105.
340 Ibidem.
341 Ibidem, p. 151.

the nature of Capitalism itself would be disarranged.

Adeodato clarifies that, "with Hobbes, there is a covenant among men of which the State arises, instead of being part of it. In such covenant, citizens abdicate all of their original rights, inasmuch as all citizens do the same. The State has no obligations with is citizens, since all natural rights—in the very liberal sense of Man as a free being in his state of nature—are transferred to the State, which thereafter has rights over the life and death of an individual."[342]

It is precisely because of it that, for Bobbio, "What places Hobbes against the tradition of legal naturalism is the way in which he conceives the relationship between natural laws and civil laws, that is, how valid natural laws are when compared to civil laws. With a concise formula that seems very significant to me, I would say that, for Hobbes, natural laws are those that have not come into effect in the state of nature and, in the civil state, have already ceased to be effective."[343]

Construing the right to private property as that which is granted by an absolute State would be the same as stating that, for example, there is no right to private property in the United States and in England because of a lack of positivation. Consequently, these countries could not even be classified as Capitalists.

In sum, upon functioning as a premise that structures the right to property, nationalization is divorced from Capitalism, so much so that, for the Capitalist Regime, property is initially private. Therefore, State Capitalism would be but a mere artificial coordinated effort of the market and, as such, an inefficient exception that, historically, would be overcome by Neoliberalism.

In essence, Capitalism does not fit Hobbes' philosophy, which was the basis for the concept of State giving rights to Man, even though State Capitalism is accepted as an artificial solution. Supported by John Locke's philosophy, then, the subjective natural right to property is acknowledged as an inherent right of each man and the whole man.

---

342 ADEODATO. Op. cit., p. 119.
343 BOBBIO. Op. cit., p. 42.

As the philosopher adopted by Capitalism, Locke in turn converges with Thomism and, thus, with Anthropophilic Humanism. Upon confirming and relating with Hooker's concepts, he believed that "This equality of Men by Nature, the Judicious Hooker looks upon as so evident in itself, and beyond all question, that he makes it the Foundation of that Obligation to mutual Love among Men, on which he builds the duties they owe one another, and from whence he derives the great Maxims of Justice and Charity."[344]

Due to this philosophical construction, Bobbio classifies Locke simultaneously as "a philosopher of Liberalism and Rational Christianity,"[345] emphasizing that he supported his arguments in Saint Thomas Aquinas.[346] He also states that, for Locke, there is a "fraternal or charitable law that makes us help the poor and heal the sick, among other things." Said law exists between civil and monastic law, according to which Man individually subjects a vote or covenant to his own conscience.[347] In fact, Locke assured that "no one can be a Christian without charity and without the faith that works by love and not by violence."[348]

Therefore, Capitalism is innate to each man and the whole man, corresponding to a subjective perspective of natural rights to property that is structured according to Locke's philosophy. Notwithstanding those who think the contrary, it is fully compatible with Anthropophilic Humanism in that it addresses the universality of gifts that, as the result of a legitimate accumulation by the owners of capital, are to be distributed throughout the Planet, to each man and the whole man, according to the criteria and measures of Integral Humanism.[349]

---

344 LOCKE. Op.cit., p. 383.

345 BOBBIO. Op. cit., p. 78.

346 Idem, p. 111.

347 Ibidem, p. 103.

348 LOCKE. *Carta sobre la tolerancia*, p. 4.

349 LEBRET. *O drama do século XX*, p. 116.

(2) Human Rights To Property And Free Enterprise

Capitalist economic activity is the active or passive exercise of total or partial appropriation and distribution of private property. It is not only construed as the transfer of property, but also as the right to own and use property within other spheres of powers inherent to ownership.

As we can see, this activity is initially an exercise of ownership that realizes human liberty over things. It is a private exercise, whether active or passive, of the power to appropriate or distribute individual property. It construes this ownership in its objective perspective and, consequently, as the real right to property itself. Therefore, it is clear that this economic activity is structured within the legal system by having property as the private ownership of assets and the power to appropriate and distribute properties as a consequence of individual liberty.

The respective action or omission of specifically appropriating or distributing things, especially in regards to whether they are moved around, is a permanent fixture simply known in economy as "exchanging hands" or "appropriation." In other words, it is protracted in time and reality until it ceases to exist. Such economic conduct is not contingent upon a definite character and said exchange or appropriate is sufficient. Likewise, it needs not be burdensome or entrepreneurial: every burdensome or entrepreneurial act of private appropriation or distribution is an economic activity, even though the opposite is not true. For example, when a company sells a product to a consumer, it is performing an economic activity. The same is true of financial gifts given by members of the congregation to their religious organization.

In regards to the innate human liberty of having and distributing things, it is known in economy as "free enterprise," that is, Man has freedom to appropriate of something through economic means and distribute it as it is convenient to him. This is what structures Capitalist activities.

In Brazil, free enterprise is positivated in Article 1st, Section

4, and in the introduction or Article 170 of the Federal Constitution. Hence, the ownership exercised by economic means is considered a free enterprise and structured by the authentic subjective natural right to property, whose elementary characteristic is found in the Capitalist economy.

Said right to property is classified as a subjective right because it refers to Man's natural liberty, which in turn encompasses the prerogative of a respective *erga omnes* perfection that includes others, the State, and Civil Society. And so it is because it was constituted before the birth of civil society itself, which resulted in the creation of the State.

Despite contrary opinions, it is ascertained that private property is an instituted objective right that, above all, corresponds to the external liberty from human nature in regards to subjective rights. It exists with or without a Civil Code, even in the absence of a Constitution to assure said right. Consequently, it is interrelated to Human Rights and, more objectively, to Human Dignity.

According to Locke's view, legal systems that do not accept private property violate the natural law that imposes Human Rights and are enforced artificially, despite expressing the will of the people since, as Miranda indicates, "The will of the people is subordinated to Human Dignity."[350]

This does not mean that private property is non-existent in such a State; it means that Human Rights are being violated by the respective legal system inasmuch as it does not accept its concrete realization. As in Antigone's tragedy, even though she dies because she exercised her natural right, no one denied her the application of natural law and superiority of Humanism: everyone acknowledged the tyranny and transgressions of Creon.

It is unacceptable to deny the subjective natural right to property and, consequently, the objective right respective to private property. Traversing it is an act against Human Dignity, since said right is inherent to Man, that is, a Human Right to property and free

---

350 MIRANDA. *A dignidade da pessoa humana e a unidade valorativa do sistema de direitos fundamentais,* p. 176.

enterprise. From this perspective, the subjective concept of property is broad and cannot be mistaken by the meaningful contents of its positivation, which tends to limit it to the concrete right to something and excludes all other liberties that are authentically represented in its subjectivity.

Property is, first and foremost, liberty to participate, retain, and distribute things that belong to the Planet. For this very same reason, it is considered a universal element that erects Human Rights, from the subjective natural right that corresponds to the most basic individual external liberties inherent to Humans, of which all other external liberties arise. So much so that Locke, in the second half of the 17th century, already compared property to religious liberty in his *Letters on Toleration*, for both are internal liberties that preach the opposition to tyrannical governments that do not assure the Natural Rights of Mankind.[351]

When addressing this idea, Vita indicates that, incidentally, those who advocate for the minimal intervention of the State are radically for the absolute characterization of subjective natural right to property. As a manifestation of this market fundamentalism, he observes that "Individual liberty is not Norzick's primary concern; it is the sanctity of the moral right to ownership of oneself and of external resources that have been obtained by legal means." And he adds, "This right must be thoroughly assured by a fair and liberal State, despite the disastrous consequences that may arise of it."[352]

Insofar as the right to property is concerned, as acknowledged by Locke, having it recognized does not constitute an obstacle to either the classic Capitalism philosophy, its concrete realization, or the subjective natural right of others before the property owner. Locke stated that "The same law of nature, that does by this means give us property, does also bound that property too. God has given us all things richly (1 Timothy 6:17) is the voice of reason confirmed by inspiration. But how far has he given it us? To enjoy."[353] And he

---

351 LOCKE. Op. cit., pp. 53, 58 and 60.

352 VITA. *A justiça igualitária e seus críticos*, p. 60.

353 LOCKE. Op. cit., p. 412.

emphasizes: "Whatever is beyond this, is more than his share, and belongs to others."[354]

Saint Basil the Great, a Patristics scholar, echoed the same message when he taught us that "The bread you keep belongs to the hungry, the cloak you store in your closet belongs to the naked man; the shoes rotting in your house belong to those who are barefooted; the money you keep hidden belongs to the needy. Thus you are committing as many injustices as there are people to whom you can give."[355]

In more modern times, while addressing a subject that should be reflected upon by all those who think of the subjective natural right to property, Pope John Paul II warned us that "Ownership of the means of production, whether in industry or agriculture, is just and legitimate if it serves useful work. It becomes illegitimate, however, when it is not utilized or when it serves to impede the work of others, in an effort to gain a profit which is not the result of the overall expansion of work and the wealth of society, but rather is the result of curbing them or of illicit exploitation, speculation or the breaking of solidarity among working people. Ownership of this kind has no justification, and represents an abuse in the sight of God and man."[356]

Upon observing said premises, and according to Locke's concepts, despite their legal naturalist nature, we can acknowledge the positivation of property as an explicit indication of this subjective natural right, inasmuch as it is subordinated to it. Locke once said "And amongst those who are counted the civilized part of Mankind, who have made and multiplied positive laws to determine property, this original law of nature for the beginning of property in what was before common, still takes place."[357] Still according to Locke, the subjective natural right to property is inherent to Humans, but it is relative according to the Natural Law itself. Consequently, positivation finds authority to attribute a special legal discipline to make it relative,

---

354 Idem, p. 412.

355 HUSCENOT. *Os doutores da igreja*, p. 54.

356 *Centesimus Annus*, item 43.

357 Idem, p. 411.

but without demeaning its core.

Making proper reservations to assure the essence of the subjective natural right to property, said relativity is acceptable and positivation precisely functions as a way to make it explicit. As an example,, Article 170, Section 2 of the Brazilian Federal Constitution recognizes private property and then later, on Section 3, attributes a social function to it with the express purpose of assuring a dignified existence to everyone, pursuant to the principles of social justice. The constituent assembly was indeed going into that direction, because the introduction to Article 5 assures the sanctity of property, which is also specified in Section 22 with the list of respective fundamental rights, in which "right to property is assured." Further on, in Section 23, it sets forth that "property shall fulfill its social function."

Within this spectrum, it is possible to apply Anthropophilic Humanism to Capitalism. Even though it openly recognizes the subjective natural right to property, said right is classified as a Human Right and limited by Fraternity Law. For instance, the aforementioned Article 170 of the Federal Constitution, which is the source of economic order in the country, expressly attributes a purpose to it upon assuring a dignified existence to all, pursuant to the principles of social justice, thus positivating the duty to economic fraternity within a Capitalist Brazil.

During a lecture in Brazil, Alexy referred to the Brazilian Constitution and, recognizing the positivation of fundamental rights in the Brazilian constitutional catalogue, he introduced precisely this example of an estimated judgment between right to property, as set forth in Article 5, Section 22, and the social function stated in Section 23.[358]

Consequently, based on Locke's concepts, it is undeniable that

---

358 *Constitucionalismo discursivo*, pp. 50-51. Upon mentioning this example, Alexy said, "However, deliberation as part of a proportionality exam is the core issue found in the fundamental rights dogma and the principle foundation for a fundamental rights catalog to be widened. In some cases, this issue is clearly evident. For example, when Article 5, Section 22 assures property and, immediately after it, on Section 23, it is added that property must serve its social function."

the subjective right to property, just as the basic freedom of Humans, is a subjective natural right for the instrumentalization of a human essence that, despite not being absolute, can be realized and, thus, is found in the sphere of Human Rights and subject to their multidimensional deliberation.

According to Aristotle, "Property is a necessary instrument to life."[359] Pope John XXIII acknowledged private property as Man's natural right, including ownership of means of production,[360] but without neglecting the universal destination of said property, as preached by Anthropophilic Humanism.

It was not by chance that the 1791 Declaration of the Rights of Man and of the Citizen, which was a result of the French Revolution, and the U.N. Universal Declaration of Human Rights of 1948 have recognized the right to property as an individual human right classified among the so-called negative liberties. Suppressing the natural right to property is certainly equivalent to mutilating the essential dignity and self-determination of each man and the whole man at its very core. A clear example of such violence can be seen on Chapter 2 of the Declaration of Rights of the Working and Exploited People, dated January 12, 1918. Upon abolishing private property, the Communist government announced its intention "to mercilessly crush the resistance of the exploiters" and make efforts towards "achieving at all costs, by revolutionary means, a democratic peace between the nations."

Ergo, this is the subjective natural right to property, which in our days has supported Civil Rights. This doctrine is widely accepted as the very platform for the negative liberties that are part of the first dimension of said rights, which are composed themselves of internal liberties or those of conscience that comprise personality rights. Based on such premises, Macpherson understand that we should be "treating all the human rights as individual property rights. My

---

359 Op. cit., 16.

360 *Mater et Magistra*, item 109. The Pope reminds us that, "in the plan of the Creator all of this world's goods are primarily intended for the worthy support of the entire human race." (item 119).

point was simply that the property right is so deeply imbedded in the Western liberal tradition that we might more effectively campaign for human rights by treating them as individual property rights than by treating human and property rights as opposites. To do that requires no sleight of hand. To speak of human rights as individual property rights would indeed be to restore the original liberal meaning of property, as when Locke and his contemporaries spoke of a property in one's person, one's life and liberty, as well as one's worldly goods."[361] Expressing the meaning of such notion on individual rights, the political scientist recorded that "We shall need to recognize that the individual can be fully human only as a member of a community,"[362] and, consequently include in its proposal the subjective natural right to property.

Considering such a proposition, we are certain that external Human Rights are part of the innate subjective heritage of their holders, aligned with the objective dimensions of Human Dignity, Democracy, and Peace in order to reach each man and the whole man and achieve balance among all Capitalist property interests.

(3) Classic Economic Regimes Of Capitalism

As we have seen, upon acknowledging the subjective natural right to property, Capitalism prevailed as the economic regime of our post-modern planet, so much so that it has recognized free enterprise, private property, right to inheritance, acquired right, and perfect legal act. As the majority of nations in the globalized world, Brazil is constitutionally Capitalist,[363] since said rights are expressly set forth in the country's Federal Constitution.

There are two classic Capitalist economy regimes:

---

361 MACPHERSON. *Ascensão e queda da justiça econômica*, pp. 50-51.

362 Idem, p. 51.

363 SAYEG. *Práticas comerciais abusivas*, p. 41.

— Liberal Capitalism: The Capitalist regime originally comprises the coordination of natural market forces, thus forming the so-called Economic liberalism. It is arranged according to a market Capitalist economy in which a Liberal State (that is, a Minimal State) interferes with the economy as little as possible.

— State Capitalism: It is accepted that said coordination, despite artificial, be performed by the State. It can inclusively be a direct economic agent acting in its own name and at its own charge, thus establishing the so-called economic statism. Characterized by a Capitalist economy with centralized command, in which a Welfare State coordinates economic activities, it is controlling without rejecting private property over means of production and financial institutions.

In regards to Liberal Capitalism, the market economy promoted by a Liberal State is based on four pillars of natural order, as Rossetti explains: (1) "The rationality of Men of economy [as] an assumption that individual economic agents are always rationally driven [to] maximize their revenue and, by investing their revenue, to achieve the highest possible level of satisfaction;"[364] (2) "The virtues of individualism [based on the] concept that combining individual rights resulting from the rationality of each economic agent is the true expression of collective interests. In seeking their own interests, each one of them is acting towards the realization of social interests;"[365] (3) "The automation of market power, [since] markets are internally endowed with powers that keep them operating correctly."[366] In other words, they have natural mechanisms that bring harmony to the interests of different economic agents, and (4) "The competition adjustment"[367] as an instrument of competition among economic agents and a means to transfer the best productive practices to the respective

---

364 ROSSETTI. *Introdução à economia*, pp. 312-313.
365 Idem.
366 Ibidem.
367 Ibidem.

passive subjects of the economic activity.

As we can see, Liberal Capitalism leads to market economy and have its foundations on verifications of the natural order, the well-known "invisible hand"[368] mentioned by Adam Smith,[369] thus constituting *laissez-faire*, which could be understood as "leave us alone!" Upon defining an economic order, Rossetti[370] also establishes the following dominant traits: (1) Minimal State; (2) Private Property; (3) Free Enterprise, and (4) Market as the center of economic coordination.

Friedman and other liberals think that "Government is necessary to preserve our freedom, it is an instrument through which we can exercise our freedom; yet by concentrating power in political hands, it is also a threat to freedom."[371] The classic liberal concept is better represented in economy by the motto "the best government is the one that governs the least,"[372] which is attributed to Liberal Americans dating back to the Independence of the United States, especially Thomas Jefferson's ideology.[373] To extreme liberals, as Thoreau, such ideology would be even more radical: "The best government is the one that governs not at all."[374]

On the other end of the spectrum, still according to Rossetti, State Capitalism has a centralized economy that is inserted in the idea

---

368 SANDRONI. *Dicionário de economia do século XXI*, p. 511: "Invisible hand. A concept developed by Adam Smith in *The Wealth of Nations*, meaning an invisible coordination that assures consistency of individual plans in a society where a market system is predominant. According to Smith, individuals only seeks their own intrests and, in fact, are led by an invisible hand towards achieving a result that was not originally in their plans. The result achieved would then correspond to the interests of society."

369 SMITH. *Investigación sobre la naturaleza y causas de la riqueza de las naciones*, p. 402.

370 ROSSETTI. Op. cit., p. 313.

371 FRIEDMAN. *Capitalismo e liberdade*, p. 12.

372 THOREAU. *A desobediência civil e outros escritos*, p. 13.

373 Idem.

374 Ibidem.

of a Welfare State, which in turn is based on other pillars of an artificial order: (1) The ostensible control of economic dynamics by the government; (2) "The juxtaposition of political and economic power [through which] government centralizes powers"[375] of a political and economic nature, at the same time, and consequently distributes economic resources based on politics, and (3) "The sovereignty of the planner,"[376] as an imperative to determine the economic guidelines to be followed by the market, including "supremacy of compulsory management measures, compared to an incentives system based on the pursuit of individual interests."[377]

Therefore, State Capitalism is structured in Keynes' concepts, as opposed to the market economy, and has the following dominant traits: (1) Intervening State; (2) Private Property; (3) Realization of Subjective Natural Rights to Property; (4) Free Enterprise, and (5) State as the center of economic coordination in favor of its economic policy.

On the Capitalist economic thought, Keynes argues that "the postulates of the classical theory are applicable to a special case only and not to the general case, the situation which it assumes being a limiting point of the possible positions of equilibrium. Moreover, the characteristics of the special case assumed by the classical theory happen not to be those of the economic society in which we actually live, with the result that its teaching is misleading and disastrous if we attempt to apply it to the facts of experience."[378]

Keynes used to say that there was not a favorable market environment to support Liberal Capitalism within the economic reality, for it could only be applied without any damages within a competitive Capitalism with perfect competition. Competitive Capitalism is characterized by plurality of competitors within the same sector, product consistency, market atomicity, mobility of production factors, and price transparency in an economic scenario in which no one has

---

375 ROSSETTI. Op. cit., p. 327.

376 Idem.

377 Ibidem.

378 KEYNES. *A teoria geral do emprego, do juro e da moeda*, p. 23.

a preponderant influence over the market all by themselves, where perfect competition is a necessary condition that leads to self-regulation through the free dynamics of the economic law of supply and demand.[379]

We stated that, back in the 1990s, the trend was for the global market to become more concentrated and, in Brazil, it had become particularly concentrated. This foreknowledge proved to be exact.[380] Future is the master of reason and, despite the fact that these Capitalism models were applied, none of them provided sufficient answers to the demands of Humanity and the Planet.

Capitalism must be protected from liberals and Keynesians alike. Thus the mission of the contemplations herein: unveiling another Capitalist economy discipline based on the multidimensional realization of Human Rights in order to universally fulfill Human Dignity.

(4) The Inconveniences Of Neoliberalism

The economic doctrine has acknowledged that the economic fact, product of an economic activity, necessarily leads to repercussions that somehow give color to the economy fabric, whether in a Liberal State, State Capitalism, or half-way point between them. Such repercussions are known as externalities; they may be positive, when they serve a purpose, or negative, when they are undesirable. They are private when they reach the interests of a person in particular, within their individual scope. They are public when they reach a group (primary target) or the interests of the State (secondary target). They are universal when they act upon all Humans, Mankind, and the Planet.

As an example of negative private externality, we have the effect that a product sold by a company to the consumer has over their competitor. Such economic activity has a negative repercussion over

---

379 SAYEG. op. cit., p. 61.
380 Idem.

the competitor because that company in particular has not performed its activity in relation to said consumer. As a negative externality over a primary target, we have the pollution caused by a company during its industrialization process, releasing chemical waste to the environment.

Notwithstanding the negative externalities generated by the economic fact, economic Liberalism understands that such externalities are, in principle, absorbed by the market, resolved by the competition, or offset by the positive externalities that may arise. While an economic agent creates a negative externality upon polluting the environment while manufacturing their products, this very same agent also gives room to a positive externality when creating employment opportunities, for example.

Therefore, as Adam Smith and David Ricardo state, Liberal Capitalism proposes and justifies a free market that is subject to its own dynamics. According to Adam Smith, "It is not from the benevolence of the butcher, the brewer, or the baker, that we expect our dinner, but from their regard to their own self-interest. We address ourselves, not to their humanity but to their self-love, and never talk to them of our own necessities but of their advantages."[381]

Subsequent to this liberal theory, the market regulates itself through competition and the consequent natural profit, especially in regards to prices, seeing that as David Ricardo once indicated, "every Capitalist wishes to transfer their funds from a less profitable activity to a more profitable one, which does not allow the price of merchandise to remain well above or below the natural price for too long. This competition adjusts the exchange value of merchandise in such a way that, after paying wages for the production work required, and after all other expenses needed for the capital investment to fulfill its efficient purpose, the remaining or exceeding value in each activity will be proportional to the capital value that has been applied."[382]

However, according to Brue,[383] those theorists known as "so-

---

381 SMITH. Op. cit., p. 17.

382 RICARDO. *Princípios de economia política e tributação*, pp. 78-79.

383 BRUE. *História do pensamento econômico*, p. 393 and following.

cial welfare economists," Arthur Cecil Pigou being the most promi-
nent of them, understood that the government would be responsible
for leveling the respective public marginal costs and benefits, thus
promoting a State Capitalist economy.

This State Capitalism is the foundation of the so-called Welfare State, which practices governmental economic statism to act
artificially in the market, thus compensating or correcting negative
externalities through taxes, subsidies, or regulations.

It could not be any different and such ideas have provoked a
reaction from part of market economy advocates and, consequently,
that of Liberal Capitalism, which promotes economic Neoliberalism.
As Brue[384] recalled, in 1959 Ronald Coase (who would earn a Nobel
in Economics in 1991) published an article that confronted Pigou's
analysis on externalities and indicated that the role of the government
should be restricted to defining property rights and reducing transaction costs.

Brue[385] comments on Coase's interpretation, according to
which externalities would have been reciprocal: The [Pigou] approach
has tended to obscure the nature of the choice that has to be made.
The question is commonly thought of as one in which A inflicts harm
on B and what has to be decided is: How should we restrain A? But
this is wrong. We are dealing with a problem of a reciprocal nature.
To avoid the harm to B would inflict harm on A. The real question
that has to be decided is: Should A be allowed to harm B or should
B be allowed to harm A? The problem is to avoid the more serious
harm." In conclusion, Brue adduces that, for Coase, "When one of the
parties has rights to property that are adversely affected by the action
of another, both parties will be motivated to negotiate an acceptable
outcome."[386] Pinheiro and Saddi remind us that such an interpretation, known as Coase Theorem, "has introduced a way of thinking in
which there is an efficiency principle behind each rule presented."[387]

---

384 Idem, p. 402.
385 Ibidem.
386 Ibidem.
387 PINHEIRO. *Direito, economia e mercados*, p. 143.

Incidentally, as a precedent for the Supreme Federal Court in regards to Paraná State Law # 10,248/93, which makes it mandatory that consumers be present at the time propane gas cylinders are weighed at their door, ADI 855 and other formal foundations also had the rule of efficiency applied to them to have them considered unfeasible, damaging, and consequently contrary to the principle of reasonability, thus being ruled unconstitutional.

Therefore, according to liberal theorists, the presence of the State in solving reciprocal externalities becomes undesirable; it should only take place to define rights to property and reduce transaction costs, as Coase once stated. A solution would then be left up to the market devices and at the mercy of interested parties, considering the rationale behind the *homo economicus*, so that the respective efficiency could be maximized in the name of their individual and Hedonistic interests, which are a result of public benefits, since if each one of us play our parts while driven by our own individual interests, it will necessarily have a good result on the collective.

This economic theory wound up promoting the development of a philosophy known as the Economic Analysis of Law with the School of Chicago, which advocates for having the State as the sole party responsible for defining property rights and reducing transaction costs, thus creating an environment and instruments for free negotiation among stakeholders. Thereinafter, everything must be in the private scope of stakeholders, who will align their interests by naturally promoting the respective positive externalities (benefits) and absorbing, resolving, or offsetting negative externalities without additional costs to the population or the State. The resulting group of positive externalities, despite the fact that they are found in the private scope, implicate both primary and secondary public benefits as well as universal ones.

Consequently, it was thereby proclaimed that the Welfare State had become unnecessary in countries where, despite past crises, an economic health and structure had been restored to absorb negative externalities through a natural economy dynamics by generating wealth, creating jobs, and collecting taxes. In other words, these would basically include members of the European Union, Japan and the United States.

Due to its burdensome characteristics, the Welfare State that had been installed in those countries as a war-related effort after World War II started to diminish proportionally to how their economy started to prove that it could support itself, that is, as they consistently started to meet universal demands according to the natural order and restored their economic liberalism. In other words, Europe and Japan allowed the market to follow its natural course while facing negative externalities, being controlled by Adam Smith's so-called "invisible hand" after their economies reached maturity once again, especially today, when they have serious reservations about the global financial crisis of 2008. Evidence of such is the persistent agricultural protectionism in Europe, which even before the aforementioned crisis has interfered with multilateral negotiations in global trading.

The Welfare State has also proved to be unsustainable in peripheral countries due to the lack of national wealth and tax revenues required to meet internal and external demands while resolving negative externalities at the same time. That was the case in Brazil, Mexico, and Argentina, among other countries. It was not by chance that international organizations, especially the IMF and the World Bank, started to pressure these countries into having Neoliberal thoughts and the Capitalist interest of economic globalization prevail in their countries as well.

While reflecting on Latin America, Berreneche ponders that *"el Estado de Bienestar, la matriz de desarrollo estado-céntrica, se agotó en la década de 1980. No fue el ocaso de las experiencias autoritarias y de gobierno de excepción en Latinoamérica lo que apuró su fin: fue la crisis de la deuda externa en 1982. Ese mismo año, después de endeudarse significadamente, México comunicó al mundo que no podía seguir haciendo frente a sus compromisos externos. Otros países latinoamericanos pronto siguieron sus pasos. Mientras tanto, una combinación de nuevas ideas económicas preponderantes y el alumbramiento de otro orden internacional posguerra fría se unieron para proclamar al mundo que la nivelación de las cuentas fiscales de los países latinoamericanos, el pago de sus compromisos externos y una nueva plataforma para su crecimiento económico jamás se realizarían si los estados de la*

región continuaban con su política intervencionista, expansiva e asfix-
iante de la iniciativa privada. Se crearon así las condiciones, ideológicas
primero y políticas después, para el lento pero firme predominio del par-
adigma neo-liberal que reinó durante la década de 1990".[388]
The concept of a Welfare State was worn out and lost its hegemony during the final decades of the 20th century due to two different
factors: (1) In the main Capitalist States, economic strength allowed
the State to shrink. Naturally, with a generalized prosperity, public
benefits in favor of the population were generated, as aligned with
what Adam Smith had classically preached. (2) In peripheral States,
in addition to the Neoliberal wave, those countries were unable to
honor their commitment and pay off their national and international
debt while, at the same time, covering the costs of demands associated
with negative externalities.

Therefore, the Liberal Capitalism preached by Adam Smith
and David Ricardo, as Bjork reports and as seen prior to the Welfare
State wave, restored the control of national economies and became
known as Neoliberalism. Brue narrates that, by the end of the 20th
century and while promoting the dissemination of economic Neoliberalism under the platform of a Liberal State, "advocates for the
ideas from Chicago helped to convince the general population and
elected officials that a competition market system free of government
intervention generates the utmost economic freedom that, in turn,
generates the utmost individual and collective wellbeing."[389] For this
school of thought in particular, this is so because having private desires and interests met, or merely seeking to have them met, wind up
maximizing positive externalities in favor of everyone.

As Stiglitz and Charlton clarified, ""the notion that trade -free
trade, unencumbered by government restrictions—as welfare en-
hancing is one of the most fundamental doctrines in modern economics, dating back at least to Adam Smith (1776) and David Ricardo
(1816)."[390] Neoliberals have reached a point that, due to their exacer-

388 BARRENECHE. *Prólogo,* p. 19.

389 Idem, p. 485.

390 STIGLITZ; CHARLTON. *Livre mercado para todos,* p. 12.

bated exaltation of individualism, they denounce any public forces or even the civil society. As we can construe from Ayn Rand's paradigmatic position, "Any group or 'collective,' large or small, is only a number of individuals. A group can have no rights other than the rights of its individual members. In a free society, the 'rights' of any group are derived from the rights of its members through their voluntary, individual choice and contractual agreement."[391] This is exactly what Henry Thoreau had in mind when he stated that "The government cannot have any rights over me and my properties beyond those I have granted."[392]

According to economic rationality, if State intervention goes beyond the clear definition of property rights and the role of assuring transactions instruments, it will wind up generating an additional cost while providing artificial resolutions for negative externalities; it will create other negative externalities that will be significantly unfair due to this unessential burden and its traditional lack of economic efficiency. This is the theory that supports Economic Liberalism as a more efficient system with minimal State, private property, free enterprise, and market as the center of economic control, while its natural order tries to resolve negative externalities for the benefit of primary and secondary target interests, as well as universal interests.

A significant share of Law professionals have followed this Neoliberal Capitalist ideology and recovered classic jurisprudential positions, such as "the courts of the United States under the leadership of the Supreme Court did attempt to place substantive checks on legislative power. The essence of the judicial argument was that it was improper for legislatures to pass legislation which would tend to confiscate part of the exchange value of property or to interfere in the bargaining process between individuals and groups. The argument

---

391 *The virtue of selfishness*, p. 119. Unofficial translation of: "any group or 'collective,' large or small, is only a number of individuals. A group can have no rights other than the rights of its individual members. In a free society, the 'rights' of any group are derived from the rights of its members through their voluntary, individual choice and contractual agreement."
392 THOREAU. Op. cit., p. 39.

had its roots in John Locke and Adam Smith or at least the jurists' understanding of these writers. An underlying assumption was that economic freedom and property were 'natural rights' guaranteed by the Constitution and that the existing distribution of property and freedom were the results of a natural process with which it was unconstitutional and unwise for government to interfere."[393]

It was within this philosophical-economic context that Richard Posner, judge of the U.S. Court of Appeals for the Seventh Circuit and Professor of Law at the University of Chicago, released his 1972 *Economic Analysis of Law*, in which he stated that market economy is a tool that is able to analyze a vast group of legal demands. He also proposed to apply Neoliberal economic efficiency to concrete, numerous, and diversified legal issues. Evidently, such legal analysis was made according to the perspective of the Chicago School of Economics, which is characterized by economic neoliberalism. Among other aspects, Posner states that self-interest should not be mistaken for selfishness and that other people's miseries may become part of our satisfactions.[394]

Basically, the legal-economic analysis made by the Chicago School of Economics preaches that Law, which is neutral when faced with negative externalities, should move towards a monetarist and utilitarian economic rationality, thus defining property and reducing transaction costs from the point of view of an individual's self-interest, as it is the basic of economic activities. While incessantly aiming at satisfying his own desires and meeting his own individual, hedonistic goals, said individual would become part of the planet's economic scenario and align his interests with that of others, thus generating the respective positive externalities. Considering this aspect, Liberal Capitalism is positive "as a maximization of economic process and, consequently, general wealth, thus allowing markets to work its miracles."[395]

Undoubtedly, powerful market forces enhance Capitalist pos-

---

393 BJORK. *A empresa privada e o interesse público*, p. 71.
394 POSNER. *El análisis económico del derecho*, p. 11 and following.
395 Idem, p. 23.

itivity within a free environment and, therefore, tend to yield good economic results and increase the collective wealth and prosperity. Stiglitz and Charlton acknowledge that "trade is good for development."[396] Thus, "Bringing together survey material from a range of industrial countries, Inglehart shows values of economic achievement and economic growth do fade with increasing prosperity. Self-expression and the desire for meaningful work are replacing the maximizing of economic rewards."[397]

Facing its best performance and implying the increase of general prosperity, Liberal Capitalism solves the economic problem. Once he is free from it, Man tends to forget individualism and naturally moves toward fraternity and the remaining virtues. As quoted by Giddens, David Green emphasizes that "The virtues of civil society, if left to its own devices are said to include: Good character, honesty, duty, self-sacrifice, honour, service, self-discipline, toleration, respect, justice, self-improvement, trust, civility, fortitude, courage, integrity, diligence, patriotism, consideration for others, thrift and reverence. To the modern ear, the writer says, these having 'a ring of either antique charm'—but this is because state power has suppressed them through sabotaging civil society."[398]

The historical confirmation of such fact happened in 2007 in Australia, a country with one of the highest Human Development Indexes (HDI) in the planet, when the opposition led by Kevin Rudd won the election after receiving a great majority of the votes against John Howard's neoliberals, who had been in power for eleven years. According to the BBC, "During the campaign, Labor sought to Capitalise on the Howard administration's refusal to sign the Kyoto protocol on climate change. Mr Howard campaigned on his record of sound economic management."[399]

After all, the Neoliberal doctrine restores Liberal Classical Capitalism to remove from the State the task of correcting or com-

---

396 STIGLITZ; CHARLTON. Op. cit., p. 11.

397 GIDDENS. Op. cit., p. 31.

398 Idem, p. 22.

399 BBC.Brasil.com (http://www.bbc.co.uk), 11/25/2007. Visited on 08/11/2008.

pensating for negative economic externalities in order to leave them to the market forces. However, as a result of it and the influence of economic Liberalism, the economic analysis of law is instrumental only in the main countries of Capitalism, and the United States in particular. Even so, there are reservations in regards to culture, conjecture, and economic structure, for these countries have been forced to make this analysis flexible when faced with the global financial crisis of 2008.

Advocating for economic liberalism in these main countries does not pose any difficulties since, despite the economic rationality behind seeking individual interests that generate wealth as a means to achieve collective prosperity, these countries promote social welfare, thus assuring an economic, political, social, and cultural evolution toward the realization of Human Rights in their second and third dimensions. In sum, Liberalism and its transposition into Law are convenient in sovereign nations that do not experience a severe deficit in realizing said rights, for the tendency in Liberalism is to keep the wealthy wealthier and the poor poorer.

Prior to 2008, Alan Greenspan was considered the *"Wall Street Wizard"* for being a great advocate for Neoliberalism. As the President of the Federal Reserve, Greenspan led the global commercial liberalization towards the end of the 20th century during the neoliberal economic globalization phenomenon.

Greenspan said that, "While central planning may no longer be a credible form of economic organization, it is clear that the intellectual battle for its rival—free-market Capitalism and globalization—is far from won. For twelve generations, Capitalism has achieved one advance after another, as standards and quality of living have risen at an unprecedented rate over large parts of the globe. Poverty has been dramatically reduced and life expectancy has more than doubled. The rise in material well-being—a tenfold increase in real *per capita* income over two centuries—has enabled the earth to support a sixfold increase in population. Yet, for many, Capitalism still seems difficult to accept, much less fully embrace."[400] And he adds, "There is no de-

---

400 GREENSPAN. Op. cit., p. 258.

nying Capitalism's record. Market economies have succeeded over the centuries by thoroughly weeding out the inefficient and poorly equipped, and by granting rewards to those who anticipate consumer demand and meet it with the most efficient use of labor and capital resources. Newer technologies increasingly drive this unforgiving Capitalist process on a global scale. To the extent that governments 'protect' portions of their populations from what they perceive as harsh competitive pressures, they achieve a lower overall material standard of living for their people."[401]

When commenting on the Index of Economic Freedom calculated by the Heritage Foundation in a joint venture with The Wall Street Journal, Greenspan recalled proudly that "The index for 2007 lists the United States as the most 'free' of the larger economies."[402]

Incidentally, in the preamble of the agreement that instituted the World Trade Organization (OMC), which is the most typical of Neoliberal institutions, it is expressly written that the organization was created *"reconociendo que sus relaciones en la esfera de la actividad comercial y económica deben tender a elevar los niveles de vida, a lograr el pleno empleo y un volumen considerable y en constante aumento de ingresos reales y demanda efectiva y a acrecentar la producción y el comercio de bienes y servicios, permitiendo al mismo tiempo la utilización óptima de los recursos mundiales de conformidad con el objetivo de un desarrollo sostenible y procurando proteger y preservar el medio ambiente e incrementar los medios para hacerlo, de manera compatible con sus respectivas necesidades e intereses según los diferentes niveles de desarrollo económico."* Further, it recognizes that *"es necesario realizar esfuerzos positivos para que los países en desarrollo, y especialmente los menos adelantados, obtengan una parte del incremento del comercio internacional que corresponda a las necesidades de su desarrollo económico."*[403]

In regards to economic liberalism, Pope Paul VI says that, "We must in all fairness acknowledge the vital role played by labor

401 Idem.
402 Ibidem, p. 266.
403 http://www.wto.org/spanish/docs_s/legal_s/legal_s.htm

systemization and industrial organization in the task of development"[404] because, as he had mentioned earlier, "In God's plan, every man is born to seek self-fulfillment, for every human life is called to some task by God."[405]

According to Friedman, back when the United States followed State Capitalism, people's "pocketbooks were being hit with inflation and high tax rates."[406] As a matter of fact, Friedman justifies Liberalism clearly and logically as the Capitalist economy model that promotes overall prosperity and fights poverty. That is why he states that Liberal economists "showed deep concern with threats to freedom and prosperity represented by the increase in government mismanagement and the triumph of Keynesian ideas."[407]

However, in the face of Anthropophilic Humanism, Friedman unwarrantably does not mention the issue of having a sustainable planet. Moreover, he literally recognizes that Liberalism is slow in fighting poverty and implementing prosperity,[408] while the opposition is concerned with poverty, feeling "anxious" and "impatient with the delay"[409] of their benefits.[410]

Ergo, the inconveniences of Neoliberalism: they are patient or tolerant with poverty, but indifferent to the fate of the planet, which is an unacceptable issue for Anthropophilic Humanism. In fact, globalization has put Humanity at risk, to the point that the following alert has been made: "Globalization is also single-mindedness and poverty of spirit, the reconstitution of monstrous profits in the detriment of jobs, and the authorized—if not demanded—growth of social inequalities."[411]

The effective realization of Human Rights in their second and

---

404 PAULO VI. Op. and item cits.

405 Idem, item 15.

406 Idem, p. 7.

407 FRIEDMAN. Op. cit., p. 5.

408 Idem, p. 184.

409 Ibidem, p. 183.

410 Ibidem.

411 LONGCHAMP. *Globalização: o novo nome do desenvolvimento?*, p. 128.

third dimensions is not certain, much less immediate; nor do the positive results from Liberal Capitalism come fast to increase collective prosperity while fighting poverty, especially in the so-called peripheral countries, where there are large social and environmental deficits and a high rate of fraud and misappropriation of government funds.

The issue with the uncertainty and delay in achieving positive externalities of the public order in regards to the destitute lays in realizing that these people are left behind in their pursuit for a dignified life. Human needs are much more pressing and it is imperative that we save Capitalism from Capitalists themselves. The 2008 crisis in the U.S. and global financial systems is proof of that. On that account, back in the 1960s, Pope Paul VI already called for celerity, stating that "The critical state of affairs must be corrected for the better without delay."[412] Thirst, hunger, and death do not wait a single day longer.

It is unacceptable that humans beings are being discarded in their path towards a dignified living as if they were mere numbers, or "casualties of war." That is exactly what happens when the Neoliberal agenda is followed to solve negative externalities, especially concerning exclusion, poverty, and the degradation of the planet. This situation is unallowable and allows us to understand the reason why Alan Greenspan was called a "fraud" by some of his critics. Among them are Ravi Batra, who said that "Greenomics oppresses the poor of today, supply-side economics those of tomorrow. Which is worse? They are both cowardly and nefarious, because they shift the tax burden from the haves to the have-nots. They both reward the opulent and trample the destitute. Contrary to popular belief, it's Greenomics, not supply-side economics, that has largely shaped the government policy since 1981, because the tax rises of 1982, 1983, 1990, and 1993 infuriated the supply-siders, but had Greenspan's blessings. Greenomics has been followed in the United States ever since 1981."[413]

Greenspan indeed talks about a "creative destruction." He seems to advocate for transposing Darwin's law of natural selection to economy and, consequently, the Darwinian philosophy christened

---

412 PAULO VI. Op. cit., item 32.

413 GREENSPAN. *A fraude*, p. 107.

by Herbert Spencer as "survival of the fittest."[414] He supports that, "assisted by the wave of deregulation since the mid-1970s, today's U.S. economy remains the most competitive large economy in the world, and American culture still exhibits much of the risk taking and taste for adventure of the country's earlier years."[415] Thus, the former President of the Federal Reserve seems to admit that, in fact, the survival of the fittest is the law that must prevail in the savage environment of economic freedom.

However, due to the fraudulent mismanagement of financial institutions, the 2008 global financial crisis came in the aftermath of a Neoliberal Capitalist attitude, putting the U.S. and the global economy in checkmate. This crisis led to massive material unpleasantness, as well as the intolerably aggravating social exclusion of an inestimable number of people worldwide. It impaired the UN Millennium Development Goals. That is the other side of the Neoliberal coin.

The United States claim to be a free economy that keeps the State away from the task of correcting negative externalities. Nevertheless, when faced with the 2008 global financial crisis in its own financial system, which was triggered by the real estate market due to default on mortgage payments, the Republican administration of George W. Bush, followed by the Democratic administration of Barrack Obama, abandoned Neoliberalism and nationalized companies, whether they were financial institutions or not, to pragmatically create the concept of corporations that are "too big to fail." Their particular purpose was to bail these companies out, injecting an exorbitant amount of public money into them, as well as several other private financial institutions, with the excuse of preventing the collapse of the economy, which would lead to massive unemployment and the loss of incalculable savings and private insurance accounts among other damages, as Treasury Secretary Henry Paulson had announced.[416] Furthermore, the U.S. government assumed and intervened into the negotiation of default mortgage payments, refinancing them.

---

414 Idem, p. 269.

415 Ibidem, 270.

416 PAULSON JR *À beira do abismo financeiro*, p. 15.

All these measures took U.S. Capitalism away from the Neo-liberal agenda, which was abandoned hurriedly when faced with the imminent economic collapse. The same happened in European economies. Considering such an alarming situation, with the exceptional accumulation of negative externalities of the private and public orders, even the main countries of Capitalism have been abandoning Liberal thinking unceremoniously, bringing upon their governments the task that had been originally attributed to the market, and doing so in an artificial manner while using public funds. This is, without a doubt, the correct approach.

In their actions and attempts, these governments executed what the Pontifical Council had called *Justitia et Pax*: *"existe y debe buscarse tenazmente la posibilidad de contribuir a una salida sostenible de la crisis financiera, también construyendo las condiciones para que los ahorros que se generan se dediquen verdaderamente al desarrollo, es decir, a la creación de ocasiones de trabajo"*.[417] And so, in the aftermath of the 2008 crisis, market self-regulation and Neoliberalism as we've known them have come to an end around the globe.

Undoubtedly, Neoliberalism does not suffice when it comes to realizing Human Rights and their corresponding purpose of achieving Human Dignity.

(5) Capitalism And Anthropophilic Humanism

Despite its positive effects, market economy as the basis of a Neoliberal State has its wicked side. Marked by hedonism and individualism, it does not consider the harmonization of Human Rights directly in their first dimension, nor does it consider them more widely in their second and third dimensions. However, as Porto Oliveira has pondered, it is imperative that we recognize that "Upon embracing all beliefs, forms and lifestyles, the Neoliberal model is increasingly guided by the respect for individualities and plurality, thus indicating

---

417 *Un nuevo pacto financiero internacional*, p. 23.

in its very format the respect for Human Dignity."[418]

Notwithstanding such liberty and respect for plurality, market economy is not compassionate enough to establish Fraternity, since its very environment is the savage state of nature subjected to a law of natural selection in which the fittest will survive and the weakest will perish. In its plenitude, the Liberal model is pure savagery, thus not appropriate for the current civilization status of Humanity.

In such a philosophical terms, Friedman states that "The only social responsibility of a company is to deliver profit."[419] For Liberal Capitalists, the extent and magnitude of negative externalities do not come into play; inasmuch as they comply with the Positive Law, they are businesses. Even armed conflicts can become an attractive business, as Galbraith denounced when referring to the Vietnam War: "It was occupationally appropriate that both the armed services and the weapons industries should accept and endorse hostilities. To repeat, this was taken for granted. Again the spurious distinction between a private and a public sector. Here, clearly evident, the corporate interest in the rewarding contracts."[420]

Consequently, in order to address the legal monetarist purposes that determine the results of natural selection by the market, a Neoliberal economy disregards any direct and specific purpose to realize Human Rights in all their dimensions, thus resulting in inequality and social exclusion, as well as the degradation of the planet.

Incidentally, Hegel says that, "When the standard of living of a large mass of people falls below a certain subsistence level—a level regulated automatically as the one necessary for a member of society—and when there is a consequent loss of sense of right and wrong, of honesty and self-respect that makes a man insist on maintaining himself by his own work and effort, the result is the creation of a rabble of paupers and a concentration of disproportionate wealth."[421]

Social exclusion is especially unacceptable, once "poverty is

418 OLIVEIRA. Op. and p. cits.

419 AMY UELMEN. Op. cit., p. 73.

420 GALBRAITH. *A economia das fraudes inocentes*, p. 76.

421 HEGEL. Op. cit., p. 208.

seen as lack of social responsibility,"[422] as Ammann declared. Making the situation worse, as Bauman has reported when referring to the Neoliberal State from the U.S. paradigm, "Increasingly, being poor is seen as a crime; becoming poor, as the product of criminal predisposition's or intentions—abuse of alcohol, gambling, drugs, truancy and vagabondage. The poor, far from meriting care and assistance, deserve hate and condemnation—as the very incarnation of sin."[423] The sociologist also says that, "As the New York Herald Tribune put it on 25 December 1994, the Americans—conservatives, moderate, Republican—consider it their right to blame the poor for their fate and simultaneously condemn millions of their children to poverty, hunger and despair.[424]

Therefore, we must move past the Neoliberal paradigm. As Stiglitz and Charlton accurately stated, "In a world in which many see global poverty—by some estimates there are more than two billion people living on less than a dollar a day—as the world's most pressing problem."[425] In fact, the World Bank published the following information in August 2008, even before unveiling the international economic crisis it was experienced at the moment: "*1.4 billion live on less than $1.25 a day.*"[426] This means that, when Neoliberalism had reached its utmost global acceptance, almost one quarter of the world population at the time, estimated in six billion people, was living under the extreme poverty line. In the face of said crisis, today's numbers are even more compromising in regards to global dignity.

If the planet collapses, so will Humanity. Not only the mass of poor, but Humans in general are negatively affected by the disregard of market economy towards the Planet, as seen during the environmental catastrophe of April 20, 2010 in the Gulf of Mexico, which

---

422 AMMANN. *Cidadania e exclusão social: o mundo desenvolvido em questão*, p. 133.

423 BAUMAN. Op. cit., pp. 59-60.

424 Idem, p. 60.

425 STIGLITZ; CHARLTON. Op. cit., p. 13.

426 web.worldbank.org, on 09/09/2008. Translation: "1.4 billion live with less than $1.25 a day".

THE HUMANISTIC CAPITALISM

was caused by the explosion of the Deepwater Horizon oil platform owned by British Petroleum (BP) and led to a massive oil spill in the water, as well as severe harm to the ecosystem and economy in the region. The explosion was due to failure in the oil well cap, which was not replaced by a more reliable system because the procedure would imply an added cost of a few hundred thousand dollars.

In addition to the environmental degradation, Humanity also suffers with geographical restriction, since migrants from emerging and developing countries are banned from entering developed countries and become permanent residents. Actually, borders are designed mainly to protect wealth and work as dam for poverty. Additionally, *Guia mundial de estatísticas* shows that approximately 91% of violence-related deaths worldwide take place in countries with low or medium income, while the remaining 9% occur in the developed countries[427] that are inaccessible to migration movements. For this reason, and despite the fact that it is seductive, nutritious, and generous, market economy is also cruel and inhumane.

If on the one hand Neoliberalism fosters overall prosperity and supports democracy, showing that market economy is nevertheless the best model, on the other hand it excludes "the normal circuits of social exchanges"[428] and it is conniving with the disrespect for Human Rights in their second and third dimensions, especially when the State and Civil Society do not enjoy a political, economic, social, and cultural reality that favors the confrontation of negative externalities produced.

Undesirable effects ultimately affect the three dimensions of Human Rights without distinction, going beyond these negative externalities of the public order. They reach the changing nature of individual rights, which need to be harmonized by solidarity and largely hurt Humanity and the Planet to the point that they, too, wind up giving room to negative externalities of the universal kind, thus creating an imbalance in individual rights when they fail to converge with the

427 *Guia mundial de estatísticas*. São Paulo, 2008, p. 118.
428 CASTEL. *As armadilhas da exclusão*, p. 22.

Thomistic thought.[429]

Upon establishing the Christian social doctrine, Pope Leo XIII warned us that "wealthy owners and all masters of labor should be mindful of this—that to exercise pressure upon the indigent and the destitute for the sake of gain, and to gather one's profit out of the need of another, is condemned by all laws, human and divine. To defraud any one of wages that are his due is a great crime which cries to the avenging anger of Heaven."[430] Therefore, radical fundamentalism makes no sense, for the supremacy of a Neoliberal way of seeing and dealing with the world reveals the discouraging mark of selfishness, of guilty action and omission, sometimes even willfully, when it is indifferent to its social and global effects that imply a direct assault on the Law of Universal Fraternity.

In turn, Anthropophilic Humanism commands Capitalism to move forward from Neoliberalism and imposes on law certain restrictions and very serious care in the theoretical application of economic analysis of law in the face of negative externalities, as well as of the horizontal unbalance of individual rights.

In fact, market economy only works when it does not collide with Anthropophilic Humanism, which can only been verified in structural, conjunctural, and cultural conditions capable of supporting and correcting, with their own natural forces, the respective undesirable effects, as Stiglitz had warned.[431] Well, these ideal conditions, in practical terms, are impossible to certify. As a matter of fact, this is the same premise supported by Keynes: In order to work seamlessly, market economy implies a perfect world, which is unnatural and even utopic.

Moreover, each country has its own reality. Anthropology has

---

429 ARIAS. *La filosofia tomistica e l´economia politica*, p. 57, verbis: This is explained by someone with authority to interpret Saint Thomas Aquinas' thoughts: *"Si osserva la profonda divergenza fra la visione tomística e quella economistica delle rendite di consumo, di scambio e di monopólio. L´analisi economistica è puramente e freddamente utilitária. È, come sempre, la psicologia dell´egoismo".*

430 Leo XIII, Encyclical *Rerum Novarum*, item 20.

431 STIGLITZ. *A globalização e seus malefícios.*

indicated, with sufficient scientific grounds, the existence of multi-culturalism and global diversity, thus revealing that each nation has its own particular features in terms of politics, economy, society, and culture. This reality cannot be ignored, especially in order to verify the conditions that each society has in place to support and structure Neoliberal Capitalism.

For example, Greenspan comments that "Japan is probably the most culturally uniform society of the major industrial powers."[432] Furthermore, "from the end of World War II to 1989, Japan succeeded in developing one of the world's most successful Capitalist economies."[433]

Russia is another iconic case during its transition to a Capitalist economy. According to Stiglitz,[434] in a clear inoculation of economic Neoliberalism, the assistance offered by the International Monetary Fund to Russia was contingent upon a re-structuration that would follow the market economy system, including the privatization of state companies and economic activity. These guidelines led to their severe failure to thrive, while the value of the national currency plummeted and social exclusion intensified. Currently, even though they still have a Capitalist regime, Russia operates in its own way. Its internal market and national financial system function according to State Capitalism.

Likewise, Brazil is another example among the Top Ten countries with the largest Gross Domestic Product in the world. We are unable to withstand Economic Neoliberalism for many reasons, such as concentration of wealth, oligopolized economy, insufficient industrial foundation, significant part of the population living in poverty, and national debt, not to mention the lack of employment, health, food, drinking water, basic sanitation, housing, education, pension and social security funds, and the enormous deficit in the realization of Human Rights in their second dimension. It is also worth mentioning that Brazil imports technology, despite the fact that its institutions

---

432 GREENSPAN. Op. cit., p. 279.

433 Idem.

434 STIGLITZ. Op. cit., p. 209 and following.

are clearly inconsistent. On the one hand, there is a lack of material resources and professional background, which overwhelms workers with a heavy workload and leads to abuse of authority. On the other hand, there is corruption, embezzlement, and cronyism, which has a negative impact on the realization of Human Rights. More specifically, it hinders the right to pacification; political, economic, social, and cultural development; eradication of poverty; actions against hunger; reduction of inequalities; offer of essential services, and environmental preservation, all of them included in the third dimension of Human Rights.

Incidentally, the House of Representative recorded in 2000, in the beginning of the third millennium, that civil society in Brazil already denounced that "the Brazilian Government keeps treating social politics in a way that is completely divorced from the progress of economic policies, for they continue to prove insufficient in reversing the current situation of hunger and social exclusion with the required celerity that would promote inclusion."[435] More recently, according to the 2010 Human Development Reports compiled by the United Nations Development Programme,[436] Brazil was featured[437] as a country with high human development as per the Human Development Index (HDI). However, Brazil is in 73rd place, behind Chile (45th), Argentina (46th), and Uruguay (52th), being the second worst ranked country in Mercosur after Paraguay, which was in 96th. The aforementioned Report provides figures on poverty in Brazil, confronted with a population of 185,712,713 people as per the preliminary results of the 2010 Census performed by the Brazilian Institute of Geography and Statistics (IBGE) and published in IBGE Resolution # 6 of November 3rd, 2010.

The report registered that 21.5% of the Brazilian population

---

435 House of Representatives, Human Rights Commission, "O Brasil e o Pacto Internacional de Direitos Econômicos, Sociais e Culturais" in *Relatório da sociedade civil sobre o cumprimento, pelo Brasil, do PIDESC* [Civil Society Report on Brazil's Compliance with ICESCR], Brasília: 2000.

436 http://www.pnud.org.br.

437 Table 1, pp. 151-155.

lived under the poverty line. It represented 39.9 million people who, in regards to the multidimensional poverty index[438], are deeply deprived of health, education, and a dignified quality of life. That is the mass of poor in Brazil. The report also observed that 5.2% of the population has a purchasing power of up to $1.25 USD per day, which means that 9.65 million Brazilians are living in extreme poverty.

The Applied Economics Research Institute (IPEA) highlighted that, in 2008. "Brazil shows less inequality, but it remains far away from developed countries. The speed in which inequality decreases in Brazil (0.7 point) is higher than that of all countries analyzed, except for Spain, which achieved a slightly higher rate (0.9 point) in the Gini Scale. Sergei Soares concluded that this rate is adequate, but the challenge is to keep it consistent throughout the decades in order to achieve the same inequality rate of Canada, for example. If we keep the same inequality decrease rate observed in the past five years, we will achieve the Mexican rate within six years, the American rate within twelve years, and the Canadian rate within twenty-four years."[439]

Due to the reckless and fraudulent management of economy and financial systems, not even the United States can withstand Neoliberalist deviations, as it was unveiled in 2008.

Consequently, according to economic relations in general, particularly in countries like Brazil, Anthropophilic Humanism reacts to Neoliberalism; in the legal arena, it reacts to the theory of Economic Analysis of Law with the School of Chicago that, under Neoliberal colors,[440] cannot be applied indiscriminately. This economic analysis is a typical legal remedy with undesirable side effects; if it is prescribed without discrimination, it causes unbearable injury to overall Human Dignity, thus causing serious damage to the realization of Human Rights in their first, second, and third dimensions. Therefore, even if the analysis provided by the School of Chicago contributed to economic growth, it would not cease to be a clear promoter of count-

---

438 Table 5, pp. 169-171.

439 http://www.ipea.gov.br em 09/09/2008.

440 SAYEG. *Aspectos contratuais da exclusividade no fornecimento de combustíveis automotivos,* p. 224.

er-development due to incompatibility between development and the irrecoverable negative externalities caused by the natural action of a growing market.

With this statement, we do not intend to loathe market economy itself and, within the legal arena, the economic analysis of law that, nevertheless, is supported in Brazil by quality authors such as Coelho.[441] However, we do state that proper adjustment is necessary to move beyond it. The fact was confirmed by Stiglitz and Charlton, for whom "trade liberalization can promote development, but [...] the results of different trade policies have varied across countries."[442]

Capitalism must advance towards a Humanistic market economy that, consequently, would establish a Humanistic analysis of Economic Law. Even though, before a concrete case, Coase Theorem accurately takes into consideration a natural arrangement arising of the antagonistic clash of interests due to the confirmation that externalities are reciprocal, and they are indeed, this Theorem ultimately is correct only when the clash of interests creates externalities that are reasonably equivalent to what is achieved, to the extent and magnitude of what is achieved. That is, the reciprocity of said externalities must be reasonably balanced or equivalent for the Theorem to work as efficiently as it proclaims to be. Otherwise, it is halting under the perspective of harmonization, pursuant to the natural Fraternity Law. In the event that said equivalence does not take place, the Law of Universal Fraternity shall set free everything that, in contraposition, Neoliberal Fundamentalism enslaves, for there will be no harmonization, and only resignation and desolation will be verified, as emphasized by the motto attributed to Lacordaire: "Between the strong and the weak, it is freedom which oppresses and the law which sets free."[443]

Considering the unbalance found in legal business structures, which in the Capitalist field are celebrated within these social environments of non-equivalent reciprocal externalities, individual rights will not be properly harmonized either. And it is so because, due to

---

441 COELHO. *Dignidade da pessoa na economia globalizada*, pp. 1237-1248.
442 STIGLITZ; CHARLTON. Op. cit., p. 13.
443 Pensador.uol.com.br.

its non-equivalence, the weakest position cannot exercise Human Rights multidimensionally as they fall upon the current scenario, thus threatening the respective edification of a structural changing universality, interdependence, and indissociability towards the fulfillment of Human Dignity in its multiple dimensions.

(6) The Humanistic Capitalism

Throughout the decades, the United Nations Development Programme has reinforced the idea that people are the real wealth of nations. The wealth of a country isn't restricted to its economic growth and the insufficient criteria of greatness facilitated by the calculation of its Gross Domestic Product (GDP). As proposed by Gadrey and Jany-Catrice, its verification must "offset evaluations based purely on economic progress [with] 'socioeconomic' indexes that take into account, at the same time, economic, human, and social criteria, as well as environmental criteria, as it happens in many of these nations."[444]

In developed nations, people are engaged in political, economic, social, and cultural evolution, thus gaining access to a quality of life that, in the very least, fulfills the minimum standard of living, where there is respect for Humanity and the Planet. The minimum concept of living does not arise of the mere theoretical reflection of law scholars. Above all, it is about having an instrument to implement Human Rights,[445] as it happened in 2010 when the UN, through a General Assembly resolution, declared that access to drinking water and basic sanitation were human rights and added them to the list found in their Universal Declaration.

Thus, developed nations are inclusive and emancipating for each man and the whole man; they take men into consideration and respect their insertion into the Planet.

In response to a purely Neoliberal focus on market economy,

---

444 GADREY; JANY-CATRICE. *Os novos indicadores de riqueza*, p. 17.

445 BALERA. *A dignidade da pessoa humana e o mínimo existencial*, p. 1359.

that is, a focus that is not interested in the fate of Humanity or the enormous mass of excluded individuals, thus not taking into consideration the alarming poverty and depletion that we see in the planet today, Vanderborght and Van Parijs have advocated for the concept of basic income.[446] Brazilian efforts as the "Allowance Program" that is part of the "Zero Hunger" initiative have revealed themselves as a significant instrument of governmental planning to directly transfer income to the poor, even though some value must be attributed to human work. While we fail to achieve a full employment scenario, these programs will remain necessary. As Romar once said, "Work dignifies man."[447] However, in the absence of work and employment opportunities (as we know, they are not very many!), we cannot criticize such efforts of income transfer to the poor, especially considering the poverty we see today. Economic exclusion violates Human Dignity and it is equivalent to being condemned to exile, even though those who are excluded have not committed any crime.

Unruled economic Neoliberalism, without a Humanistic calibration, is incapable of both correcting negative externalities and properly conciliating externalities, especially those of a private nature that are non-equivalent and reciprocally considered. Said calibration is needed and must fall upon the universality of exercising subjective natural rights to property, making them relative, instead of following the Neoliberal view, in which such exercise tends to be absolute.

Paulo Netto and Braz confirm the effects of pure Neoliberalism economy in Brazil, recording that great capital application still demands democratic dimensions (should we not say humanistic dimensions as well?) of State intervention into the economy.[448]

Despite advocating for a free market, Rajan and Zingales support that, after two decades of massive privatization, radical deregulation and generalized liberation, there is clear evidence that markets became too free and that Capitalism should be saved from Neoliberal

---

446 VANDERBORGHT; VAN PARIJS. *Renda básica de cidadania*, p. 35.

447 ROMAR. *Direito do trabalho e dignidade da pessoa humana*, p. 1287.

448 NETTO. *Economia política*, p. 227.

Capitalists.[449] Incidentally, these authors gave such warning before the 2008 crisis.

However, we can see that, despite being unable to fulfill their obligations in regards to paying off their debt and, at the same time, meeting the demands of Human Rights, peripheral countries shall not immerse themselves in Neoliberalism while disregarding the respective social and environmental deficits that come with it, under the penalty of infringing upon the dignity of Humans and the Planet, for they are both supported by the natural Fraternity Law that imposes the realization of Human Rights in all their dimensions. Opportunely, we would like to emphasize that this reflection is not affiliated with the Neoliberal model, nor does it sympathize with State Capitalism or much less with Socialism or Communism.

In effect, in order not to become a system that oppresses individuals in their preexisting rights, as Locke once warned us, the Natural Law of Fraternity does not renounce the insurmountable limits of sustainably recognizing individual liberties. In other words, it does not forget the first dimension of Human Rights; however, even individual rights must be horizontally assured against the unbalance that they cause in the commutative plane. The negative unbalance in reciprocity between externalities, including those of a private nature, is unacceptable. As Senise Lisboa defines, the Law of Universal Fraternity must also be applied objectively, through solidarity in a horizontal angle, to reciprocity in the private, non-equivalent externalities. In regards to the concrete application of dignity to Humans, Camillo and Mac Cracken state that, "Today, effectively, balance is sought in contracts."[450]

Therefore, offering a proportional solution to the availability of economic resources, considering negative externalities as well as the negative unbalance in externality reciprocity, especially those of a private nature, the realization of Human Rights in their first, second, and third dimension resolves the primordial issue of global economic

---

449 RAJAN; ZINGALES. *Salvando o Capitalismo dos Capitalistas*, p. 339.

450 CAMILLO. *Aplicação concreta do princípio da dignidade da pessoa humana – Limites para contratar*, p. 1033.

management in alignment with the Natural Law of Fraternity. Thus, it is not limited to an individualistic market economy that is monetarist and utilitarian, generates wealth, forms an individual savings, or oppresses balanced individual rights.

Indeed, the State must act decisively in order to correct undesirable scenarios, especially in regards to human poverty and planet degradation. As Martinez indicates, *"Otro principio es que la proporción de gasto social versus el gasto publico sea cada vez mayor, me explico, si el estado tiene que preocuparse de los más desvalidos, el grueso cada vez mayor de los gastos del estado debe orientarse a las áreas sociales"*.[451] We would add 'in favor of planet sustainability as well.' Therefore, under the control of the economic order, for its efficient allocation to preferably fulfill Human Dignity for this and future generations, the availability of efforts and economic, public, and private resources must be subjected to the indispensable Anthropophilic Humanistic judgment.

In sum, in alignment with the Natural Law of Fraternity, Capitalism must organize the exercise of the subjective natural right to property in order to realize Human Rights in their first, second, and third dimension, thus universally fulfilling the objective right to Dignity for each man and the whole man in this and future generations. This would be an economic Liberalism renewed by Anthropophilic Humanism and outlined according to the concrete situation experienced by each country in regards to market economy, pursuant to the political, economic and social reality, as well as the local and global culture.

As Geertz[452] once said, the one thing that all men have in common is that they are all different. However, they identify themselves in Humanity and, consequently, in the common Dignity that includes the dignity of the Planet.

Once people's way of life is guaranteed, a legal-economic re-

---

451 MARTINEZ. *Humanismo e economia: ética e responsabilidade social*, p. 41.

452 GEERTZ. Op. cit., p. 37: "If we want to discover what man amounts to, we can only find it in what men are: and what men are, above all other things, is various."

gime that is driven by Anthropophilic Humanism and inserted within a market economy must then assure bare necessities to all in order to fulfill Human Dignity, notably in regards to externality equivalence, including externalities of a private nature. These bare necessities include education, health, work, food, drinking water, housing, basic sanitation, leisure, safety, social security, assistance to children and the destitute, thus securing a dignified planet that is free, peaceful, supported, and developed.

In this scenario, an important precedent took place on February 28, 2008 with Special Appeal # 152,229 0/1-01[453] at the Full Court of Appeals in the State of São Paulo, under Reporting Judge and President of the Court Vallim Bellocchi. Intuitively and unanimously, the Natural Law of Fraternity was recognized and apply in regards to health, while consubstantiated by Natural Law as a bare necessity in favor of the Brazilian people, as the expression of Human Dignity. The Judiciary Branch was also ordered to grant fulfillment in the face of a concrete case.

Upon ordering said attribution to the Judiciary Branch, within the scope of Public Law and in a concrete and futile case about a court-ordered debt payments against the State Department of Treasury, the Full Court of Appeals in the State of São Paulo teleologically rendered sacred the Anthropophilic Capitalist State that is the object of the reflections herein.

In turn, within the scope of Private Law, there is an iconic precedent by the Court of Justice in the State of São Paulo in regards to the horizontal enforcement of the Law of Universal Fraternity in private relations. In Civil Appeal # 991,06,054960-3, Reported by Appeals Court Judge Moura Ribeiro and adjudged on September 30, 2010 by the 11th Private Law Chamber, the reciprocity between negative private externalities was balanced, as we can see in the summary, for it was ordered that "The severe illness of a son with leukemia, which ultimately took his life, is a fact that derails the financial life of any family and can be classified as an act of God, thus allowing for the

---

453 Decision available on the Court of Justice in the State of São Paulo (TJSP) website.

removal of default interest on bad debts included within the period in which such malady took place."[454]

Consequently, a Humanistic economic analysis is thereby proposed, advancing the Neoliberal concept of Capitalism towards that which is based on a Humanistic market economy. In the event that an unbalance in negative externalities is observed and reciprocally considered, in spite of market forces, should the matter not be satisfactorily resolved in favor of the multidimensional realization of Human Rights, said unbalance must be resolved supplementarily by the State, by Civil Society, or by each man and the whole man, horizontally, as assured by the Legal Branch.

Civil Society and Free Man are supplementarily accountable for the responsibility of the State in regards to the multidimensional realization of Human Rights, for the 1st Article of Universal Declaration of Human Rights breathes the spirit of Fraternity into everyone.[455] Under such circumstances, recognizing the subjective natural right to property is placing it in favor of Human Rights in its tridimensional perspective, in which liberty is further consolidated with Equality and Fraternity. Therein lies the purpose of Anthropophilic Capitalism, which is basically a Capitalism that observes and respects Human Rights.

Therefore, as we can see, market economy in a Neoliberal State focuses strictly on recognizing negative liberties with the absolute primacy of Human Rights in their second dimension, in abstract hope that their third dimension will consequently be realized to confer an exorbitant freedom upon economic agents; nevertheless, it does not provide a sufficient answer, despite the fact that it should not be disregarded altogether. That is why we must move forward without ever loathing negative liberties.

The predominant task of a Neoliberal State consists of making the environment favorable to the free and efficient allocation of available economic resources, as assured by the legal rule of economy.

---

454 Idem.

455 Jesus's message is clear: *"Behold, I make all things new"* (The Apocalypse of Saint John, 21:5).

However, according to Sen, "Capitalist ethics are limited in a sense of economic inequality, environmental protection and need for cooperation that operates outside the market."[456]

We also need to keep in mind that a Social Welfare State, despite being Capitalist and focusing on recognizing the primacy of Human Rights in their second dimension over those of their first dimension, does not provide an adequate answer to the lack of economic efficiency and sufficiency of the State itself. In fact, it is far worse than Neoliberal Capitalism.

Neoliberal Capitalism must not retreat back to a Keynesian economy; on the contrary, we must advance in the face of State Capitalism as well. Market economy must evolve, be seasoned by the predominance of realizing Human Rights in all their dimensions in order to achieve the Dignity of Humans and the Planet. In effect, Europe is already aware that Capitalism is evolving towards a social market economy of the social-democratic nature, in which Human Rights of the first dimension are predominant and further consolidated by those of the second dimension.

Nevertheless, social market economy is restricted solely to Capitalism with a social balance and does not observe other phenomena beyond such reality. In other words, its confrontation encompasses negative externalities of a public nature, thus excluding from its model any corrections to an unbalance in negative externalities of universal and private natures; that is, it keeps a vile abstract hope that Human Rights will be realized in their third dimension and that Coase Theorem will become the absolute truth within the private scope.

It is up to Capitalism to promote the multidimensional realization of Human Rights in the first, second, and third dimensions, which must be consolidated in and of themselves and become all-encompassing to the point that they can positively achieve the complete global perspective of its demands in which economies are included. It must provide a simultaneous and concrete answer in regards to correcting and, if all possible, compensating negative externalities in all

---

456 SEN. *Desenvolvimento como liberdade*, p. 299.

their dimensions as well. Such is the view of a Humanistic Capitalism focused on consolidating Human Rights in their first, second, and third dimensions and able to shelter all other dimensions that time and history may yet reveal in order to achieve the overall Dignity of Humans and the Planet.

Hence, according to these terms, it is legally defensible and enforceable that a Capitalist economy solution must be revealed under the ideal three-part consolidated ideal of Liberty, Equality, and Fraternity. This solution must render Liberty and Equality sacred as they are proportionally set by Fraternity within an inter-consolidation chain in favor of each man and the whole man. Thus, Capitalism would be construed and governed according to the view of Human Rights that are multidimensionally consolidated and acknowledged in order to achieve the Dignity of Humans and the Planet.

Achieving the Dignity of Humans and the Planet is the direct, explicit, and concrete goal of Humanistic Capitalism, construing the concept of full life according to the ideal of Fraternity, inserted into a Humanistic market economy under the predominance of a relative individualism and conditioned in such a way for everyone to have their respective Human Rights assured in all their dimensions, according to the biocultural human condition and with individual liberties and access to dignified levels of subsistence in a dignified Planet.

Therefore, Fraternity will act, so to speak, as the conductor that harmonizes a choir with two voices: Liberty and Equality will sing the song of Human and Planet Dignity that encompasses each man and the whole man, living in the brotherhood created by the multidimensional realization of Human Rights and the due respect for its inherent biocultural diversity, as Edgar Morin explains.[457]

We are not preaching Socialism, much less Communism. For Humanistic Capitalism, Equality is not a goal or an end; it is the foundation that assures a balance between the negative externalities that are reciprocally considered, especially the access of each man and the whole man to all levels of subsistence and a dignified planet as well. This is the foundation through which each person, based on their

---

457 MORIN. *O paradigma perdido.*

own individual liberty and according to their will, should be able to infinitely develop their personal potential. Thus is the legal economic regime of a Humanistic Capitalism that institutes a humanistic market economy build upon the idea of Liberty prevailing, as calibrated by Equality and under the domain of Fraternity, within the broad perspective of a multidimensional realization of Human Rights, which at the same time assure a dignified planet and access to dignified levels of subsistence to each man and the whole man.

(7) Rethinking Locke And Capitalism

God is the Father; Jesus Christ, the Son. He is love personified, the love He gives to us, his brothers. We know we are one and the same.[458] There is a universal connection among all of us and, likewise, among everyone and everything related in the planet,[459] as proven by

---

458 In the universal prayer, Jesus says: "...so that they may all be one, as you, Father, are in me and I in you, that they also may be in us..." (*Holy Gospel of Jesus Christ according to John*, 17, 20-21).

459 Let us observe how this beautiful reality is summed up in *The Book of the Prophet Daniel* (Chapter 3, Verses 57-87), when the three young men prayed: "57 All ye works of the Lord, bless the Lord: praise and exalt him above all for ever. 58 O ye angels of the Lord, bless the Lord: praise and exalt him above all for ever. 59 O ye heavens, bless the Lord: praise and exalt him above all for ever. 60 O all ye waters that are above the heavens, bless the Lord: praise and exalt him above all for ever. 61 O all ye powers of the Lord, bless the Lord: praise and exalt him above all for ever. 62 O ye sun and moon, bless the Lord: praise and exalt him above all for ever. 63 O ye stars of heaven, bless the Lord: praise and exalt him above all for ever. 64 O every shower and dew, bless ye the Lord: praise and exalt him above all for ever. 65 O all ye spirits of God, bless the Lord: praise and exalt him above all for ever. 66 O ye fire and heat, bless the Lord: praise and exalt him above all for ever. 67 O ye cold and heat, bless the Lord, praise and exalt him above all for ever. 68 O ye dews and hoar frost, bless the Lord: praise and exalt him above all for ever. 69 O ye frost and

physics and biology. In the 6th century, Thales of Miletus said that everything is water, which is indeed the universal conductor of life. We are the children of water, a predominant element in the composition of the planet and the species that inhabit it.

Jesus is truth and was aware of it when preaching that we should love our neighbors as we love ourselves. Expanding His proposal to the legal arena, we encounter Natural Law of Fraternity. As the expression of the Law of Universal Fraternity, the Law of Fraternity imposes the realization of Human Rights in their multiple dimensions so that universal Human Dignity can be achieved.

---

cold, bless the Lord: praise and exalt him above all for ever. 70 O ye ice and snow, bless the Lord: praise and exalt him above all for ever. 71 O ye nights and days, bless the Lord: praise and exalt him above all for ever. 72 O ye light and darkness, bless the Lord: praise and exalt him above all for ever. 73 O ye lightnings and clouds, bless the Lord: praise and exalt him above all for ever. 74 O let the earth bless the Lord: let it praise and exalt him above all for ever. 75 O ye mountains and little hills, ye the Lord: praise and exalt him above all for ever. 76 O all ye things that spring up in the earth, bless the Lord: praise and exalt him above all for ever. 77 O ye fountains, bless the Lord: praise and exalt him above all for ever. 78 O ye seas and rivers, bless the Lord: praise and exalt him above all for ever. 79 O ye whales, and all that move in the waters, bless the Lord: praise and exalt him above all for ever. 80 O all ye fowls of the air, bless the Lord: praise and exalt him above all for ever. 81 O all ye beasts and cattle, bless the Lord: praise and exalt him above all for ever. 82 O ye sons of men, bless the Lord: praise and exalt him above all for ever. 83 O let Israel bless the Lord: let them praise and exalt him above all for ever. 84 O ye priests of the Lord, bless the Lord: praise and exalt him above all for ever. 85 O ye servants of the Lord, bless the Lord: praise and exalt him above all for ever. 86 O ye spirits and souls of the just, bless the Lord: praise and exalt him above all for ever. 87 O ye holy and humble of heart, bless the Lord: praise and exalt him above all for ever. (Please refer to *A Bíblia Sagrada*, official translation from the National Conference of Bishops in Brazil, 3rd edition, 2006). It is still significant that in 1225 Canticle of the Sun (*Canticum Fratris Solis vel Laudes Creaturarum*), Saint Francis of Assisi also exalts the integral reality of creation, attributing it to God, the Creator.

As mentioned before, according to Charles Darwin, as well as recent DNA researches and evolutionary biology, all species come from a common element, to which Anaximander had already referred in the 6th century b.C: a seed for the tree of life. More deeply, physicists also explain with the Big Bang Theory that the planets and starts in the universe, including Earth and everything it contains, were created from a common element known as "elementary particle" or "God particle." And so is life, as given by God. As Darwin explained, life adapted to nature to preserve itself and evolve. "Natural selection, we must not forget, only operates for and in the benefit of each being,"[460] which determines the survival of the fittest and the elimination of the weakest.[461] It was thanks to this law that life multiplied itself organically and evolved, among all species, until it culminated in a biologically superior being, Man, who was made at God's image. In this scenario, no Man can be excluded by other man as though natural selection did not apply to him.

However, man is not fully perfect: ethical perfection was not added to biological perfection. Consequently, the human spirit, as Jung once said, is constantly torn between Fraternity and Existentialism, which makes Man disregard his neighbors and the planet. Jung commented that "Since primordial times, Man was born to Earth with a healthy animal instinct that battles with his soul and demons."[462]

However, in His infinity mercy, God brought a perfect human to Earth: His only-begotten child, Jesus Christ. Jesus impresses Humanity so with His perfection that the calendar is divided in a time before Him and a time after Him. The perfection personified by Jesus can be summed up in a single word: Love. Jesus is perfect in love,[463]

---

460 DARWIN. *El origen de las especies*, p. 171.

461 Idem, p. 115.

462 JUNG. Op. cit., p. 38.

463 POPE BENEDICT XIV, op. cit., item 1, proclaims that "God is love, and he who abides in love abides in God, and God abides in him" (1 Jn 4:16). These words from the First Letter of John express with remarkable clarity the heart of the Christian faith: The Christian image of God and the resulting image of mankind and its destiny. In the same verse, Saint John also offers a kind of summary

the Supreme Gift, as Saint Paul said. Upon remembering that we are brothers, we are therefore related to God, to everyone and everything.

Curiously, Darwin appears in this context to explain that "The more important elements are love, and the distinct emotion of sympathy. Animals endowed with the social instincts take pleasure in one another's company, warn one another of danger, defend and aid one another in many ways [...]. As they are highly beneficial to the species, they have in all probability been acquired through natural selection."[464] Upon stating that "The capacity to love is inscribed in our DNA," Watson eloquently confirms that "a secular Paul would say that love is the greatest gift of our genes to Humanity."[465]

"Know thyself" was one of the Delphic maxims inscribed in the forecourt of in Ancient Greece. Therefore, as the result of natural selection applicable to all species, especially Man as the organically perfect being, moral sentiments and fraternal love in particular grow as He evolves and understands the universal connection that there exists, even though it is only intuitively. Thus, as each man and the whole man are bathed in Fraternity, they grow spiritually towards integral perfection and closer to Jesus Christ, the Perfect Man whom we may call "the Man of Love," to ultimately meet God. The "God particle" does indeed connect everyone and everything.

As the element that reflects the substance of Christ and God by actively taking part in the creation of the universe and is an agent of Fraternity, each man and the whole man give meaning to the Law.

Transposed to Law, be it by quantum physics, Jungian psychoanalysis or Judeo-Christian cultural concepts, Humanistic reflection upon each man and the whole man shall lead to the true understanding of Human Rights, whose dimensions are intersubjectively related to everyone and everything there is, which are the object of this study.

Pontes de Miranda observes that "The feeling of liberty is a biological phenomenon, which cannot be suppressed, just as the

---

of the Christian life: "We have come to know and to believe in the love God has for us."

464 DARWIN. Op. cit., p. 539.

465 WATSON; BERRY Op. and p. cits.

spine, nervous system, and eyes cannot be suppressed from superior animals."[466]

Negative liberties, as innate human liberties that reflect the substance of internal liberties (related to consciousness) and external liberties (subjective natural right to property) correspond to Human Rights of the first dimension. This is so because God gave Man life on the planet; life belongs to Man so that he can live it in the planet and for the planet. And that is why there is free will, the expression of divine concession to Mankind. According to Dante Alighieri: "This freedom (or this principle of all our freedom) is the greatest gift given by God to human nature."[467] And the poet completes his thought stating that "free will is free judgment in matters of volition."[468] Therefore, with free will, negative liberties integrate the Law of Universal Fraternity, allowing each man and the whole man to realize their Human Rights in their first dimension.

In fact, following such view, the Law of Universal Fraternity demands that Man be responsible towards one another and mutually help one another. As the spirit evolves, it leads to Human Rights of the second dimension, which consist of positive liberties, such as employment, housing, basic sanitation, health, food, drinking water, education, leisure, assistance to children and the destitute, and social security. These are called social rights, which structure Man externally and materially so that he can be free and independent, elevated as sufficient to the exercise of negative liberties and individual rights.

For Hegel, "Society has the right and duty of acting as trustee to those whose extravagance destroys the security of their own subsistence or their families. It must substitute for extravagance the pursuit of the ends of society and the individuals concerned."[469] This is the minimum guarantee of life that, despite accepting programs of direct income transfer to the poor (as in the "Allowance Program" that exists in Brazil) does not necessarily limit themselves to delivering money.

---

466 MIRANDA.*Introdução à política scientifica*, p. 145.

467 ALIGHIERI. Op. cit., p. 45.

468 Idem, p. 44.

469 HEGEL. Op. cit., p. 206.

Pursuant to Decision # 509 of 2002 by the Portuguese Constitutional Court,[470] "It is important, however, to differentiate between a right that is recognized as not being private, while being considered essential to the preservation of a critical income for a minimally dignified existence, as stated in the aforementioned judgment, and the right to demand from the State such minimally dignified existence, namely through contributions, as a result of German doctrines and jurisprudence. The latter states that 'claims to a compensation that ensures existence arises of the principle of Human Dignity, combined with the principle of a Social State,' while including 'sufficient social contributions' to the assurance of minimal existence, according to the terms of the law and under social security assistance (Horst Dreier, Grundgesetz Kommentar, Band I, Mohr Siebeck, Tübingen, 1996, pages 62 and 125-126). That is, 'the State is bound to assist citizens who have to means by providing social contributions,' the 'minimal prerequisites' to 'a humanly dignified existence' (BverfGE, 82, 60 (85)."

Notwithstanding negative and positive liberties, as men interact with one another to take part in their evolution in different ways, protecting themselves from harm, they also seek spiritual evolvement with Human Rights of the third dimension: right to protection, preservation, and evolution as inherent to Humans, including the right to a dignified Planet that is free, peaceful, sustainable, and developed.

These last two Human Rights dimensions, the second and the third, were not included in Locke's reflections. The philosopher lived in the 18th century, which was permeated by Enlightenment and Individualism, and only had a notion of individual natural rights. Aquini highlights that "18th century letters had the main concern to be a bastion for the defense of individuals before the will of sovereignty or the excessive power of authority. Therefore, they were concerned with defining individual liberty rights in particular."[471] Under the light of quantum physics, Darwin's naturalism, Jungian psychoanalysis, and the Judeo-Christian culture, however, we can identify these other two

---

470 Conselheiro Luís Nunes de Almeida, Pleno, on 12/19/02, judgement available online at http://www.tribunalconstitucional.pt.
471 AQUINI. *Fraternidade e direitos humanos*, p. 43.

dimensions, which are consolidated with the first in a universality of elements that are interdependent and indissociable.

This triad into which Human Rights are branched reflects the following substance: (a) a natural private right corresponding to individual rights and needs, as applicable, to achieve harmony in solidarity and encompassing Human Rights in their first dimension, especially in order to balance negative externalities that may be horizontally misaligned; (b) a natural public right that corresponds to the aforementioned positive rights, that is, Human Rights in their second dimension, and (c) a natural universal right that corresponds to the right to protection, preservation, and evolution of Humans in the Planet and of the Planet itself, that is, Human Rights in their third dimension. In turn, this scenario influences and modifies how the state of nature is controlled and, consequently, the forces that coordinate Capitalism and the market, the same forces that act under the control of Adam Smith's "invisible hand" in a savage context and allow for the natural selection of economic agents, among them *homo economicus*.

Upon considering its multidimensional characteristics, this perspective evolves by rethinking Locke's philosophy. We start with his philosophy with the purpose to keep such interdependent and indissociable universality that is consolidated in a reflexive balance. Our aim is to go further by pondering rights beyond individual rights, thus also including positive liberties and universal interests, whether vertical or horizontal, through solidarity and the Law of Universal Fraternity, in order to achieve Human Dignity and the Dignity of the Planet.

Uniting Men around civil society and establishing a State that will preserve and defend negative liberties, as Locke put it, freedom of religion and property, we thereby have the basis of Human Rights in their first dimension and, from them, the subsequent interdependent and indissociable dimensions described herein ultimately revealed themselves.

Hence, using the evolution of each man and the whole man as a vector, we must make Capitalism compatible with the manifestation of Fraternity that imposes the multidimensional realization of Human Rights in order to fulfill the universal Dignity of Humans and the Planet. This thought would not contradict Locke's philosophy; it would give life to it through the Law of Universal Fraternity.

VI
THE HUMANISTIC LEGAL AUTHORITY
OF CAPITALISM

(1) Existence And Concept

A Humanistic legal authority over Capitalism is a task attributed to the Three-Dimensional Humanistic view of Economic Law.

Any doubts regarding the constitutional statute of Economic Law has been overcome by what is set forth in Article 24, Section 1 of the Federal Constitution: "The Union, the States, and the Federal District are responsible for concurrently legislating over: I – Economic [...] Law."

Eros Grau clarifies that "There is no longer a place for the academically purposeless debate on whether Economic Law does exist. Any argument that denies it has, for some time now, been qualified in the same category as those arguments that cannot find a Law to base its demands."[472]

The same scholar has taught us that the perspective of Economic Law "is supported by a different view [unlike the traditional view] and by a different method [unlike the orthodox method] for legal assessment and classification; its methodological function is to establish connections and, consequently, organize legal regulations re-

---

472 *A ordem econômica na Constituição Federal de 1988*, p. 130.

garding the phenomenology of large social and economic changes of our current times."[473]

Once the issue on whether it exists is finally overcome, there is still much discussion to be had on the Economic Law concept. Nelson Nazar professes that "Economic Law is intended to organize economy."[474] In turn, Celso Bastos brings forward the fact that "ergo, it is the Law of Economy."[475]

In the introduction to Article 170 of the Federal Constitution, "economic order" is expressly referred to as meaning that economy is organized by a fundamental norm itself. In other words, it is subjected to a legal authority. Hence, a legal authority over economy is recognized and we can say that it determines the Economic Law concept. That is, Economic Law has the legal authority over economy. This concise concept fulfills the purpose of this discipline without hesitation.

Economic Law, as Nusdeo indicates, is found between "two simple observations of daily life: On the one hand, human needs tend to multiply themselves indefinitely; on the other hand, the resources required to address them are strictly limited and finite. In one word, they are 'scarce.'"[476] The same scholar recorded that, "Due to these two realities identified above, every society establishes relationships that tend to order and control the use of these scarce resources."[477] He adds, "Therefore, Economy and Law are indissociable, for the basic relationships created by society when applying such scarce resources have an institutional character, that is, they are a legal nature."[478]

Since economy as a whole is the object of Economic Law, this branch of Law encompasses overall legal and economic issues, whether it is a normative economy that includes economic doctrines and policies, or a positive economy that comprises economic analy-

---

473 Idem, p. 131.
474 NAZAR. *Direito econômico e o contrato de trabalho*, p. 190.
475 BASTOS. *Curso de direito econômico*, p. 52.
476 NUSDEO. *Curso de economia*, p. 41.
477 Idem.
478 Ibidem, p. 42.

sis and applied economics. In a few words, Economic Law includes macroeconomy and microeconomy, both scopes into which economy itself is divided. Macroeconomy is a general principle, the behavior of economic systems; microeconomy is respective to meta-individual results and implications of economic activities. Therefore, we cannot accept attempts to conceptualize Economic Law while disregarding economy in its entirety.

More specifically, we must reject the narrow views of those who only give heed to the State's intervention into economy upon stating that Economic Law is merely Public Economic Law, thus only a chapter in Administrative Law. Well, economy is much broader than the State's intervention into economic activities! Likewise, we must also reject positions that consider Economic Law as Macroeconomy Law. Economy is also about microeconomy and vice-versa. We say the same of those who align said subject solely with microeconomy, such as Competition Law and Regulation Law: Economic Law goes beyond them. It addresses the overall economy.

As mentioned above, Article 170 of the Federal Constitution refers to Economic Constitutional Order, while Article 24, Section 1 indicates a sub-constitutional positive Economic Law that is the object of Normativity by the Union and the States.

However, prior to the positivated authority over economy, there is a natural legal economic order that arises of a Human Nature that is intrinsic to the Planet and guided by negative liberties; it is the expression of Human Rights in their first dimension, notedly the subjective natural right to property. Then, if it is guided by Human Rights in their first dimension, this natural Economic Law that we have elucidated in the reflections herein is also structured, through indissociability and interdependence, on the other dimensions of Human Rights, thus imposing the realization of all of them in order to fulfill Human Dignity and the dignity of the Planet.

Regarding Brazil, following the precepts of natural Economic Law, the purpose of assuring everyone a dignified existence is positively explicit in the introduction to Article 170 of the Brazilian Magna Carta. Consequently, the Constitution expresses a Humanistic legal nature and, hence, the multidimensional nature of the Constitutional Economic Order.

According to Roque Carraza, "The Constitution of 1988 made a clear decision to opt for Human Dignity."[479] The author also adds that, "In the same sense, in Article 1st, Section 3 [...] the Democratic State of Law is founded on Human Dignity. Additionally, in the introduction to Article 170 it clearly states that the purpose of an economic order is to assure everyone a dignified existence."[480] Precisely and correctly because of that, Matsushita demonstrated[481] that the principles of Article 170 of the Federal Constitution are a development of the aforementioned constitutional device and proclaim a fundamental right, despite the fact that they do not topographically belong to the list stated in Article 5.

Therefore, supported by Locke, we can state that there is a preexisting natural Economic Law with broad authority over the subjective natural right to property, a basic external liberty of human beings of which other external liberties arise. Among these other external liberties, we have a free enterprise that gives legal discipline to economy and is tied to the multidimensional realization of Human Rights in order to assure a dignified existence to Man, Mankind, and the Planet.

This is the reasoning according to which we support that the natural Economic Law makes a crosswise cut into the sub-constitutional positive legal order. Once again, in Brazil, it is so through the constitutional positivation of the Economic order. Consequently, its purpose is to assure a specific and necessary effect on economic relations, Human Rights, and all their dimensions.

Thereby, we have a natural legal order that is Humanistic and Universal, having authority over economy and being reassured, in Brazil, by a fundamental Humanistic legal order. According to the intertextuality of a positivated law, this Humanistic legal order interpenetrates the sovereign legal orders of each country, shaping the

---

479 CARRAZZA. *O princípio constitucional da dignidade da pessoa humana e a seletividade no ICMS. Questões conexas*, p. 1103.

480 Idem.

481 MATSUSHITA. *Análise reflexiva da regra matriz da ordem econômica.*

legal protection of *homines economici* worldwide as a way to realize Human Rights multidimensionally to fulfill Human Dignity and the dignity of the planet.

(2) Natural Sources

Natural Economic Law has its own sources in the legal humanistic arena, which arise of a Law of Universal Fraternity that imposes the realization of Human Rights in all their dimensions and the fulfillment of Human Dignity and the dignity of the planet within the economic scope. Its purpose is to permeate the intertextuality of a positivist plane through a quantum method, through the Constitution of each sovereignty, until laws have been passed to rule the economic order, thus encompassing private, public, and universal economic relations.

Human Rights are declared as they reveal themselves. In turn, the role of positivation in Human Rights is clear: To make the respective contents explicit in order to assure their realization, preferably transforming them into Fundamental Rights of a Constitutional nature. However, in the event that positivation infringes upon said rights, they must remain in existence and effect. They are clauses truly set in stone: Inasmuch as each man and the whole man inhabit the Universe, Human Rights will not cease to exist. And, despite not being explicit, their natural order permeates positivation through intertextuality, to the point that this order may renounce the force of such infringing legislation.

As Article 1st of the Universal Declaration of Human Rights reveals, people "are endowed with reason and conscience and should act towards one another in a spirit of brotherhood." There is no room in natural Economic Law for criticism against Legal Humanism. Nowadays, we cannot ignore the fact that Human Rights are in effect and enforced, in all their dimensions, within Capitalism. There is no Capitalism without Human Rights.

Once again, since Capitalism is the work of man, it is structured upon negative liberties, that is, Human Rights in their first dimension, and also situated within the Legal Humanism field. In this scenario, if on the one hand Human Rights in their first dimension provide legal support to Capitalism, on the other hand the indissociability and interdependence of these rights demand that Capitalism be contingent upon the remaining dimensions and their interrelated consolidation.

Since it represents a perspective on Human Rights, "acting in the spirit of brotherhood" is not a mere moral obligation towards Capitalism. It is imperative that we bring Fraternity to the realm Economic Law.

Ultimately, notwithstanding their recognition in the law, Human Rights and the resulting Capitalism exist. Comparato indicates that, "If the Individual Rights doctrine, as a prerogative associated with Human Nature itself, made Locke one of the founders of modern theories on Human Rights, the way he advocated for rights to private property makes him one of the founding fathers of bourgeois civilization and one of the patron saints of Capitalism system."[482] It is clear that, according to Locke's philosophy, Human Rights are intrinsically related to Capitalism and, once Capitalism is recognized, said rights must be compulsorily respected. Ergo, Anthropophilic Humanism based on Jesus Christ inserts itself into legislation and encompasses Capitalism. Consequently, the sources of Natural Law of Fraternity must be enforced and come into effect within Capitalism, for it constitutes the aforementioned Three-Dimensional Humanistic view of Economic Rights.

And that is why we believe it to be an insurmountable paradox that Capitalists have the audacity to deny or disregard the absolute quality of Human Rights in all their dimensions. The aforementioned rights become an indissociable and interdependent bundle; we cannot accept some and deny others. They are the innate, indissociable core of elements that are intrinsic to each man and the whole man, inherent to the planet, thus becoming part of the universal legal order, including economic behavior.

---

482 LOCKE. Op. cit., p. 220.

It does not matter that some countries refuse to sign treaties and international declarations; they are all subject to Human Rights by Natural Law. *Veritas et ratio quae similitudine oritur.*[483] In fact, these Capitalists pretend not to see or disregard their accountability because they maybe do not want to be called upon to pay the bill. Respecting Human Rights thoroughly means having expenses and many Capitalists simply do not accept it. That is why people used to think that Human Rights are incompatible with Capitalism, and they have been proven wrong to think that way. Under this light, Human Dignity is improperly perceived as a right that comes with a cost, despite opinions to the contrary.

Human Rights, and more notedly Human Dignity, shall not be construed according to the perspective of a right that comes with a cost, despite their economic impact being verifiable. These are different objects and criteria.

Consequently, the natural Laws of Fraternity applied to Capitalism compulsorily lead to the realization of Human Rights in all their dimensions in order to fulfill Human Dignity. They interpenetrate positive legal texts, including national constitutions. In Brazil, it happens seamlessly, to the point that it is rendered sacred as a fundamental right, the principal rule of the economic order associated with the assurance of a dignified life for everyone. In Brazil, it suffices to apply the quantum method and permeate legal intertextuality, whether it is through Natural Law or the Federal Constitution as a principal rule of the economic order.

The Constitution of a nation, albeit a sovereign one, and its positive laws must be adapted to the natural laws that arise of intertextuality positivation within Capitalism. The Brazilian Supreme Federal Court has begun to create precedents for this subject, as we can see in Binding Abridgement # 25, which abolished the civil arrest of an unfaithful depositary, notwithstanding the fact that it provided in the Constitution. This position had already been addressed in Brazil when it was applied to monocratic instances, such as by District Judge

---

483 In vernacular: *Truth is reason that is born from similarity.*

Evandro Portugal.[484]

Therefore, we must identify the natural Laws of Fraternity, which are the sources of the Three-Dimensional Economic Law: 1) Private Natural Law, 2) Structuring Natural Law, and 3) Universal Natural Law. Despite unwritten, its contents are elementary and comply with the intertextuality of positivated Economic Law applied by the quantum method.

Private Natural Law is the non-positivated recognition of Human Rights in their first dimension within Capitalism, that is, negative liberties and the internal and external liberties of Man. The latter two are a result of the subjective natural right to property, for they correspond to the free man and assure rights that are constituted by the state of nature. Originally, is Man is free, his property is private. This natural law is the basis for Capitalism and makes it an innate economic regime. That is why Capitalism does not need to be recorded in a positive normative charter. We must emphasize that it exists notwithstanding any positivation and that is why, even in the absence of a supranational positivating sovereign power, free international economic relations are legally arranged and governed by a Capitalist system. We must note that economic globalization is legally arranged and Capitalist in nature. It is so in England, a country that has not even positivated its laws in a Constitution, as well as in the United States, where their Constitution recognizes property without directly positivating it, as we have discussed earlier.

Now, Structuring Natural Law is the non-positivated recognition of Human Rights in their second dimension within Capitalism, that is, the positive liberties of Man, which are economic, social, and cultural Human Rights corresponding mainly to the State. The State has a determinant role in assuring positive liberties, but it also has a complementary duty to collaborate with Man, Mankind, and Civil Society. For free men to exercise their negative liberties, everyone, especially the State, must maintain the necessary structure for

---

484 Decision to deny citizen's arrest of an unfaithful depositary, Record # 3,792/07, Araucária Civil Court, Paraná State Justice, which was not published in the State Gazette due to the attorney's personal knowledge.

the respective task among those who have it, while providing such structure for those who do not. It is a well-known fact that it is not possible to exercise Human Rights in their first dimension without a minimum structure, without the minimum existential requirements in which the so-called positive liberties are included. Once again, the Federal Constitution in Brazil gives us an example of explicit Human Rights in Constitutional Amendment # 31, Article 79 of the Temporary Constitutional Provisions Act, with provides for the "right to access dignified subsistence levels." Consequently, it positively unveils the right to have our bare necessities assured. After all, Human Rights in their second dimension provide the foundations for the Human Rights in their first dimension to be exercised.

Finally, Universal Natural Law is the non-positivated recognition of Human Rights in their third dimension within Capitalism. These are the rights that each man and the whole man, as well as the Planet itself, must be concerned with, notwithstanding the rights in their first dimension and their structuring facilitated by their second dimension. In sum, they are related to protection, preservation, and evolution rights for the Earth and Humankind itself. As a consequence of these rights, Human Rights become an inherent part of the Planet. In fact, Ecuador's Constitution of 2008[485] expressly renders Nature sacred as *Pacha Mama*, which in the indigenous Kichwa language translates into "subject of rights." Ultimately, in their third dimension, "Rights are conceived and no longer targeted at the individual or the collective, but at Humankind itself."[486] We would add

---

485 "Art. 71 – *La naturaleza o Pacha Mama, donde se reproduce y realiza la vida, tiene derecho a que se respete integralmente su existencia y el mantenimiento y regeneración de sus ciclos vitales, estructura, funciones y procesos evolutivos. Toda persona, comunidad, pueblo o nacionalidad podrá exigir a la autoridad pública el cumplimiento de los derechos de la naturaleza. Para aplicar e interpretar estos derechos se observaran los principios establecidos en la Constitución, en lo que proceda. El Estado incentivará a las personas naturales y jurídicas, y a los colectivos, para que protejan la naturaleza, y promoverá el respeto a todos los elementos que forman un ecosistema.*"

486 Santiago Guerra, *Processo constitucional e direitos fundamentais*, p. 46.

the Planet as their target as well. Basically, these are the rights to a dignified planet, which translates into a free, peaceful, developed, and sustainable world.

Inasmuch as they integrate the intertextuality of Positive Law, when it suffices to apply the quantum method, Natural Laws do not have to subject to one another. Human Rights do not cancel each other out and, as a consequence, nor do Natural Laws, for their enforcement is consolidated as well. Therefore, Natural Laws must be applied as an entire set, even though current complexities in our lifestyles in this Planet may lead to a permanent clash between Human Rights of one dimension with those of the remaining dimensions, or even clashes within the same dimension. Potentially, this tension creates an unbalance in the realization of rights, which must be aligned horizontally in private relations as well. Santiago Guerra reminded us that "In order to resolve the clash between several interests in certain groups and those of individuals and the State, we cannot simply find support in broad regulations that have been already created, for these clashes are so diversified and unpredictable, whence the procedures that cannot be bypassed to reach unexpected solutions."[487]

The answer to alignment is proportionality since, as Santiago Guerra indicated, "it is what allows for a coexistence of divergent principles; we can even say that there is a mutual implication between them and proportionality, for principles provide values to be balanced, or these principles could not be applied in any way."[488] Proportionality is crucial to have Natural Laws applied to the economic realm. It is a principle of Natural Law since, as Dante Alighieri once said, "Law is a real and personal proportion of man to man, which, when preserved, preserves society; when destroyed, it ruins society."[489]

We can say that the natural principle of proportionality is a result of Men assembled together after leaving the state of nature. Hence, it is a necessary instrument to private life and its interrelations, as well as to civil society constitution and State creation. And,

---

487 GUERRA FILHO. Op. cit., pp. 159-162.

488 Idem, p. 135.

489 ALIGHIERI. Op. cit., p. 67.

when assembled together, Men entered into a social contract whose purpose is to assure a peaceful coexistence in harmony, a coexistence that is inclusive and egalitarian while, at the same time, libertarian. It is not by chance that, before States were created, a notion of justice had already resulted from this assembly among Men. Justice is then represented by the symbol of a scale, which brings balance, or "common sense" for the laymen. That is why people say that judges must have common sense, thus expressing the natural principle of proportionality.

In effect, proportionality is not a sterile and merely formal deliberation without a concrete destination to guide appliers of the law, leaving its path to their subjective criteria. Considering the clash of Human Rights, we cannot use proportionality as a pretext to recognize one right and simply destroy all others. On the contrary, proportionality must be applied in such a way that, in a reflexive balance, it encompasses and assures the essential core of Human Dignity in the face of all Human Rights being collided against.

Appeals Court Judge Vallim Bellocchi, with the São Paulo Court of Justice, created an important precedent[490] with a decision to suspend the effects of a public civil verdict. Among other arguments, upon the request of the municipality of Santa Rosa de Viterbo and with the purpose to ensure the local economy and employability of residents, Judge Bellocchi suspended an environmental demand that ordered the demolition of a plant in order to restore a rainforest in an area considered degraded. He did so on the grounds of proportionality, considering the clash between the aforementioned Human Rights of the third dimension, in regards to environmental protection, and that population's economic and social Human Rights of the second and third dimensions.

---

490 Request to suspend public civil action sentence, Record # 167.533.0/1-00, published in Online Legal Gazette (DJE) of São Paulo on 09/10/2008, p. 22.

(3) Legal Nature

Santos, Gonçalves and Leitão Marques state that Economic Law is "the study of legal ordinance (or regulation) specific to the organization and governance of economic activities by public authorities and (or) private authorities with the ability to edit or contribute to editing general rules binding economic agents."[491] We must keep in mind that there is also a civil society and humanity that are not public or private entities and could have this same ability, which is inherent to Universal Law, for these legal associations go beyond public or private authorities. They belong to the planet and, why not, are universal. It suffices to say that, from a legal perspective, the economic globalization phenomenon is neither private nor public: It belongs to the planet.

And it should not be considered of a private international nature either, for the traditional philosophy of International Law, which assigns all economic relations to the private scope, has been overcome as well. How could WTC laws be private, if its contentious role in governing world trade is established among countries? Even in national legislations, how could it be private if we notoriously know nowadays that Human Rights encompass economic and social rights, as well as those of a third dimension?

These economic relations are not public either, since they include planet-related issues that go beyond the States themselves, especially in regards to the sovereignty or comparison of States. In a geopolitical setting, economy evolves from local, national, regional, continental, and hemispherical levels until it reaches the status of a planet-wide economy, perhaps universal too, encompassing Human Rights of the first, second, and third dimensions, as well as all other dimensions that may be unveiled in the future.

Therefore, could Economic Law be merely public or private? It is much broader than that. In fact, it belongs to each man and the whole man, protecting everyone (both *homo economicus* and *homi-*

---

491 SANTOS; GONÇALVES; MARQUES. *Direito económico*, pp. 15-16.

nes economici) and everything. Ultimately, it protects the planet itself. That is why it falls upon economic relations between countries and people worldwide, whether they are neighbors or located at opposite sides of the Earth, notwithstanding any physical contact.

The reference made by Article 174 of the Federal Constitution to public and private sectors in the economy does not restrict the economic order to these sections, which are public and private in the face of economic agents, not in the face of those protected by the economic order, which are everyone and everything. Hence, we can see that the economic order controls the private and public sectors of economy, that is, private individuals and the State as economic agents. However, it cannot be mistaken for the multidimensional protection offered by the Economic Law, whose purpose is to assure a dignified existence to everyone, as explained in the introduction to Article 170 of the Federal Constitution.

More emphatically, due to the Law of Universal Fraternity applied to Capitalism, the goal of an economic order is to realize Human Rights in all their dimensions, consolidating them one by one and assuring a full life to free Man, Mankind, and the Planet. Thus, it is the pursuit of a corresponding objective of dignity for Humans and the Planet. Considering such purpose, we can understand that the economic order is not protecting only private interests, nor is it protecting public interests solely. It protects everyone and everything, including universal interests. Bagnoli explains that "By engaging the rights of individuals within society and private relations within a collectivity, Economic Law breaks away from the traditional restrains imposed by Private and Public Law."[492]

It is clear then that the economic order, that is, Economic Law, does not belong precisely to Private Law or Public Law. Likewise, it is not lined by the exclusive nature of Universal Law either. One thing is certain: it tends to protect universal interests, but it does not exclude the protection of public and private interests. We must understand that, as a matter of protection, what we see is the consolidation of Private, Public, and Universal natures within an economic environment.

---

492 BAGNOLI. *Direito econômico*, p. 20.

Therefore, we can say for sure that Economic Law has a tri-dimensional nature. It is, at the same time, private, public, and universal. It legally governs economy through Human Rights in all their dimensions. In the words of De Lucca, it is "a kind of third-generation Law."[493]

(4) The Importance Of Defending The *Homo Economicus*

As we can see, Humanistic Capitalism as a legal and economic authority has the purpose to achieve the multidimensional realization of Human Rights in order to assure the dignity of Man, Mankind, and the Planet.

Anthropological studies on "the other," as "defined [...] in terms [...] of economy,"[494] show that the post-modern man shapes his lifestyle according to the market, considering the impersonal mass relationships provided by a Capitalistic economy, thus being part of the so-called Capitalist Society. In turn, this economic insertion integrates Human Nature itself as a way to express the external liberties of each man and the whole man. The instinct of ownership that is so characteristic of Human Nature is a sign of current developments in primal survival instincts.

Under this light, which we may classify as an anthropological and economical take on the subject, Man must be qualified as *homo economicus*.[495] In a Capitalist Society, *homines economici*[496] express their primal survival instincts through economic actions and they are, naturally, individualistic, competitive, and massified. Consequently, Men are disjoined and isolated and that is why they do not have an organic bond among themselves.

At first, no relationship among *homines economici* can be

---

493 DE LUCCA. *Direito do consumidor*, p. 467.

494 AUGE. Op. cit., p. 23.

495 In vernacular: *Economic Man*.

496 In vernacular: *Economic Men*.

formed horizontally, for they may spend hours, days, months, and years next to one another without ever getting to meet each other. They are part of a shapeless and uncoordinated mass of human being, who find mobilization extremely difficult because they are not aligned in a social and economic environment and act on their primal instincts, according to the original state of nature.

Among *homines economici* there is only a direct and isolated relationship due to the legal and economic relations of an impersonal and dehumanized nature, which "does not create a unique identity, nor relationship, but only loneliness and resemblance,"[497] thus surely leading to a "ethnology of loneliness."[498] Such relationship does not create an organic social group, but a mass of lonely individuals amid a multitude of peers, without any deeper interrelations, controlled by horizontal impersonality. Gathering *homines economici* together is certainly a Herculean task, if not utopia.

As we can see, *homo economicus*, considered individually, are alone in the crowd and in an absolutely insignificant position, at the mercy of a market that potentially disregards his Human Rights of first, second and third dimensions. They are captives of Capitalism because, as Weber once said, "The Capitalistic economy of the present day is an immense cosmos into which the individual is born, and which presents itself to him, at least as an individual, as an unalterable order of things in which he must live. It forces the individual, insofar as he is involved in the system of market relationships, to conform to Capitalistic rules of action."[499]

In this Capitalism, money is the core value. For Max Weber, such distortion means that "Man is dominated by the making of money, by acquisition as the ultimate purpose of his life. Economic acquisition is no longer subordinated to man as the means for the satisfaction of his material needs."[500] McFarlane supports this argument: "For what Weber saw was that it is not money in itself, it is not mar-

497 AUGE. Op. cit., p. 95.
498 Idem, p. 110.
499 WEBER. *A ética protestante e o espírito do Capitalismo*, pp. 47-48.
500 Idem, p. 46.

kets by themselves, it is not even particular accounting systems that are significant, it is the use and purposes to which these are put. It is not money which is the root of Capitalism, but the love of money."[501] According to this environment, *homo economicus* is unacceptably in second place. Money is the priority in this odd situation that has been elevated to "a process of economic survival of the fittest."[502] It is its center of gravity, or as Weber puts it, "the *summum bonum* of this ethic, the earning of money and more money."[503]

Homo economicus reacts by isolating himself in individualism. For this type of man, as Pope John Paul II once warned us, "The so-called "quality of life" is interpreted primarily or exclusively as economic efficiency, inordinate consumerism, physical beauty and pleasure, to the neglect of the more profound dimensions—interpersonal, spiritual and religious—of existence."[504] Following such view, Man becomes, almost instinctively, an economic predator of Man and the Planet. He is the hunter and the prey at the same time. According to Richard Leakey, it is well known that "the notion that the physique of early *Homo* reflected the active pursuit of meat—that is, as a hunter in search of prey."[505] Keeping it in perspective, *homo economicus* is, at the same time, a predator (as an active economic agent) and prey (as a human that is subjected to the savage market economy.)

Therefore, considering the high level of massification, impersonality, and misalignment with *homo economicus*, that is, the dehumanization of market economy, it is clear that this type of man is vulnerable and exposed, as a prey, and consequently, his condition makes the Planet vulnerable as well. By elevating individualism and hedonism in the name of liberty, Anthropocentric Humanism winds up corroborating the idea that money is a priority, thus placing *homo economicus* in second place, by himself, at the mercy of the power of money and as a victim of Anthropocentrism itself, which must be

501 MCFARLANE. *A cultura do Capitalismo*, p. 271.

502 Idem, p. 47.

503 WEBER. Op. cit., p. 46.

504 JOHN PAUL II, Encyclical *Evangelium Vitae* of March 25, 1995, item 23.

505 LEAKEY. *A origem da espécie humana*, p. 66.

reshaped, but never denounced, by Humanistic Capitalism as a manifestation of Anthropophilic Humanism.

As a result, there is a long-lasting fight among *homines economici* within Capitalism. And they also fight against the planet, in a state of nature made of savage manifestations during their perpetual pursuit of ownership or consumption as the end to their means. Souza and Clark conclude that "In the post-modernity of the 21st century, genocide is yet to be completely eradicated. Men are executed by weapons of war or by political and economic means that eliminate millions of people all at once or in installments."[506]

Physical violence and the abuses and omissions of Capitalism stand side by side, promoting economic injuries and disregarding the planet. We only need to think about the crowds of people who have no food, jobs, a roof over their heads, medical insurance... Likewise, we see global warming as the product of human pollution, which maximizes the damages caused by natural events. Economic violence has the potential to cause the break-down of Mankind and the Planet. Against this perspective, the Law of Universal Fraternity arises and it is capable of structuring the Humanistic Legal Authority over Capitalism through the multidimensional realization of Human Rights in the economic regime.

(5) Gravitational Incidence

Humanistic Capitalism is part of Martin Luther King's dream of a brotherhood.[507] This is the same dream that Barack Obama called "The Audacity of Hope."[508] It is now becoming a reality in the Brazil-

---

506 SOUZA. *Questões polêmicas de direito econômico*, p. 35.

507 Martin Luther King delivered in his speech: "I have a dream: that one day this nation will rise up and live out the true meaning of its creed: We hold these truths to be self-evident; that all men are created." *I Have a Dream*, public speech on August 28, 1963 at the steps of Lincoln Memorial in Washington D.C.

508 OBAMA. Op. and p. cits.

ian legal system, for the Constitution determines that we must build a free, fair, compassionate society, that is, a Fraternal Society. This dream becomes an international legal principle with the Vienna Declaration and Program of Action, which sets forth in Item 10 that "the human person is the central subject of development," thus indicating that States "should cooperate with each other in ensuring development and eliminating obstacles to development."

Constitutional commands are not pieces of rhetoric or mere symbolisms to demand the eradication of marginalization and poverty and the reduction of social inequalities. It is for the good of everyone, without discriminating against gender, color, social status, or religion, and it must be promoted in an efficient manner. Everyone should have an income, a job, food, drinking water, education, health, housing, basic sanitation, leisure, social security, as well as assistance to expectant mothers, children, and those in need. Ultimately, it is about assuring the access to a dignified subsistence. As Pope John Paul II emphasized, "There is no justification then for despair or pessimism or inertia. Though it be with sorrow, it must be said that just as one may sin through selfishness and the desire for excessive profit and power, one may also be found wanting with regard to the urgent needs of multitudes of human beings submerged in conditions of underdevelopment, through fear, indecision and, basically, through cowardice."[509] As in the Pontifex's prophecy, the darkest night of the economic and financial crisis is upon us and it was merciless with the poor and those in need.

The main demand that must be addressed by Humanistic Capitalism is, undoubtedly, achieving the development of each man and the whole man, as well as the dignity of the Planet. The internal logic of Humanistic Capitalism must necessarily lead society to the ideal of full development, which is broader than simply economic development. We must not forget Pope John Paul II's warning: "Development which is merely economic is incapable of setting man free, on the contrary, it will end by enslaving him further."[510] The complete

---

509 *Solicittudo Rei Socialis*, item 47.
510 Idem, item 46.

development of nations, as mentioned above, cannot be considered solely in its economic dimension, as practitioners of every shape and size would like. It is, more fittingly, a matter of justice demanding the growth of each man and the whole man and respect for the Planet.[511]

In effect, in 1967 Pope Paul VI already advocated for the development of nations, "This is particularly true in the case of those peoples who are trying to escape the ravages of hunger, poverty, endemic disease and ignorance; of those who are seeking a larger share in the benefits of civilization and a more active improvement of their human qualities; of those who are consciously striving for fuller growth."[512] He adds, "So today we earnestly urge all men to pool their ideas and their activities for man's complete development and the development of all mankind."[513]

Along the same lines, the UN General Assembly published in 1986 the Declaration on the Right to Development, whose introduction stated the following: "Bearing in mind the purposes and principles of the Charter of the United Nations relating to the achievement of international co-operation in solving international problems of an economic, social, cultural or humanitarian nature, and in promoting and encouraging respect for human rights and fundamental freedoms for all without distinction as to race, sex, language or religion." The Declaration also recognized that "development is a comprehensive economic, social, cultural and political process, which aims at the constant improvement of the well-being of the entire population and of all individuals on the basis of their active, free and meaningful participation in development and in the fair distribution of benefits resulting therefrom."

Development is a continuous process and the UN demands that everyone participate in it: Government and governed society, States, and international organizations. Their purpose is to assure that the dignification of Humans and the Planet is not further delayed.

---

511 BALERA. Apresentação do volume em homenagem aos 40 anos da encíclica *Populorum Progressio*.

512 PAULO VI. Op. cit., item 1.

513 Idem, item 5.

In Sengupta's words, "the right to development was elaborating on a concept of development that did not deny the importance of the growth of income and output which provides the basis for the expansion of resources and therefore of the opportunities for development. However, they should be realized in a way that ensures fair distribution, equal access to resources, and the expansion of fundamental freedoms of the individuals." These freedoms, as Sen now puts it, "should be seen as a central development aim, not just an instrument for achieving other aspects of development."[514]

Both perspectives, one constructive and the other instrumental, are revealed in the first paragraph of Article 1st of the Declaration on the Right to Development, which addresses the on the continuous evolution of each man and the whole man: "The right to development is an inalienable human right by virtue of which every human person and all peoples are entitled to participate in, contribute to, and enjoy economic, social, cultural and political development, in which all human rights and fundamental freedoms can be fully realized."

Sen argues that "development can be seen as process of expanding the real freedom that people enjoy. Focusing on human freedoms contrasts with the narrower views of development, such as identifying development with the growth of Gross National Product, or with the rise in personal incomes, or with industrialization, or with technological advance, or with social modernization. The growth of GNP or individual incomes are obviously very important means of expanding the freedoms enjoyed by members society. But freedoms also depend on other factors, such as social and economic arrangements (for example, access to education and health care,) as well as civil rights."[515] Therefore, the right to development as a Human Right is part of the innate core of Humans, since "The human person is the central subject of development and should be the active participant and beneficiary of the right to development," pursuant to what is revealed in the first paragraph of Article 2 in the aforementioned Declaration.

---

514 SEN. Op. cit., p. 19.
515 Idem, p. 17.

In Brazil, Article 3, Section 2 of the Federal Constitution literally renders sacred national development as one of its fundamental objectives. Support on such order, Ishikawa ponders that development has been positivated "as a fundamental right, in order to assure and protect not only civil and political rights, but those of an economic, social, and culture nature as well."[516] Consequently, right to development is a subjective natural right to multiple ownership of Man, Mankind, and the Planet. It imposes progress toward Humanistic Capitalism, supported by the demand that, despite being Capitalistic, the economic order must realize Human Rights in all their dimensions in order to universally fulfill the Dignity of Humans and the Planet.

As a result, Capitalism must correspond to "individual liberty with commitment,"[517] thus realizing Human Rights in order to fulfill Human Dignity. Hence, everyone, Men with one another and the Planet itself, will promote development and legally impose the subjective natural right to demand Fraternity from all, especially from those who are affluent, the State, the international community and civil society, in sum, of Humanity as a Universal Society.

Paragraph 2, Article 2 of Declaration on the Right to Development records that "All human beings have a responsibility for development, individually and collectively, taking into account the need for full respect for their human rights and fundamental freedoms as well as their duties to the community, which alone can ensure the free and complete fulfillment of the human being, and they should therefore promote and protect an appropriate political, social and economic order for development." As a legal obligation, Silveira concluded that "it becomes a duty toward all inhabitants of the planet, especially toward the destitute."[518]

We no longer measure the development of a nation by its Gross Domestic Product (GDP), but by its Human Development In-

---

516 ISHIKAWA. Op. cit., p. 139.

517 SEN. op. cit., p. 320.

518 SILVEIRA. *O direito ao desenvolvimento na doutrina humanista do direito econômico*, p. 323.

dex (HDI)[519], for the wealth of a nation, as we have seen, is not limited to its economic aspects. National wealth is also found in the social, political, and cultural evolution of a country.

Therefore, every individual must be inserted into this process of political, economic, social, and cultural development. Social responsibility takes a broader perspective in addition to what is related to political rights. It is the manifestation of a full and universal democracy that, naturally, is part of a social contract and, why not, of a global society, whose objective contents promote Human Dignity and the constant fight against all forms of exclusion, whether they are political, economic, social, or cultural.

On the other hand, we must emphasize that the multidimensional realization of Human Rights, aimed at fulfilling the Dignity of Humans and the Planet in its objective dimensions of democracy and peace, is not absolute. It is limited within the scope of what is materially possible and the concrete meaning of different development levels among nations as measured by the HDI. This material limitation encompasses economic, social, and cultural policies that involve costs that must be covered. We must find harmony between the realization of Human Rights in all their dimensions and the reserves available, not only in the relationships between Men and the State, but in private relations as well. It is evident that this harmony comes as a result of applying the principle of proportionality.

Compelled by the duty to Fraternity, within reasonable limits and according to available reserves, we are all responsible according to the multidimensional perspective of realizing Human Rights

---

519 In Brazil, the UN Development Programme clarifies in its website that "The purpose of elaborating a Human Develop Index (HDI) is to offer a counterbalance for another indicator that is used very often, the Gross Domestic Product (GDP) per capita, which only takes economic development into consideration. Created by Mahbub ul Haq with the help of Indian economist Amartya Sen, recipient of the Nobel Prize in Economics of 1998, HDI aimes at becoming a general, synthetic measurement for human development. It does not encompass all aspects of development, not does it represent how 'happy' people are or indicates 'the best place in the world to live.'" http://www.pnud.org.br/idh, on 09/23/2008.

through the dignification of Humans and the Planet. Nevertheless, paternalism and populism are intolerable. Neither should we accept ungrounded pretexts on available reserves in order to deny the multidimensional realization of Human Rights. In other words, available reserves must be applied with caution, for they are not a shield, but as a relief against Humanistic Fundamentalism. We must make it clear that all efforts are made in the name of the highest possible level of multidimensional realization of Human Rights. As a result, the burden of proof is on those calling upon the available reserves, who must then clarify the need for their use.

A logical deliberation on the Human Rights to be realized is a determining factor on their interpretation. Mendes has taught us that, regarding this subject, "legal deliberations concern the ultimate test on the principles of proportionality in its strict sense. The exercise of deliberation is sensitive to the idea that, even though all norms have the same hierarchical status within a constitutional system, each principle set forth in a constitution may have different abstract weight."[520]

Supported by the premises of development, reasonability, and proportionality, a Three-Dimensional Humanistic view of Economic Law uses the Law of Universal Fraternity through its legal authority over economy to give prestige to the three-dimensional core of Human Rights. It draws, at the same time, on the simultaneous and pondered application of natural private laws, which are universal and structuring, within an unbreakable gravitational performance on the concrete case, as it happened with the spheres that Galileo dropped from the Tower of Pisa in 1589.

In this well-known historical and scientific event, Galileo did an empirical experiment when he dropped two spheres of different masses from the top of the Tower of Pisa and recorded that both were drawn by the same velocity, notwithstanding their weight. With the application of the law, Human Rights will have the same gravitational pull on Humanistic Capitalism, with the support of a Three-Dimensional Humanistic view of Economic Law. Through intertextuality in the corresponding Positive Law, it promotes an interpenetration

---

520 MENDES; COELHO; BRANCO. *Curso de direito constitucional*, p. 285.

of the multidimensional legal realization of Human Rights with economic relations, thus making it possible for the Capitalist environment to be driven by Anthropophilic Humanism, with the support of a quantum method that will apply the respective normative text and metatext.

The solution in each concrete case will, thus, correspond to the fulfillment of Human Dignity's objective right. Once a certain level of universal evolution has been achieved, thus realizing Human Rights, such standard will become part of a subjective natural property to be enjoyed by all beneficiaries, thus becoming opposable and implying in the prohibition of retrogression. As soon as these political, economic, social and cultural rights are realized, Humans will have acquired their right to property in its subjective aspect.

Earned rights cannot be removed or reduced and any measures aimed at doing so should be opposed by the State itself if it somehow competes against the State itself. Locke once warned us that "Just and moderate governments are everywhere quiet, everywhere safe; but oppression raises ferments and makes men struggle to cast off an uneasy and tyrannical yoke."[521]

As for fundamental rights, retrogression is prohibited by the systemic legal support positivated in the Brazilian constitution. In constitutional terms, according to Afonso, we can see that "upon analyzing the wording in Article 5, Section 41, which says that the Law will punish any attempt to discriminate against fundamental rights and liberties, we can also fit here the principle of no social retrogression into our order, since such device addresses the exact principle in question and even prescribes punishment against any retrogression in regards to fundamental rights and liberties."[522] As we can see, constitutional order rendered sacred systemic protection through its own realization. Once fundamental rights are realized, the catalog of such rights, in Brazil, renders protection sacred in a truly Autopoiesis. From this perspective, such protections must be extended to Human

---

521 Idem, p. 60.

522 AFONSO. *A busca do pleno emprego e a proteção contra a despedida arbitrária*, p. 189.

Rights and their multidimensional impact within the Capitalist scope, as they reveal themselves, considering the fact that they incorporate the subjective public property of Man, Mankind and the Planet. For this reason, they cannot be simply undermined by a third party, by the State or by Civil Society.

VII
THE PROPOSAL

Joining The Humanistic Capitalism

The reflections herein propose, within the Philosophy of Law, a Humanistic doctrine over Economic Law to introduce the Three-Dimensional Humanistic view of Economic Law as a more suitable response to the predominance of a Capitalist market economy, thus recognizing the subjective natural right to property that is the basis of all other external liberties, especially free enterprise.

Recognizing property in the subjective field necessarily implies its respective relativization, in order to realize Human Rights in their first, second, and third dimensions, as well as any other dimensions that may reveal themselves, as they are consolidated among themselves, with the purpose to fulfill the Dignity of Humans and the Planet. It implies a Capitalist economic regime with a humanistic market economy, which calibrates the subjective natural right to property and the resulting free enterprise to assure the full innate rights of each man and the whole man in the name of everyone and everything. Within private legal relations, it includes a horizontal angle, since negative balances among reciprocal externalities must be resolved.

Likewise, we are certain that the best answer to Liberal Capitalism is the realization of Capitalism with Human Rights. It is not about denouncing Capitalism, nor destroying negative liberties, which are part of the human essence and assured by the subjective natural right to property that ultimately encompasses external Human Rights in their first dimension.

Consequently, a Three-Dimensional Humanistic view of Economic Law creates a reflexive balance between Capitalist regime and Fraternity in favor of everyone and everything, especially the Planet and those who are economically excluded. The basis for such right is the Anthropophilic Humanism constituted by Legal Culturalism, which is part of Natural Law.

Therefore, through normative Legal Humanism, this perspective of Natural Law becomes part of the positive legal norm through its inoculation in the intratextuality that is part of the significant contents of Constitution and the laws intertwined with metatext.

This Humanistic thought find support in Jesus Christ. It balances the individualism and hedonism found in Capitalism with Human Rights in all their dimensions, under the anthropological light that irradiates from the proposal of our Master. Before being equal, we are all brothers; therefore, Man is moved from the center of all things to the diffuse medium of all things.

Disregarding Anthropocentric Humanism in favor of an Anthropophilic nature, such Economic Law aims as building the environment for a Humanistic market economy, in which Human Rights are recognized and realized in all their dimensions, thus corresponding to the objective right to Dignity for Humans and the Planet.

Anthropophilic Humanistic is, then, the supporting foundation for Humanistic Capitalism, through which Human Rights in their first, second, and third dimensions will be realized upon promoting, according to the current reality, a Humanistic market economy that is governed by the Three-Dimensional Humanistic view of Economic Law.

It is, after all, a fourth path that makes a commitment to each man and the whole man to realize Human Rights in all their dimensions, whose purpose is to universally fulfill Dignity for Humans and the Planet.

As it is applied to the Capitalist legal rule of economy, by overcoming a merely formal and material equality before the law, it sees a universal connection between everyone and everything in the "God particle," thus placing a Brotherhood of Men at the diffuse medium of all things.

By implication, Man, Mankind, and the Planet must be fraternally protected, thus the realization of Human Rights in all their dimensions within Capitalism arises of a natural duty to Fraternity, as the subjective natural right that benefits the destitute, in special, and is demanded not only of the State, but also horizontally of civil society and every Men to encompass all private individual relations.

Fraternity is the pillar that governs the Three-Dimensional Humanistic view of Economic Law and, consequently, Humanistic Capitalism, which is structured by the Humanistic philosophy of Economic Law. Fraternity is no longer seen as a merely moral virtue that emerges as a legal obligation of the State, civil society, and free men towards everyone and everything, especially the socially excluded and the Planet. It is applied by a quantum method due to its tri-dimensional gravitational incidence, according to the perspective of development, reasonability, and proportionality.

In conclusion, we would like to invite our readers to join our proposal: Let us understand and govern Capitalism through an Anthropophilic Humanistic perspective, which demands the realization of Human Rights in all their dimensions in order to control market economy, as best as possible, according to the reality, as well as the objective right to Dignity that is assured to Humans and the Planet, thus building a universally fraternal society. The *Omega* (Ω).

Bibliographical references

ABDALLA, Maria Cristina. *Bohr, o arquiteto do átomo*. São Paulo: Odysseus, 2006.

ADEODATO, João Maurício. *A retórica constitucional*. São Paulo: Saraiva, 2009.

_____. *Ética e retórica*. São Paulo: Saraiva, 2006.

_____. *Filosofia do direito*. São Paulo: Saraiva, 2005.

AFONSO, Túlio Augusto Tayano. *A busca do pleno emprego e a proteção contra a despedida arbitrária*. Master Degree Thesis at Universidade Presbiteriana Mackenzie, São Paulo, 2005. Unpublished.

ALEXY, Robert. *Constitucionalismo discursivo*. Porto Alegre: Livraria do Advogado, 2007.

ALIGHIERI, Dante. *Da monarquia*. Rio de Janeiro: Ediouro-Tecnoprint, [s.d.].

AMMANN, Safira Bezerra. "Cidadania e exclusão social: o mundo desenvolvido em questão". *In: Revista Serviço Social & Sociedade*. n. 76, ano XXIV. São Paulo: Cortez, 2003.

ANDRIGHI, Fátima Nancy. "A tutela jurídica do consumidor e o respeito à dignidade da pessoa humana". *In*: MIRANDA, Jorge; SILVA, Marco Antonio Marques da (orgs.). *Tratado luso-brasileiro da dignidade humana*. São Paulo: Quartier Latin, 2008.

AQUINI, Marco. "Fraternidade e direitos humanos". *In*: CASO, Giovanni; CURY, Afife; CURY, Munir; SOUZA, Carlos Aurélio Mota de (orgs). *Direito & fraternidade*. São Paulo: LTr, 2008.

AQUINO, Santo Tomás de. *Suma teológica*. São Paulo: Loyola, 2002.

_____. *Tratado da justiça extraído da suma teológica*. Porto: Resjuridica, [s.d.].

ARENDT, Hannah. *A condição humana*. Rio de Janeiro: Forense Universitária, 2008.

_____. *O conceito de amor em Santo Agostinho*. Lisboa: Instituto Piaget, 1929.

ARIAS, Gino. *La filosofia tomistica e l'economia politica*. Milano: Vita i Pensiero, 1934.

ARISTÓTELES. *A ética – textos selecionados*. São Paulo: Edipro, 2003.

_____. *A política*. São Paulo: Edipro, 1995.

ARRUDA, Eloísa de Sousa. "O papel do ministério público na efetivação dos tratados internacionais de direitos humanos". *In*: MIRANDA, Jorge; SILVA, Marco Antonio Marques da (orgs.). *Tratado luso-brasileiro da dignidade humana*. São Paulo: Quartier Latin, 2008.

AUGÉ, Marc. *Não-Lugares – Introdução a uma antropologia da supramodernidade*. São Paulo: Papirus, 1994.

BAGNOLI, Vicente. *Direito econômico*. São Paulo: Atlas, 2005.

BALERA, Wagner. *Comentários à Declaração Universal dos Direitos Humanos*. Brasília: Fortium, 2008.

_____. "A dignidade da pessoa humana e o mínimo existencial". *In*: MIRANDA, Jorge; SILVA, Marco Antonio Marques da (orgs.). *Tratado luso-brasileiro da dignidade humana*. São Paulo: Quartier Latin, 2008.

_____. *Apresentação em homenagem aos quarenta anos da Carta encíclica Populorum Progressio*. São Paulo: Centro de Documentação Eletrônica Beato João XXIII, [s.d.].

BARRENECHE, Osvaldo. "Prólogo". *In*: BAGGIO, Antonio M. (org.). *El principio olvidado: la fraternidad*. Buenos Aires: Ciudad Nueva, 2006.

BARROW, R. H. *Los romanos*. México: Fondo de Cultura Económica, 1980.

BASTOS, Celso Renato. *Curso de direito econômico*. São Paulo: Celso Bastos, 2003.

BATRA, Ravi. *Greenspan, a fraude*. São Paulo: Novo Conceito, 2006.

BAUMAN, Zygmunt. *O mal-estar da pós-modernidade*. Rio de Janeiro: Zahar, 1998.

BECHO, Renato Lopes. *Filosofia do direito tributário*. São Paulo: Saraiva, 2009.

BENACCHIO, Marcelo. "Direito subjetivo – situação jurídica – relação jurídica". *In*: LOTUFO, Renan; NANNI, Giovanni Ettori (orgs.). *Teoria geral do direito civil*. São Paulo: Atlas, 2008.

BENTO XVI. *Carta encíclica Deus Caritas Est*. 25 de dezem-

bro de 2005. Available at: http://www.joaosocial.com.br/enciclicas/
deuscarisest.html, viewed on April 20, 2010.

_____. *Carta encíclica Caritas in Veritate, sobre o desen-
volvimento humano integral na caridade e na verdade.* 29 de junho
de 2009. Available at:
http://www.joaosocial.com.br/enciclicas/Caritas%20in%20
Veritate.htm. Viewed on June 29th, 2010.

_____. *Introdução ao cristianismo.* São Paulo: Loyola,
2006.

BETHENCOURT, Francisco. *História das inquisições.* São
Paulo: Companhia das Letras, 2000.

Bíblia Sagrada, tradução oficial da Conferência Nacional dos
Bispos do Brasil, 3ª edição, 2006.

BJORK, Gordon C. *A empresa privada e o interesse público.*
Rio de Janeiro: Zahar, 1971.

BOBBIO, Norberto. *Liberalismo e democracia.* São Paulo:
Brasiliense, 2006.

_____. *Locke e o direito natural.* Brasília: UnB, 1997.

BOHR, Niels. *Física atômica e conhecimento humano.* Rio de
Janeiro: Contraponto, 2008.

BONAVIDES, Paulo. *Ciência política.* São Paulo: Malheiros,
2006.

_____. *Curso de direito constitucional.* São Paulo: Mal-
heiros, 2008.

BORK, Robert H. *The antitrust paradox.* New York: Free

Press, 1993.

BOURDIEU, Pierre. *O poder simbólico*. Rio de Janeiro: Bertrand Brasil, 2007.

BOUZON, Emanuel. *Código de Hammurabi*. Rio de Janeiro: Vozes, 1992.

BRITTO, Carlos Ayres. *O humanismo como categoria constitucional*. Belo Horizonte: Fórum, 2007.

BRUE, Stanley. *História do pensamento econômico*. São Paulo: Thomson, 2006.

BULGARELLI, Waldírio. *O direito dos grupos e a concentração de empresas*. São Paulo: Universitária, 1975.

Câmara dos Deputados, Comissão de Direitos Humanos. O Brasil e o Pacto Internacional de Direitos Econômicos, Sociais e Culturais. *Relatório da sociedade civil sobre o cumprimento, pelo Brasil, do PIDESC*. Brasília: 2000.

CAMILLO, Carlos Eduardo Nicoletti; MAC CRACKEN, Roberto Nussinkis. "Aplicação concreta do princípio da dignidade da pessoa humana – Limites para contratar". *In*: MIRANDA, Jorge; SILVA, Marco Antonio Marques da (orgs.). *Tratado luso-brasileiro da dignidade humana*. São Paulo: Quartier Latin, 2008.

CANOTILHO, José Joaquim Gomes. "O círculo e a linha – Da liberdade dos antigos à liberdade dos modernos na teoria republicana dos direitos fundamentais". *In*: MIRANDA, Jorge; SILVA, Marco Antonio Marques da (orgs.). *Tratado luso-brasileiro da dignidade humana*. São Paulo: Quartier Latin, 2008.

CARRAZZA, Roque Antonio. *Imposto sobre a renda*. São Paulo: Malheiros, 2005.

_____. "O princípio constitucional da dignidade da pessoa humana e a seletividade no ICMS. Questões conexas". *In*: MIRANDA, Jorge; SILVA, Marco Antonio Marques da (orgs.). *Tratado luso-brasileiro da dignidade humana*. São Paulo: Quartier Latin, 2008.

CARVALHO, Paulo de Barros. *Direito tributário, linguagem e método*. São Paulo: Noesis, 2008.

CASTEL, Robert. "Armadilhas da exclusão". *In*: ____; WANDERLEY, Eduardo W.; BELFIORE-WANDERLEY, Mariângela. *Desigualdade e a questão social*. São Paulo: EDUC, 2007.

COELHO, Fábio Ulhoa. "Dignidade da pessoa humana na economia globalizada". *In*: MIRANDA, Jorge; SILVA, Marco Antonio Marques da (orgs.). *Tratado luso-brasileiro da dignidade humana*. São Paulo: Quartier Latin, 2008.

COMPARATO, Fábio Konder. *A afirmação histórica dos direitos humanos*. São Paulo: Saraiva, 2004.

_____. *Ética*. São Paulo: Companhia das Letras, 2006.

COURTIS, Cristian. "La eficacia de los derechos humanos en las relaciones entre particulares". *In*: SARLET, Ingo Wolfgang (org.). *Constituição, direitos fundamentais e direito privado*. Porto Alegre: Livraria do Advogado, 2006.

CUNHA, Paulo Ferreira da. *Geografia constitucional*. Lisboa: Quid Juris, 2009.

DARWIN, Charles. *A origem do homem e a seleção sexual*. Belo Horizonte: Itatiaia, 2004.

_____. *El origen de las especies*. México: EDAF, 2000.

DE LUCCA, Newton. *Direito do consumidor*. São Paulo:

Quartier Latin, 2008.

DOMMEN, Edouard. "Feliz aniversário, Sísifo". *In: Globalização e fé*. Bauru: EDUSC, 2000.

DWORKIN, Ronald. *Uma questão de princípio*. São Paulo: Martins Fontes, 2005.

_____. "A igualdade importa?" *In*: GIDDENS, Anthony (org.). *O debate global sobre a terceira via*. São Paulo: UNESP, 2007.

EINSTEIN, Albert; INFELD, Leopold. *Evolução da física*. São Paulo: Zahar, 2008.

FELICE, Flavio Felice. *L'economia sociale di mercato*. Roma: Rubbettino, 2008.

FERNANDEZ, Atahualpa. *Fraternidade: a "terceira" virtude ilustrada*. Available at: <http://www.uj.com.br>. Viewed on October 18th, 2009.

FIGUEIREDO, Marcelo. "O respeito à dignidade humana e a eutanásia". *In*: MIRANDA, Jorge; SILVA, Marco Antonio Marques da (orgs.). *Tratado luso-brasileiro da dignidade humana*. São Paulo: Quartier Latin, 2008.

FINKELSTEIN, Cláudio. *O processo de formação de mercados de bloco*. São Paulo: Thomson, 2003.

FONSECA, João Bosco Leopoldino da. *Cláusulas abusivas nos contratos*. Rio de Janeiro: Forense, 1993.

FORGIONI, Paula A. *Os fundamentos do antitruste*. São Paulo: RT, 1998.

FRIEDMAN, Milton. *Capitalismo e liberdade*. São Paulo:

Nova Cultural, 1985.

FURTADO, Celso. *Formação econômica do Brasil*. São Paulo: Nacional, 1977.

FUTUYMA, Douglas J. *Biologia evolutiva*. São Paulo: Funpec, 2003.

GADREY, Jean; JANY-CATRICE, Florence. *Os novos indicadores de riqueza*. São Paulo: Senac, 2006.

GALBRAITH, John Kenneth. *A economia das fraudes inocentes*. São Paulo: Companhia das Letras, 2004.

GEERTZ, Clifford. *A interpretação das culturas*. Rio de Janeiro: LTC, 1990.

GIDDENS, Anthony. *A terceira via – reflexões sobre o impasse político atual e o futuro da social-democracia*. Rio de Janeiro: Record, 2005.

_____. *A terceira via e seus críticos*. Rio de Janeiro: Record, 2001.

_____. "A questão da desigualdade". *In:* ___ (org.). *O debate global sobre a terceira via*. São Paulo: Unesp, 2007.

GILBERT, Adrian. *Enciclopédia das guerras*. São Paulo: M. Books, 2005.

GOYARD-FABRE, Simone. *Os fundamentos da ordem jurídica*. São Paulo: Martins Fontes, 1999.

GRAU, Eros Roberto. *A ordem econômica na Constituição Federal de 1988*. São Paulo: Malheiros, 2003.

GREENSPAN, Alan. *A era da turbulência*. Rio de Janeiro: Elsevier, 2008.

GRUNBERGER, Richard. *Historia social del tercer reich*. Barcelona: Ariel, 2007.

GUERRA FILHO, Willis Santiago. "Dignidade humana, princípio da proporcionalidade e teoria dos direitos fundamentais". *In*: MIRANDA, Jorge; SILVA, Marco Antonio Marques da (orgs.). *Tratado luso-brasileiro da dignidade humana*. São Paulo: Quartier Latin, 2008.

_____. *Para uma filosofia da filosofia*. Ceará: UFC, 1999.

_____. *Processo constitucional e direitos fundamentais*. São Paulo: RCS, 2005.

_____. *Teoria da ciência jurídica*. São Paulo: Saraiva, 2009.

_____. *Filosofia, uma introdução*. Teresópolis: Daimon, 2009.

Guia mundial de estatísticas. São Paulo: On Line, 2008.

GUIMARÃES, Antônio Márcio da Cunha. *Tratados internacionais*. São Paulo: Aduaneiras, 2009.

HAWKING, Stephen; MLODINOW, Leonard. *Uma nova história do tempo*. Rio de Janeiro: Ediouro, 2005.

HEGEL, G. W. F. *O belo na arte*. São Paulo: Martins Fontes, 1996.

_____. *Princípios de filosofia do direito*. São Paulo: Martins Fontes, 2003.

HOBBES, Thomas. *Do cidadão*. São Paulo: Martins Fontes, 2002.

_____. *Leviatã ou matéria, forma e poder de um estado eclesiástico e civil*. São Paulo: Abril Cultural, 1979.

HOBSBAWM, Eric. *Era dos extremos*. São Paulo: Companhia das Letras, 1995.

HUGON, Paul. *Economistas célebres*. São Paulo: Atlas, 1955.

_____. *História das doutrinas econômicas*. São Paulo: Atlas, 1952.

HUSCENOT, Jean. *Os doutores da igreja*. Lisboa: Paulus. 1997.

ISHIKAWA, Lauro. *O direito ao desenvolvimento como concretizador do princípio da dignidade da pessoa humana*. Master Degree Thesis at Pontifícia Universidade Católica. São Paulo, 2008. Unpublished.

JOÃO PAULO II. "Carta encíclica Dives in Misericordia". 30 de novembro de 1980. *In: João Paulo II, o profeta do ano 2000*. 2ª ed. São Paulo: LTr, 1999.

_____. "Carta encíclica Laborem Exercens, sobre o trabalho humano, no 90º aniversário da Rerum Novarum". 14 de setembro de 1981. *In: João Paulo II, o profeta do ano 2000*. 2ª ed. São Paulo: LTr, 1999.

_____. *Carta encíclica Sollicitudo Rei Socialis, sobre a solicitude social da Igreja*. 30 de dezembro de 1987. Available at:http://www.joaosocial.com.br/ enciclicas/
sollicitudo.html. Viewed on June 26th, 2010.

_____. *Carta encíclica Centesimus Annus, no centenário da Rerum Novarum.* 1° de maio de 1991.
Available at:http://www.joaosocial.com.br/enciclicas/ centesimus_annus.html. Viewed on July 4th 2010.

_____. *Carta encíclica Evangelium Vitae, sobre o valor e a inviolabilidade da vida humana.* 25 de março de 1995.
Available at:< http://www.vatican.va>. Viewed on June 20th 2008.

_____. *Carta encíclica Ex Corde Eclesiae sobre as universidades católicas.*
Available at:< http://www.vatican.va>. Viewed on September 23rd 2008.

JOÃO XXIII. *Carta encíclica Mater et Magistra, sobre a evolução contemporânea da vida social à luz dos princípios cristãos.* 15 de maio de 1961.
Available at: http://www.joaosocial.com.br/enciclicas/materetmagistra.html. Viewed on September 29th 2008.

_____. *Carta encíclica Pacem in Terris, sobre a paz cristã.* 11 de abril de 1963. Available at:http://www.joaosocial.com.br/enciclicas/pacem.html. Viewed on June 23rd 2010.

JUNG, C. G. *Os arquétipos e o inconsciente coletivo.* Rio de Janeiro: Vozes, 2008.

KANT, Immanuel. *A metafísica dos costumes.* Bauru: Edipro, 2007.

_____. *Ideia de uma história universal de um ponto de vista cosmopolita.* São Paulo: Martins Fontes, 2003.

KELSEN, Hans. *La paz por médio del derecho.* Madri: Trotta, 2003.

KENNEDY, James; NEWCOMBE, Jerry. *E se Jesus não tivesse nascido?* São Paulo: Vida, 2003.

KERSHAW, Ian. *El mito de Hitler.* Barcelona: Paidós, 2008.

KEYNES, John Maynard. *The end of laissez-faire.* Londres: Hogarth Press, 1926.

_____. *A teoria geral do emprego, do juro e da moeda.* São Paulo: Atlas, 2007.

LALANDE, André. *Vocabulário técnico e crítico da filosofia.* São Paulo: Martins Fontes, 1999.

LAUBIER, Patrick de. *As três cidades.* São Paulo: LTr, 2002.

LEAKEY, Richard. *A origem da espécie humana.* Rio de Janeiro: Rocco, 1995.

LEÃO XIII. *Carta encíclica Rerum Novarum, sobre a condição dos operários.* 15 de maio de 1891.
Available at: http://www.joaosocial.com.br/enciclicas/ revum_novarum.html. Wiewed on May 1st 2010.

LEBRET, Louis-Joseph. *Princípios para a ação.* São Paulo: Duas Cidades, 1959.

_____. *Manifesto por uma civilização solidária.* São Paulo: Duas Cidades, 1962.

_____. *O drama do século XX.* 2ª ed. São Paulo: Duas Cidades, 1966.

LEPENIES, Wolf. "A intolerância – terrível virtude". *In:* BARRET-DUCROCQ, Françoise (org.). *A intolerância.* Rio de Janeiro: Bertrand Brasil, 2000.

LEWANDOWSKI, Enrique Ricardo. "A formação da doutrina dos direitos fundamentais". *In*: MIRANDA, Jorge; SILVA, Marco Antonio Marques da (orgs.). *Tratado luso-brasileiro da dignidade humana*. São Paulo: Quartier Latin, 2008.

LIMA, Carolina Alves de Souza; MARQUES, Oswaldo Henrique Duek. "O princípio da humanidade das penas". *In*: MIRANDA, Jorge; SILVA, Marco Antonio Marques da (orgs.). *Tratado luso-brasileiro da dignidade humana*. São Paulo: Quartier Latin, 2008.

LIMA, Roberto Kant de; VARELLA, Alex. *Ensaios de antropologia e de direito*. Rio de Janeiro: Lúmen Júris, 2008.

LIGÓRIO, Santo Afonso Maria. *A prática do amor a Jesus Cristo*. São Paulo: Santuário, 1996.

LIPOVETSKY, Gilles. *A sociedade da decepção*. São Paulo: Manole, 2007.

LOCKE, John. *Dois tratados sobre o governo*. São Paulo: Martins Fontes, 2005.

_____. *Carta sobre la tolerancia*. Madri: Tecnos, 2005.

LONGCHAMP, Albert. "Globalização: o novo nome do desenvolvimento?" *In*: *Globalização e fé*. Bauru: Edusc, 2000.

LOSURDO, Domenico. *Hegel, Marx e a tradição liberal*. São Paulo: Unesp, 1998.

LUCAS, Davison de. *Por um mundo melhor*. São Paulo: Qualidade Total, 1998.

LUGON, Luiz Carlos de Castro. *Ética, diretos humanos e princípios constitucionais*.
Available at:<http://www.trf4.jus.br/trf4/upload/arquivos/

emagis_atividades/ccp5_ lugon.pdf>. Viewed on September 29th 2008.

MCFARLANE, Alan. *A cultura do Capitalismo*. Rio de Janeiro: Zahar, 1989.

MACHADO, Jonatas Eduardo Mendes. *Liberdade religiosa numa comunidade constitucional inclusiva*. Coimbra: Coimbra, 1996.

MACPHERSON, C. B. *Ascensão e queda da justiça econômica*. Rio de Janeiro: Paz e Terra, 1991.

MANUS, Pedro Paulo. "A dignidade da pessoa humana, o dano moral e o direito do trabalho". *In*: MIRANDA, Jorge; SILVA, Marco Antonio Marques da (orgs.). *Tratado luso-brasileiro da dignidade humana*. São Paulo: Quartier Latin, 2008.

MARITAIN, Jacques. *Humanismo integral*. São Paulo: Nacional, 1941.

MARTINEZ, Gutemberg Martinez. *Humanismo e economia: ética e responsabilidade social*. n. 84. São Paulo: Bem Comum, 2005.

MARTINS, Ives Gandra da Silva. "A dignidade da pessoa humana desde a concepção". *In*: MIRANDA, Jorge; SILVA, Marco Antonio Marques da (orgs.). *Tratado luso-brasileiro da dignidade humana*. São Paulo: Quartier Latin, 2008.

MATSUSHITA, Thiago. *Análise reflexiva da regra matriz da ordem econômica*. Dissertação de mestrado apresentada e aprovada na Pontifícia Universidade Católica. São Paulo, 2007. Não-publicada.

MELLO, Marco Aurélio. "Liberdade de expressão, dignidade humana e estado democrático de direito". *In*: MIRANDA, Jorge; SILVA, Marco Antonio Marques da (orgs.). *Tratado luso-brasileiro da dignidade humana*. São Paulo: Quartier Latin, 2008.

MENDES, Gilmar Ferreira; COELHO, Inocêncio Martines; BRANCO, Paulo Gustavo Gonet. *Curso de direito constitucional.* São Paulo: Saraiva, 2008.

MEZZAROBA, Orides. *Humanismo político.* Florianópolis: Boiteux, 2008.

MIRANDA, Jorge. "A dignidade da pessoa humana e a unidade valorativa do sistema de direitos fundamentais". In: _____; SILVA, Marco Antonio Marques da (orgs.). *Tratado luso-brasileiro da dignidade humana.* São Paulo: Quartier Latin, 2008.

MIRANDA, Pontes de. *Introdução à política scientifica.* Rio de Janeiro: Garnier, 1924.

_____. *O problema fundamental do conhecimento.* Campinas: Bookseller, 2005.

_____. *Garra, mão e dedo.* São Paulo: Martins, [s.d.].

MONTESQUIEU. *Grandeza e decadência dos romanos.* Rio de Janeiro: Francisco Alves, 1937.

MONTORO, André Franco. *Introdução à ciência do direito.* São Paulo: RT, 1991.

MORIN, Edgar. *O paradigma perdido – a natureza humana.* Lisboa: Europa-América, 1999.

_____. *O método 5 – A humanidade da humanidade.* Porto Alegre: Sulina, 2005.

MOUNIER, Emmanuel. *O personalismo.* São Paulo: Centauro, 2004.

NALINI, José Renato. "Duração razoável do processo e dignidade da pessoa humana". *In*: MIRANDA, Jorge; SILVA, Marco Antonio Marques da (orgs.). *Tratado luso-brasileiro da dignidade humana*. São Paulo: Quartier Latin, 2008.

NAZAR, Nelson. *Direito econômico e o contrato de trabalho*. São Paulo: Atlas, 2007.

_____. *Direito econômico*. São Paulo: Edipro, 2004.

NEGRÃO, Theotonio; GOUVÊA, José Roberto F. *Código civil*. São Paulo: Saraiva, 2006.

NERI, Marcelo Côrtes; CARVALHAES, Luisa. *Miséria e a nova classe média na década da desigualdade*. Rio de Janeiro: FGV/IBRAE, 2008.

NERY JR., Nelson. "Coisa julgada e o estado democrático de direito". *In*: MIRANDA, Jorge; SILVA, Marco Antonio Marques da (orgs.). *Tratado luso-brasileiro da dignidade humana*. São Paulo: Quartier Latin, 2008.

NETO, Lira. "A absolvição do Padim". *In*: *Aventuras na história*. São Paulo: Abril, 2009.

NETTO, José Paulo; BRAZ, Marcelo. *Economia política*. São Paulo: Cortez, 2007.

NICOLAS, Marie-Joseph. *Introdução à suma teológica*. Translation published under the coordination of Carlos-Josaphat Pinto. São Paulo: Loyola, 2001.

NIETZSCHE, Friedrich. *O anticristo – maldição ao cristianismo*. São Paulo: Companhia das Letras, 2007.

NINIO, Marcelo. "Ministro alemão vê fim do poder dos EUA após crise". *In*: *Folha de S. Paulo*, 26 set. 2008. Dinheiro, p. B6.

NUNES JR, Vidal Serrano. "O ministério público e a concretização do princípio da dignidade humana". *In*: MIRANDA, Jorge; SILVA, Marco Antonio Marques da (orgs.). *Tratado luso-brasileiro da dignidade humana*. São Paulo: Quartier Latin, 2008.

NUNES, Luiz Antonio Rizzatto. "A dignidade da pessoa humana e o papel do julgador". *In*: MIRANDA, Jorge; SILVA, Marco Antonio Marques da (orgs.). *Tratado luso-brasileiro da dignidade humana*. São Paulo: Quartier Latin, 2008.

_____. *Manual de monografia jurídica*. São Paulo: Saraiva, 2008.

NUSDEO, Fábio. *Curso de economia*. São Paulo: RT, 2001.

OBAMA, Barack. *A origem dos meus sonhos*. São Paulo: Gente, 2008.

OLIVEIRA, Eutálio José Porto. "O estado, a ordem econômica e a dignidade da pessoa humana". *In*: MIRANDA, Jorge (org.); SILVA, Marco Antonio Marques da (org.). *Tratado luso-brasileiro da dignidade humana*. São Paulo: Quartier Latin, 2008.

ONU. *Declaração do Milênio das Nações Unidas*. 8 set. 2000. Available at:<http://www.mp.ma.gov.br/site/centrosapoio/DirHumanos/DecMilenioNacoesUnidas.htm>. Viewed on May 10th 2010.

PAULA, Paulo Afonso Garrido de. "Criança e dignidade da pessoa humana". *In*: MIRANDA, Jorge; SILVA, Marco Antonio Marques da (orgs.). *Tratado luso-brasileiro da dignidade humana*. São Paulo: Quartier Latin, 2008.

PAULO VI. *Carta encíclica Populorum Progressio*. 26 de março de 2010. Published in honor of its 40th anniversary under the coordination of Wagner Balera, Centro de documentação eletrônica Beato João XXIII. São Paulo, [s.d.].

PAULSON JR., Henry M. *A beira do abismo financeiro*. Rio de Janeiro: Elsevier, 2010.

PERI GUEDES, Marco Aurélio. *Estado e ordem econômica e social – A experiência constitucional da República de Weimar e a Constituição Brasileira de 1934*. Rio de Janeiro: Renovar, 1998.

PINHEIRO, Armando Castelar; SADDI, Jairo. *Direito, economia e mercados*. Rio de Janeiro: Elsevier, 2005.

PINHO, Débora. *O homem que parou o maior exército do mundo*. 22 out. 2009. Available at:< http://www.conjur.com.br>. Viewed on October 24th 2009.

PINTO, Eduardo Augusto Alves Vera Cruz. "Os tribunais militares e o estado democrático de direito". *In*: MIRANDA, Jorge; SILVA, Marco Antonio Marques da (orgs.). *Tratado luso-brasileiro da dignidade humana*. São Paulo: Quartier Latin, 2008.

PINTO, Nelson Luiz; FINKELSTEIN, Cláudio; CEZAR, Leonel. "Manifesto de instituição da escola humanista de direito econômico". *In*: *Revista de Direito Internacional e Econômico*. n. 1, Porto Alegre: Síntese, 2002.

PIO XI. *Carta encíclica Quadragesimo Anno, sobre a restauração e aperfeiçoamento da ordem social em conformidade com a lei evangélica*. 15 maio de 1931. Available at:http://www.joaosocial.com. br/ enciclicas/quadragesimo_ano.html. Viewed on June 13th 2010.

PISIER, Evelyne. *História das ideias políticas*. São Paulo: Manole, 2004.

Pontifício Conselho "Justitia et Pax". *Un nuevo pacto financiero internacional*. Roma: Tipografia Vaticana, 2008.

POSNER, Richard A. *El análisis económico del derecho*. México: Fundo Mexicano de Cultura, 2000.

PUSSOLI, Lafaiete. *Humanismo de Jacques Maritain e sistema jurídico brasileiro.* PHD dissertation at Pontifícia Universidade Católica. São Paulo, 1999. Unpublished.

RADBRUCH, Gustav. *Filosofia do direito.* Coimbra: Armênio Amado, 1979.

RAJAN, Raghuram G.; ZINGALES, Luigi. *Salvando o Capitalismo dos Capitalistas.* Rio de Janeiro: Elsevier, 2004.

RAND, Ayn. *The virtude of selfishness.* New York: Centennial, 1964.

REALE, Miguel. *Filosofia do direito.* São Paulo: Saraiva, 2008.

_____. *Teoria do direito e do estado.* São Paulo: Saraiva, 2000.

_____. *Noções preliminares de direito.* São Paulo: USP, 1973.

RESTA, Eligio. *O direito fraterno.* Santa Cruz do Sul: Edunisc, 2004.

RICARDO, David. *Princípios de economia política e tributação.* São Paulo: Abril Cultural, 1982.

RIPERT, Georges. *Aspectos jurídicos do Capitalismo moderno.* São Paulo: Freitas Bastos, 1947.

_____. *O regime democrático e o direito civil moderno.* São Paulo: Saraiva, 1937.

ROCCARO, Giuseppe. "Humanismo e Islã: consummatio

modernitatis e contemporaneidade. Nos traços de um ato ideológico". *In*: RI JUNIOR, Arno Dal; ORO, Ari Pedro (orgs.). *Islamismo e humanismo latino*. Rio de Janeiro: Vozes, 2004.

ROMAR, Carla Teresa Martins. "Direito do trabalho e dignidade da pessoa humana". *In*: MIRANDA, Jorge; SILVA, Marco Antonio Marques da (orgs.). *Tratado luso-brasileiro da dignidade humana*. São Paulo: Quartier Latin, 2008.

ROSSETTI, José Cabral. *Introdução à economia*. São Paulo: Atlas, 2006.

ROVIGHI, Sofia Vanni. *História da filosofia contemporânea*. São Paulo: Loyola, 2004.

SANDRONI, Paulo. *Dicionário de economia do século XXI*. Rio de Janeiro: Record, 2005.

SANTOS, Antônio Carlos; GONÇALVES, Maria Eduarda; MARQUES, Maria Manuel Leitão. *Direito económico*. Coimbra: Almedina, 1995.

SAVAGE, Nigel; BRADGATE, Robert. *Business law*. Londres: Butterworths, 1993.

SAVAGNONE, Guiseppe. "Fraternidad y comunicación". *In*: BAGGIO, Antonio M. (org.) *El principio olvidado: la fraternidad*. Buenos Aires: Ciudad Nueva, 2006.

SAYEG, Ricardo H.. *Aspectos contratuais da exclusividade no fornecimento de combustíveis automotivos*. São Paulo: Edipro, 2002.

_____. *Práticas comerciais abusivas*. São Paulo: Edipro, 1995.

_____. "O Capitalismo humanista no Brasil". *In*: MIRAN-

DA, Jorge; SILVA, Marco Antonio Marques da (orgs.). *Tratado luso-brasileiro da dignidade humana*. São Paulo: Quartier Latin, 2008.

SCHERER, D. Odilo Pedro. *PUC em Notícias*, 1ª quinz. set. 2009, p. 2.

SENGUPTA, Arjun K. *O direito ao desenvolvimento como um direito humano*. Available at:
< http://www.itv.org.br/site/publicacoes/igualdade/direito_desenvolvimento.pdf>. Viewed on September 21th 2008.

SEN, Amartya. *Desenvolvimento como liberdade*. São Paulo: Companhia das Letras, 2000.

SENISE LISBOA, Roberto. "Dignidade e solidariedade civil constitucional". *In*: *Revista de direito privado*, nº 42. São Paulo: RT, 2010.

_____. *Manual de direito civil*. 6ª ed. São Paulo: Saraiva, 2010.

SILVA, José Afonso da. *Comentário contextual à constituição*. São Paulo: Malheiros, 2008.

SILVA, Marco Antonio Marques da. "Cidadania e democracia: instrumentos para a efetivação da dignidade humana". *In*: MIRANDA, Jorge; _____. (orgs.). *Tratado luso-brasileiro da dignidade humana*. São Paulo: Quartier Latin, 2008.

SILVEIRA, Vladmir Oliveira da. *O direito ao desenvolvimento na doutrina humanista do direito econômico*. PHD dissertation at Pontifícia Universidade Católica. São Paulo, 2006. Unpublished.

SIQUEIRA JR., Paulo Hamilton. "A dignidade da pessoa humana no contexto da pós-modernidade". *In*: MIRANDA, Jorge; SILVA, Marco Antonio Marques da (orgs.). *Tratado luso-brasileiro da dignidade humana*. São Paulo: Quartier Latin, 2008.

SMITH, Adam. *Investigación sobre la naturaleza y causas de la riqueza de las naciones*. México: Fundo Mexicano de Cultura, 1990.

SODRÉ, Marcelo Gomes. "Dignidade planetária: o direito e o consumo sustentável". In: MIRANDA, Jorge; SILVA, Marco Antonio Marques da (orgs.). *Tratado luso-brasileiro da dignidade humana*. São Paulo: Quartier Latin, 2008.

SÓFOCLES. *Antígona*. Porto Alegre: L&PM, 2007.

SOUZA, Washington Peluso Albino de; CLARK, Giovani. *Questões polêmicas de direito econômico*. São Paulo: LTr, 2008.

STIGLITZ, Joseph E. *A globalização e seus malefícios*. São Paulo: Futura, 2002.

_____; CHARLTON, Andrew. *Livre mercado para todos*. Rio de Janeiro: Elsevier, 2007.

STRATHERN, Paul. *Bohr e a teoria quântica*. Rio de Janeiro: Zahar, 1999.

SUPIOT, Alain. *Homo juridicus*. Paris: Du Seuil, 2005.

TAVARES, André Ramos. *Direito constitucional econômico brasileiro*. São Paulo: Método, 2006.

TELLES JUNIOR, Goffredo. *O direito quântico*. São Paulo: Max Limonad, [s.d.].

THOMSON, Oliver. *A assustadora história da maldade*. São Paulo: Ediouro, 2002.

THOREAU, Henry David. *A desobediência civil e outros escri-*

tos. São Paulo: Martin Claret, 2003.

TRALLI, César. *Olhar crônico.* São Paulo: Globo, 2001.

TRIBE, Laurence H. *The invisible constitution.* Nova York: Oxford University Press, 2008.

TRINDADE, Antônio Augusto Cançado. *Tratado internacional dos direitos humanos.* Porto Alegre: Sérgio Antonio Fabris, 2003.

UELMEN, Amy. "Fraternidade como categoria jurídica no direito empresarial". *In:* CASO, Giovanni; CURY, Afife; CURY, Munir; SOUZA, Carlos Aurélio Mota de (orgs.). *Direito & fraternidade.* São Paulo: LTR, 2008.

VALLE, Alberto del Castillo del. *Garantias del gobernado.* México: Alma, 2005.

VANDERBORGHT, Yannick; VAN PARIJS, Philippe. *Renda básica de cidadania.* Rio de Janeiro: Civilização Brasileira, 2006.

VARGAS, Getúlio. *A nova política do Brasil.* Rio de Janeiro: José Olympio, 1938.

VILANOVA, Lourival. *As estruturas lógicas e o sistema do direito positivo.* São Paulo: RT, 1977.

VILLEY, Michel. *Filosofia do direito.* São Paulo: Martins Fontes, 2008.

_____. *A formação do pensamento jurídico moderno.* São Paulo: Martins Fontes, 2005.

VITA, Álvaro de. *A justiça igualitária e seus críticos.* São Paulo: Martins Fontes, 2007.

VOLTAIRE. *Tratado sobre a tolerância*. São Paulo: Martins Fontes, 2000.

WAITE, Geoff. *Nietzche's corpse*. Londres: Duke, 1996.

WAMBIER, Teresa Arruda Alvim. *Nulidades do processo e da sentença*. São Paulo: RT, 2007.

WATSON, James D.; BERRY, Andrew. *DNA – O segredo da vida*. São Paulo: Companhia das Letras, 2005.

WEBER, Max. *A ética protestante e o espírito do Capitalismo*. São Paulo: Companhia das Letras, 2004.

WEINBERG, Steven. *Os três primeiros minutos – uma análise moderna da origem do universo*. Lisboa: Gradiva, 2002.

WOLKMER, Antonio Carlos (org.). *Fundamentos do humanismo jurídico no ocidente*. São Paulo: Manole, 2005.

YOSHIDA, Consuelo Yatsuda Moromizato. "Direitos fundamentais e meio ambiente". *In*: MIRANDA, Jorge; SILVA, Marco Antonio Marques da (orgs.). *Tratado luso-brasileiro da dignidade humana*. São Paulo: Quartier Latin, 2008.

Online References

– http://cbn.globoradio.globo.com. Viewed on Sept 16th 2008
– http://frases.netsaber.com.br. Viewed on Nov 1st 2009
– http://jornalnacional.globo.com. Viewed on Sept 10th 2008
– http://noticias.terra.com.br. Viewed on Sept 25th 2008
– http://pensador.uol.com.br. Viewed on Feb 19th 2011
– http://pt.wikiquote.org. Viewed on Nov 1st 2009
– http://web.worldbank.org. Viewed on Sept 9th 2008

- http://www.bbc.co.uk. Viewed on Aug 11th 2008
- http://www.cienciahoje.pt. Viewed on Sept 12th 2009
- http://www.cnj.jus.br. Viewed on Sept 10th2009
- http://www.conjur.com.br. Viewed on Mar 7th 2008
- http://www.estudosdabiblia.net. Viewed on Sept 3rd 2008
- http://www.fgv.br. Viewed on Sept 20th 2008
- http://www.frasesfamosas.com.br. Viewed on Nov 1st 2009
- http://www.google.com.br. Viewed on Sept 21th 2008
- http://www.ibge.gov.br. Viewed on Sept 20th 2008
- http://www.institutoatkwhh.org.br. Viewed on Nov 19th 2009
- http://www.internext.com.br. Viewed on July 13th 2008
- http://www.ipea.gov.br. Viewed on Sept 9th 2008
- http://www.itv.org.br. Viewed on Sept 21th 2008
- http://www.newsweek.com. Viewed on Sept 21th 2008
- http://www.onu-brasil.org.br. Acessado em: Oct 11th 2010
- http://www.philgraham.net. Viewed on Aug 13th 2008
- http://www.pnud.org.br. Viewed on Nov 30th 2010
- http://www.stf.gov.br. Viewed on Sept 23rd 2008
- http://www.tj.sp.gov.br. Viewed on Sept 23rd 2008
- http://www.trf4.jus.br. Viewed on Sept 29th 2008
- http://www.tribunalconstitucional.pt. Viewed on May 10th 2010
- http://www.tvcultura.com.br. Viewed on Nov 2nd 2009
- http://www.uj.com.br. Viewed on Oct 18th 2009
- http://www.uol.com.br. Viewed on Sept 23rd 2008
- http://www.vatican.va. Viewed on Sept 29th 2008
- http://www1.folha.uol.com.br. Viewed on Sept 8th 2008

www.ingramcontent.com/pod-product-compliance
Lightning Source LLC
Chambersburg PA
CBHW072120270326
41931CB00010B/1614